Relæ

Relæ
Christian
F. Puglisi

A
Book
of Ideas

Photography by Per-Anders Jorgensen

TEN SPEED PRESS
Berkeley

Contents

Chapter 3: Dishes

Foreword

Years ago I began planning the first of what would become several research trips in Denmark to study the resurgence of heirloom Nordic grains. In advance of the trip, I asked my friend Kille Enna—a noted chef and cookbook author who currently lives in southern Sweden—where to eat in Copenhagen. Kille is a trusted source in such matters; she is as critical as she is dear, and only suggests places exceptional enough to merit a detour in her perpetually overscheduled days. With no hesitation, and no other recommendations, she directed me to a newish place where a young chef from Noma was "doing his own thing." That was all I knew of Relæ before showing up for my first dinner there with Nick Balla (my chef and colleague at Bar Tartine in San Francisco).

I had been thoroughly enjoying my visit to Denmark so far: meeting Danish bakers and farmers, and making bread using the local, fresh-milled flours. Little did I know that Christian, the chef/proprietor whose restaurant I had just walked into, was a serious baker himself. He greeted us warmly and seated us at the bar facing into the open kitchen. The two cooks working across the bar welcomed us also, and set to making our first courses.

As dinner began, paired with classic-era Johnny Cash, Nick and I knew we were amongst friends. We settled in as exceptional bread, folded warm into a soft leather pouch, was brought from the oven in the center of the kitchen. Deep green Sicilian olive oil was measured into a shallow dish and sparkling natural wine was poured. A plate of burnt, gnarled roots appeared too: bitter-sweet, char-roasted Jerusalem artichokes, an early variant of a recipe that appears in this book. Nick and I could have made a meal of these alone.

We investigated drawers under the table which revealed our utensils, and then, quickly, the plates started to come. There are no actual servers here, belying the seemingly effortless service. What followed was one astonishingly focused dish after another. Food that was conceptual yet comforting, restrained and absolutely generous. A fascinating contrast unfolded throughout the meal: that of luxury *and* economy. Cooks set out each plate, wines were poured, and the sommelier's introductions transported us to the place the grapes were grown and wine was made. All of this at once, in less than a minute. Like a well-built track racing cycle, the evening had been perfectly engineered.

This is what one experiences as a diner at Relæ. But one also senses a complex back story, one that is relentlessly workshopped before we ever step in for dinner. Afterwards, I struggled to describe my meal to friends at home. It was not Nordic food per se—Christian sourced seaweed from Brittany, citrus and olive oil from near his childhood home in Italy. Reading the menu aloud to illuminate didn't help much:

Ox tartar, mussels, bergamot

Barley porridge, smoked almonds, and black trumpets

Pork, poached salad, and unripe fruit

Jerusalem artichokes, coffee, and passion fruit

There was something else going on here that fundamentally changed the way I looked at modern cuisine. Was it "post-regional," perhaps? Nick and I were moved by the singular voice of our dinner.

I returned to Copenhagen a few more times to visit Kille, and to work with the local grains and the bakers I had made friends with—who inspired large parts of the bread book I was working on. And each time I returned to eat at Relæ. There are many restaurants I love to eat in, but very few that I look forward to months in advance. Christian's vision has a clear and independent perspective. Dishes finally make it onto the menu after many weeks of development, wrought through a deliberate,

obsessive, and very personal approach. This book brings us to the heart of his process—from the kernel of an idea to the finish. Essentially, it offers the back story I had wondered about since that first meal at Relæ: the dynamic way concepts are hewed, honed, distilled, taken apart, and put back together in a fresh, hard-edit shorthand where flavors fit together like a Mamet dialogue. The cache of ideas presented here helps articulate the language of Christian's distinct style of cooking—and gives readers new ways to express their own ideas using the language of Relæ. For those interested in a more hands-on approach, a collection of practical, slightly radical recipes follows—comprised of healthy, vegetable-focused food that is light, yet delivers strong, satisfying, and memorable flavors.

I gave up long ago trying to describe Relæ in much detail. These days I keep it simple: "my perfect restaurant, serving the food I want to eat every day." Thankfully, this book brings us a much more detailed narrative—straight from the mind of the chef.

—Chad Robertson

Acknowledgments

In the process of making this book, I really focused in on analyzing my team's work, trying to find the most essential ideas that frequently show up in our cuisine so that you could read about and find inspiration from them. That is why I felt it appropriate to write the entire book myself. The process of analyzing and thus questioning every aspect of our work has truly helped clear up my ideas and thoughts about food. Not only has this book become a way of communicating our food and introducing you, the reader, to our cooking; it has also been an adventure to rediscover the dishes we created and try to clearly understand their qualities.

But I must admit that it was a tough process. I am used to numerous deadlines a day, with phones ringing, people demanding my attention, and something cooking in a pan at the same time. I am very good at that. You won't stress me out—the worst thing that can happen is a bit of shouting. I keep on top of things. Yet working on a book required concentrating on a single idea—one chapter, one dish—for hours and hours without interruptions. It proved to be extremely difficult for me to find and prioritize that time, and it has challenged me just as much as running two restaurants and taking care of my family. But I love being challenged. The blood, sweat, and tears I put into this book made me grow as a chef, a person, and a writer.

Even though the process of communicating this big mess that is going on in my head made me swear that I would *never* do this again several times, it has helped me further understand my own work and define my own ideas and opinions. I thank Ten Speed Press for being as focused on the details of the writing of this book as my team and I have been on every single dish we send from our kitchen, making me incredibly proud now

that the work is finally coming to an end. I also thank Tara Duggan for polishing up my kitchen English (if this sentence makes sense to you, it's because she probably rewrote it) and the entire team at the restaurant for supporting me during this period of enormous work.

It is needless to say that the love of my life, Cecilie, and our son, Louis, deserve all the praise in the world for their patience with me. They accepted my venture of writing this book—and the enormous workload it entailed—because they knew what a dream it was for me to realize. As if running two restaurants didn't challenge our lives enough. Thanks to my family, which is spread across a good portion of Europe, for introducing me to the joy of cooking from the very beginning. An enormous thank-you to my father and mother for making me understand the value of hard work, responsibility, and sacrifice, while always prioritizing my future before their own. And at the same time for making the best decision of my life for me when they pulled their roots and brought us all to Denmark, which is today our home. Thanks to Kim Rossen and Ulrik Mikkelsen for partnering up with me on these crazy adventures. Thanks to John Tam for the sparring, honest feedback, and creative contribution to all the dishes in this book. Thanks to Lisa Lov for doing a hell of a job in converting all our professional gibberish to meaningful, foolproof, and precise recipes. Thanks to all the rest of my staff for challenging me and inspiring me to do better every single day. Thanks to Katherine Cowles for holding my hand all throughout this process and to Chad Robertson for introducing me to her. Thanks to all the chefs that I have worked under, over, and next to— for the massive inspirations, lessons, and ideas with which you have influenced me.

Introduction

When I opened Relæ in 2010, the last thing I wanted was for it to be just another fine dining restaurant. Our entire philosophy is grounded in the idea that conventional fine dining—with its big round tables, waitstaff showing you the way to the toilet and constantly scraping the crumbs off the thick tablecloth, jazz music piping through the speakers—has little do with the way people actually want to eat. Rather, we want the dining experience at Relæ to be simple and unpretentious, focusing solely on gastronomy. Everything else—all those unnecessary details—is stripped away. We describe our restaurant's philosophy as "cut to the bone."

Similarly, when I sat down to write this book, I didn't want it to be a conventional cookbook that readers were expected to page through from cover to cover. I could have written it the easy way: line up fifty to one hundred recipes and scatter some pictures throughout. But my goal was not just to give you an introduction to the food we do and make it possible for you to cook it yourself. I wanted to show you the creative process behind our work and the ideas that inform the fundamentals of our kitchen.

As I was thinking about this book, I realized that all our dishes are interconnected by the ideas behind them—the practical ideas, theoretical ideas, and technical ideas. The dishes themselves are the most superficial expression of our work. Rather than just list the ingredients and step-by-step methods for each dish, I felt it was more useful to actually articulate the concepts that underlie them.

To be honest, I rarely read cookbooks, though I love to buy them. I have shelves and shelves lined with colorful covers emblazoned with big chefs' names writing about everything from nose-to-tail cooking to German fine dining.

That said, I rarely have time to read them, and whenever I do grab one, I impatiently open it up, flip through a few pages, and then close it again. Maybe I'll pick it up later and take another peek. Admittedly, I never cook from others' recipes; I want to put my imprint on everything I do. I might be interested in how Fergus Henderson cooks trotters, but ultimately I will use his work as inspiration and find my own way of cooking them.

I want you to use the recipes in this book in the exact same way. Feel free to look up a dish and cook it exactly as it is written on the page. But I would be even happier if you plunged into this book just to see how we pickle mackerel, how we plate that dish with cauliflower, and then have a go at it yourself. I want you to grab this book, open it like a deck of cards, and flip to whatever attracts you. Once a dish has captured your attention, take a look at the handful of ideas listed at the bottom of the page; hopefully *that* sparks your curiosity and leads you to another spot in the book with another list of interconnected dishes and ideas. Each dish in this book is grounded on a set of ideas—and each idea is the basis for several other dishes, dishes you can then jump to and have a look at. Everything is connected in a sort of web in which one thing springs out of another in a big hot pot of inspiration, hard work, and craft. I want you to mix and match all these ideas and thoughts. Take what you can use, throw away what you don't like, and make it your own. That is what the cooking at Relæ is about, and I hope that that's what this book inspires you to do.

Chapter 1

The Groundwork
The Initial Idea

I had been sous chef at Noma for about two years when I dropped the bomb on René Redzepi. I wanted to quit so I could go out and open my own restaurant. Since I was basically running the kitchen, I knew it would take time to find the right person to replace me, so I was giving him about four months' notice. I knew it wouldn't be good for any of us if I kept my job at Noma while secretly nailing down a location, investor, and concept. But still, I dreaded telling him.

There was nothing to dread about René's reaction, though. As he had often done before and would continue to do after I left his restaurant, he surprised me. "You know what, I can't even get mad at you," he said. "I just know your restaurant will be great. I am looking forward to it. Good luck."

I felt the relief of someone who finally revealed his greatest secret. Believe me, Noma was a great restaurant to work in. I learned so much, but it just wasn't my project. My heart was not in it anymore, and my mind was heading somewhere else—somewhere I could create my own little universe. I wanted to influence not only the kitchen's organization, the cooking, and the menu, but everything else as well. I wanted to release myself from the world of fine dining—the huge staff, fancy linens, and long tasting menus. "Coming out of the closet" allowed me talk openly about my own

ideas for the future with everyone around me. René proved to be a great ambassador and soon began pushing journalists in my direction, saying, "You know, Christian is opening his own restaurant." I was pitching journalists from all over Europe before I even got a bank to finance me, found a potential investor, or had a location. This all helped me get closer to what I really wanted. As I talked about it again and again, I found myself gaining a better understanding of what my ideal restaurant would be.

My goal was to serve inventive, intelligent cuisine based on simple, high-quality ingredients. But I wanted to serve it in an environment that made guests feel welcome and relaxed. I couldn't understand why a creative kitchen should be a slave to a luxurious dining room and its oppressive style of service. As a young apprentice, I occasionally went to the fine dining restaurants that were considered the best in the country at the time. Believe me, I was impressed. I was *in awe*. But as I grew as a chef, going deeper and deeper into cooking itself, I realized I was losing interest in all the things surrounding the plate. I can pretty much take care of finding the toilet, at least the second time I go, and I prefer pouring my own water, thank you very much. It felt like everyone was putting an array of extraneous things on top my dining experience, not to mention increasing my bill. I didn't want those things and I sure didn't want to pay for them. I dine out to savor the food, the quality ingredients, the techniques—not the chandeliers or the plush towels neatly rolled up next to the bathroom sink.

It really started to bother me when I realized that I felt more comfortable in a bistro. While I still wanted to try the cuisine of fine dining, I grew tired of sitting for hours with waiters all over my back. In my own restaurant, I wanted to combine that feeling of sitting in a crowded restaurant filled with laughter and joy with the cuisine of the greatest kitchens. I wanted to cut to the bone, strip away everything but the most essential, and put all our effort into creating great food in a relaxed atmosphere.

Without really knowing how to get started, at least financially, I sought advice from a friend who connected me to Ulrik Mikkelsen. A slick businessman with a heart that beats for the restaurant industry, Ulrik had always wanted to open a café or a restaurant but had never found the right opportunity. Then I found out that my former colleague, Kim Rossen, had quit his job as assistant restaurant manager at Noma. Kim and I quickly found common ground. He was even more tired of fine dining than I was, and the idea of serving great food to guests in a small restaurant without all the fuss had him hooked within a few weeks. He soon joined our partnership.

I felt that the first and most important criterion for the restaurant's success would be total liberty. I needed us to be free from the financial constraints of investors, and the only way to do that was to be humble, to start off simple and small. We wanted to get away from the long tasting menu—not only because it's expensive, but also because I wanted guests to be able to experience great gastronomy in

less than two hours. We settled on a four-course menu, which allowed us to turn the tables twice and get the largest number of guests, especially on weekends. To keep prices down, we opted to make vegetables the unifying theme of the menu, and we also offered a vegetarian menu. It made total sense to me to have vegetables as our focus. Their great variety would make for an interesting base to work with, and on a personal level I wanted to eat that way myself—more veggies and less meat. And the meat I did want to eat must be of a higher quality. It's a philosophy that should make sense to most people in the Western world in the beginning of the 2010s.

We needed a small spot where we could seat about forty diners around an open kitchen, but finding such a spot was nearly impossible. The open kitchen was crucial for me: I wanted total control of the restaurant, even when I was in the kitchen, and I wanted to integrate the chefs into the service as much as possible. The problem was that no establishments with an open kitchen were ever for sale, and buying a place and remodeling it was financially out of reach for us. I dragged Ulrik, Kim, and my girlfriend, Cecilie, to numerous locations without even knowing how to pay the security deposit—a worn-out Chinese restaurant, a sushi place, and even a smelly old bodega were candidates. It all seemed a bit impossible, until one day when I went for a bike ride with Ulrik around the Jægersborggade neighborhood, close to my own apartment.

Jægersborggade, for non-Danish readers, is the most famous street in Copenhagen's multicultural Nørrebro district, previously best known for drug deals. I had heard that signs of gentrification were slowly starting to appear there, as creatives were taking over

small basements to live out their dreams. On our bike ride, we saw a woman putting up posters for a street party. She put us in contact with Jonas Steenstrup, who back then was in charge of coordinating the leases available on the street. My background with big-name restaurants like Noma and elBulli piqued his interest, and we got to see the biggest lease available, a corner spot that was all of 163 square meters.

At this point, my desperation to find a location was making me restless, and I saw potential in just about everything. Even this former bikers' club, with its stained yellow walls, brown tiled floor, and dilapidated pool table, had appeal. The place had to be completely redone, but I realized that even if the place looked like crap now, this was the opportunity to build the open kitchen that would be so crucial to our style of service.

There was only one problem: Jægersborggade was struggling to move on from its past as a drug-infested nest of criminals, and the dealers were selling hash on the doorsteps of our future restaurant. That specific corner had a strategic value for the dealers, serving as a lookout for spotting police and rival gangs from all directions. It was doubtful they would let their spot go.

It wasn't my job to take care of drug dealers, but I certainly didn't want to piss them off either. Most people around me suggested looking elsewhere, but whether I was being naive or just totally desperate, I was determined to make it happen.

Next came the agonizing planning phase. We must have made dozens of pencil drawings of possible layouts of the establishment to be. After all, 163 square meters is not a lot of space. The first priority was the open kitchen, then the forty seats that would make our business viable. We also wanted a few seats at the counter, so we could serve directly from the kitchen. We decided to make the heart of the kitchen a small deck oven; I wanted to live out my dream of baking fantastic bread from Day One. We positioned the kitchen so that it was the very first thing that you saw when you walked in the door, letting us chefs welcome the guests, seat them at the table, and eventually even bring them the bill. With Ulrik we approached the bank and they finally, after a lot of convincing, approved a minuscule credit of about 300,000 Danish kroner, or about 55,000 U.S. dollars. The initial start-up costs, deposits, and so on left us with very limited funds for the interior of the restaurant, and that was very much in line with our philosophy. Kim and I ransacked flea markets and secondhand sales for furniture, until we finally realized that the small, irregular room called for custom-made tables.

We chose an oak veneer for the tables, which was cheap and had a clean look, and made sure they measured 70 centimeters by 70 centimeters. We wanted there to be enough room so that the table would not feel as if it was crammed with plates; we preferred reducing the space between the tables rather than the size of the table itself. A crowded restaurant would give us a bustling ambience, while a crowded tabletop would just be uncomfortable.

At this point both Kim and I were without a job, and we focused on those details like engineers building the space shuttle. I remember bringing the carpenter's sample of the table to my apartment for the first of many "virtual restaurant" sessions. Was the table big enough? What if we used these glasses? How big will the plates be? I remember the numerous cookbooks we stacked high in order to simulate the perfect table height for the cheap stool we had bought. We were working full-time on every single detail.

During this period I attended an aunt's funeral in Norway with my mom, and we stayed at the house where my grandparents used to live, which was built in 1729. I was amazed by an old table that had a drawer in it. My mom explained that the traditional *Gudbrandsdal* flatbread was kept there, and the idea struck me to build drawers under the tables for our bread at Relæ. Maybe we could even put the cutlery in there! Kim and I eventually dismissed the idea of putting bread there, but we did want to make full use of the limited table space. What better way to do that than by putting the cutlery under the table?

Table 0

At Relæ, we have Table 0 instead of a classic chef's table, which, at fine dining restaurants, sets a tone of exclusivity, with its extra servings of caviar, more truffles, and older vintages of wine. Since our regular menu is only four courses, when we have colleagues or friends coming in, we often want to share more with them. We set aside this table near the kitchen for them to try the new dishes we are working on and give us feedback.

When we are working on a new dish, having to put it on the table for someone really pushes us to finalize it. I really like that pressure because it forces us to come up with new and often unexpected ideas, especially when we've overthought things.

We realized that regular guests might also enjoy Table 0, so we opened it up to the public so they could experience our creative process too.

When we seat our guests at the table, we immediately ask them if they want to start off with a snack and a glass of sparkling wine. As they get settled, we ask them to pull out their drawer to find their menu and napkin. Everyone smiles at this element of surprise and it help breaks the ice, so much so that it has become a crucial part of the meal at Relæ. We also let guests pour their own water and wine.

Our bare-bones style of service and cooking and their freedom from conventions resonated very clearly with our first two sommeliers, Ulf Ringius and Anders F. S. Hansen, both of whom were also former colleagues at Noma. They wanted to focus on all-natural wines—low-intervention wines with little or no added sulfites—made by lesser-known wine makers from sometimes unknown European wine regions. *Liberty* was our mantra, so we started off with a list consisting of only a handful of wines we would like to drink ourselves, not necessarily the wines our customers expected. I'll admit I didn't think a lot about pairing wine with food prior to opening, but those guys' talents proved that we needed to handle the wine with the same care and passion as we did the food. Pairing natural wines with our food became part of the culture of our restaurant, and we've even gone so far as to start our own wine import business so that we can bring in wines previously unavailable in Denmark, educate ourselves, and work more directly with wine makers.

Our cooks bring almost all the dishes out to the tables themselves, and I am so proud that the guests can receive their food from the people who make it. If a guest ever has a question about the food, we want someone there who knows the answer.

The restaurant was roaring from the very first day, with hype and good reviews filling up the place. It made me so happy to be somewhere I could smile and have fun, all while serving food that was prepared at a very high level. In the first few months, the drug dealers refused to move even an inch, but nobody seemed to really care. We got great feedback from our peers in the industry. Fellow chefs and former colleagues praised the fact that we served gourmet food in a place with the vibe of a local joint. It was satisfying to show that we could serve clever food with a paper napkin in a tiny restaurant with incredibly simple bathroom facilities. I felt we were anti-fine dining. And because a meal at Relæ was less than 50 U.S. dollars, we had a pretty young, mixed crowd.

Relæ has evolved a lot since our first days. After about three or four years, we sort of grew up. Rather than define ourselves by what we don't do, constantly reacting against the expectations of fine dining, now we focus on the things we *want* to do.

Relæ, which is Danish for "relay," was inspired by the electrical component and the idea of making a place dynamic and powerful, and the restaurant was indeed electric from the very first day. But the lesson I learned is that a restaurant is not ready-made prior to opening. No matter how much you dig into the details and polish your ideas, no matter how much time you prepare, the beauty of running a restaurant is in the daily work of improving your menu, your staff, your surroundings, and yourself. When we opened Relæ, it was not like building a bike from scratch or finishing the manuscript for a book. Once you send it in, you are not done. You can't just ride your bike into the sunset. We had only built the frame of the place where we would realize our dreams and do things exactly as we wanted. And once that frame was in place, *then* the real work could begin, work I enjoy as much today as I did the first moment Relæ opened its doors.

Jægersborggade

The center of Copenhagen is surrounded by a few artificial lakes originally made to protect the city. The areas around those lakes are today the most populated neighborhoods of Copenhagen, with Vesterbro and Nørrebro being the youngest and most vibrant. Toward the north of the city, Nørrebro is the most densely populated and ethnically mixed borough, and our street, Jægersborggade, is nestled at its very heart.

At one point, the popular and worn-out working-class neighborhood around this street had become the center of hash sales outside Christiania. Christiania used to be a sort of "free town" where the selling of hash was unofficially tolerated, making it a tourist attraction with an Amsterdam coffee shop feel. On Jægersborggade a gang of bikers had set up shop, and I remember it being a recurring venue during a period when I was a teenager and hanging with a crowd of dubious character.

At some point in the 2000s a few local initiatives started cleaning out the basements of Jægersborggade, which were evidently in the grasp of the drug dealers controlling the criminal business going on in the street. These were brought up to a decent standard and leased to whoever wanted cheap rent for their business. The rugged ambiance of the street attracted a few creative entrepreneurs to begin with, such as the soon-to-be-famous Coffee Collective and Elsgaard, maker of classic handmade shoes. As we started considering opening our restaurant on Jægersborggade, there were great expectations for the future of the street, but things had not yet reached a fever pitch. Many considered us to be complete lunatics to think of opening a restaurant there. At the time, there were no cafés or much traffic whatsoever, so their doubt was well-founded. Still, as I tried to get to know the local business holders, their energy was contagious and everyone was extremely excited about a restaurant opening up on their street. I would not have been welcomed like this if I were opening a restaurant in one of the city's revered addresses. In the city center I would have been one among many, but there was true support to be found in Jægersborggade.

Still, at the time a few rival gangs had been going at it on each other and the ambiance was very tense in Nørrebro. Then, a month prior to our opening, a famous Danish rapper, Niarn, and a policeman were shot just feet away from Relæ's future entrance. Luckily no one got killed, but it would not be the last shooting in the street. It's easy to imagine the amount of media attention the incident created in the Danish press, which loved to tell the tale of this outlaw street in Copenhagen. The Copenhageners are used to their city being peaceful and safe, but in 2010, gang wars, shootings, and drug dealing were all hitting the headlines. Our location was at the heart of it all: it was a strategic spot for gang members on the lookout for rival gangs and police. I was confident that when we opened, the restaurant traffic would push them away. It was just a question of time, I told myself. But apparently these guys didn't notice the frenetic building that had been happening on the site for months and months, or the waiters getting the dining room ready, or the chefs prepping, or, you guessed it, the customers once we finally opened our doors. I guess those guys weren't reading our newspaper reviews.

In those early days, there was a cut-up leather couch with its yellow insides sticking out, soaking in the rain for months and blocking the biggest window by the entrance of the restaurant. It turned the front of our establishment into a living room only lacking a TV set and four walls. Those guys hung out on the couch from ten in the morning until midnight, smoking hash. Sometimes it would just be one sleepy teenager laying there, at times it would be four face-tattooed guys, a few very blonde blondes, and a fighting pit bull or two. These guys were the first people we saw when we came to work and the last as we headed home for a bit of sleep. It was hard to ignore and my temper was really put to the test in those days. I just wanted to make a restaurant, how could that not just make sense to everybody? As a kid, my temper would make me throw chairs around the classroom or fight the teachers, but I knew that the last thing that would solve this would be violence or aggression. I was scared, and I basically had to ignore that there was a pending security issue. No one ever got hurt, but we got tons of menacing threats for random things, such as when a blogger took a picture of one of the guys and got the camera taken from her. It was scary stuff, but I somehow kept myself together and it all turned out all right.

Finally all the restaurant's media attention meant that the cops felt compelled to drag away that couch. In the meantime, the street grew at a frenetic rhythm. Just before we had opened Relæ, Inge Vincents and Julie Bonde opened their pottery shops, Thinware and Uh La La, and they would provide us with tableware for the restaurant. Cafés like the nonprofit Cafe Retro and the hipster spot Lyst opened more or less at the same time as we did, and soon we also had a bar, a porridge-only restaurant called Grød, a hairdresser/retro video game shop, a chocolate maker, a butcher, a cheesemonger, and a greengrocer. The street was in the media spotlight and young students were flocking to the apartments on the street. It wasn't that rents were skyrocketing—local housing regulations meant that prices have stayed pretty stable—there was just more demand coming from this new type of low-income city dweller drawn to what the street had to offer. A Saturday flea market and annual street parties filled up the streets with thousands and thousands of people through the summer, and the few hoodlums still hanging out on a corner here and there had lost everyone's attention. With all those young hipsters, I am sure their business was proportionally growing at the same time.

Soon, colleagues were asking me about available spots in Jægersborggade, wondering if I could hook them up, so to say. As we were grinding on at both Relæ and Manfreds cooking food for up to 250 people on the busiest days and hiring more than 30 people, we watched the street change right before our eyes. One day I had drug dealers in front of me, harassing me, and then suddenly I didn't, and a lot of that was because the media attention we generated also got the police's attention. We learned that economic development might start in the heart of a street, but it is realized far from its worn-out walkways: in the hands of journalists, bloggers, and of course, hipsters.

Staff

The staff at Relæ and Manfreds are the beating heart of the restaurants. We employ around thirty skilled personnel, including cooks, waiters, sommeliers, office staff, and dishwashers. The work we all perform is physically tough, mentally stressful, and not always that well paid. Still, I have managed to gather a team around me that I am perpetually thankful for and proud of.

You often hear chefs praising produce and other raw materials as the main ingredient in great gastronomy. But they are not; it is the people. Without the fast-moving hands prepping the food, the strong shoulders bringing out the trash, and the patient minds dealing with all my ideas and opinions, we would not be anywhere today.

I drew up Relæ around the idea that I would be able to do everything myself. I had left room for a bit of expanding, a few more chefs in the kitchen and someone to take care of accounting, but to begin with I was able to do everything from putting on the stocks to updating the home page and calling in the deliveries. Maybe curiosity or the will to be independent and to influence every single part of the restaurant made me very controlling. Soon I realized that the life of a chef-proprietor was not what I had expected. I was not only a chef but also a restaurateur, and my perfectionism had me wanting to decide the color of the sign in front of the restaurant as well as how long we would marinate the mackerel for the first course or whether we would dress three or four carrots per person on the second course. I realized that if I had thought that I was busy being a sous chef and taking care of a huge kitchen brigade at Noma, that was nothing compared to my new life. All the details had always mattered to me, and now I felt that they were all up to me to decide and perfect. Luckily my staff was motivated from the beginning. I had prepared them, letting them know this was our chance to do something great and that it would require an enormous amount of work from Day One. None of the guys starting up that first day ever let me down.

Soon my trust grew in my staff and their abilities. We started up with an unclear structure of who was in charge of what, but based on their personalities, the two cooks I had hired at the time, Kristian Baumann and Jonathan Tam, rose to take their own responsibilities. Kristian was in charge of ordering, organization, and staff, and John was more focused on the creative work of the kitchen, working on new dishes and new ideas. Kim Rossen was totally in control of the front of house, and the sommeliers were doing a great job pairing wine with the food. As the days grew shorter and more intense, we were all becoming a part of something

that looked successful, and the bond between us grew tighter as we worked shoulder to shoulder. Working for so many hours under so much pressure turned staff food into what is righteously called "family meal."

The meals for the staff are as crucial for us now, when we cater to about twenty people a day, as they were when we opened up with about a third of the current employees. As soon as the restaurant opened its doors and we went into a working frenzy, I knew that the staff meal would be what I would eat most often during the week. Without necessarily indulging in steaks and truffles daily, I want to eat well. It's essential to me.

Since we obtained our organic certification, all our family meals are now made of 100 percent organic vegetables and meat. True to my own mantra of eating less meat and more vegetables, we have made Thursday our weekly vegetarian day, which means we get to eat a nice roasted Sødam chicken on Saturdays, when we also always have dessert, a glass of wine, and a bit of cheer. We seat the first guests at 5:30 p.m., so the meal has to be done by 5 p.m.

Since I became a father and my girlfriend started bringing our son, Louis, along for the staff meal as often as she can, we expanded our break to 45 minutes rather than 30. That has created a great culture where we all find ourselves with time to wind down and relax. Other members of the staff with family living close by often bring their kids as well, and the ambiance is incredibly familiar. Nobody is allowed to work during that period, and

punctuality at the buffet line is as important as being on time for work. I am often asked what it's like to raise a kid while dealing with these working hours. I admit it isn't easy all the time, but I am also proud to offer Louis this rare opportunity to regularly have a meal with up to twenty people at the table. Because this is truly our family. We may not sit at the same table for the next fifteen or twenty years, but for however many years I get to hold on to my staff, I can enjoy sitting next to a handful of the trusted people with whom I share my business, my ideas, and my thoughts every day.

I also sit next to the young ones who are starting their apprenticeship, who hand us the responsibility of making them great workers and precise cooks and who I proudly get to see grow and develop. I also get to sit next to the guests of our kitchen, the stagiaires who come to work with us for a week, a month, or even longer. These guys travel the kitchens of the world to learn and be inspired, as I did myself. Stagiaires, as they quietly scrub carrots in a corner sink, observe everything going on around them. If you really want to know what is going on in a small culinary city such as Copenhagen, those are the guys to ask, because they pick up all the details, both the good and bad, as they roam the kitchens of a city. The stagiaires are also a great reminder of how small a world we live in. There is always someone saying "hi" from In De Wulf in Belgium or Mugaritz in Spain, as careers cross paths constantly. They are the "fresh blood" in our kitchen, and the brightest among them always bring something new to us. One guy had seen a great way to ferment leeks and another one had experimented with preserving unripe plums, a technique we could use with unripe strawberries we wanted to store for the winter. At times they bring a bit of their culture too, such as when Dennis made us extraordinary bulgogi, a spicy dish from his homeland Korea, or when Andrew, a native Texan, made us Southern-style ribs on a Saturday.

I never thought that the staff would be this important to me. But working with people is the most exciting part of my life. To cook based on values that have been handed down to you in a school or inspired by a mentor gives you great satisfaction. But being in a situation where I get to hand down some of my own values and experiences is my greatest responsibility and, as I now understand it, by far my greatest privilege.

Locavorism: When It Makes Sense, and When It Does Not

I am thankful to live in this moment of gastronomy. Worldwide, chefs seem to be returning to the roots of cooking— respecting produce, manipulating things less. Ancient techniques are being dusted off and reconsidered. And with that comes a new appreciation of place: locally rooted gastronomy is often what makes the difference between a restaurant in Madrid and one in Copenhagen.

For me, the best restaurants use the best possible ingredients in the most respectful way. Creativity is just a tool to exploit them to their maximum potential. Today, there's a greater understanding of how "eating local" influences quality, since shorter distances assure us freshness. There is no doubt that when a radish is pulled from the ground mere hours before it is served, its freshness, snap, and spice is far superior than the next week or even the next day. A carrot's sweetness, an asparagus stalk's juiciness, and a tomato's aroma will all fade with time; it's incredibly important to consider these factors when planning a menu.

Still, I do not feel that I'm a part of the New Nordic movement, as I don't adhere to a dogma of using only ingredients from Denmark or the surrounding Nordic region. I am an individual, and Relæ is a unique restaurant with its own identity. What I have in common with most chefs in the locavore movement is that my staff and I carefully study each ingredient that enters our door to confirm that the quality meets our standards. We consider many more factors than just proximity, and sometimes, it might be that a local ingredient just isn't high enough quality for us. Foods that are very sensitive to freshness, such as fish, shellfish, and many types of vegetables, obviously gain from zero mileage. However, I'm proud to source the less perishable pistachios from Bronte in Sicily and citrus from the Mediterranean.

Regardless of where our ingredients come from, we keep in close contact with our purveyors and collaborators. Having a human connection with people who understand our philosophy and share our values is what really ensures quality. For example, I already loved the fresh, unadulterated flavor of the Sicilian olive oil from Frantoi Cutrera (see page 60), and when I visited the mill and saw how much care they put into sorting the fruit before pressing, I knew this was a producer our restaurant would have a long relationship with.

I was born Italian, my mother is Norwegian, and I have lived in Italy, Denmark, Spain, and France. I am a child of the globalized world, and anyone who draws up national borders and geographical restrictions on people—or vegetables—always provokes me. The question of whether our cooking is locavore, Nordic, Italian, or French is the same as asking me whether I am Italian, Norwegian, or Danish. The answer is yes to all of them. The point is, my mixed background, not the color of my passport, is what defines me as a person and a cook.

That's why it makes perfect sense to me to use imported citrus and olive oil in our cooking as well as locally sourced, newly dug carrots and potatoes. I see nothing wrong with adding a salted anchovy from Spain to slices of raw Danish beef, or mixing the bitter notes of dried black olives from Sicily with the tang and acidity of local buttermilk. Considering my upbringing, the urban setting of the restaurant, the mixed ethnicity of our staff, and our international inspirations, trying to cook strictly locally would be too simplistic. Not adhering to any dogma also forces us to stay awake and keep questioning everything we do and why we do it. That is what creates Relæ's identity.

Organic: Is a Certification All That?

Halfway through 2011, I decided that we were ready for a new challenge—or as members of my staff would put it, to make our lives more complicated—by obtaining organic certification for the restaurant.

In my personal life, I started consciously buying only organic when I started a family. Becoming a father made it more of a priority to preserve the environment for the next generation, and I wanted to protect my child from pesticides and the industrial food system as much as I could. Eventually that philosophy crept into my professional kitchen too. I wanted us to make all the right choices and I wanted our guests to know about it, not by our telling them stories but by our showing them actual proof. I wanted to not just use a lot of organic produce, I wanted our restaurant to be certified organic. The certification seemed like the clearest, least ambiguous way to signal to guests that we were making a real effort to serve them ingredients we were proud of.

In Denmark, foods that earn the iconic red Ø label have been produced, processed, or packaged following regulations that are sometimes stricter than European Union organic rules. As of 2007, Denmark had more than 2,500 certified organic farms, all of which are regularly inspected to make sure they follow rules around issues like animal welfare and pesticide use. As a food-service business, to be certified organic at the highest level means you use 90 to 100 percent organic ingredients. This meant that all the produce we would buy would have to be followed by documentation that it was certified organic, and we would need to have the certification of any producer we sourced from readily available for any routine check. Every three months, we would have to submit our own calculations on the amount of produce and food products we had acquired, and which were organic and which were not, including drinks, wine, and even staff food. The logistics behind this are, to say the least, very complicated.

I still abide by the idea that most important step toward cooking great food is to be able to choose the produce you find to be the best.

But even though we live in a time when chefs forage for carrots in a quest to move fundamentally closer to nature and agriculture, a chef is still an expert on cooking and a farmer an expert on farming. Even though I have been interested in organic farming for years, I've had only a glimpse at the load of decisions and compromises a farmer is forced to make through the year. A farmer must make those decisions while somehow balancing sustainability, quality, and economy in the same way that a chef must make similar decisions when running a restaurant.

Regardless of a farmer's good intentions and whether or not I know his first name, sometimes as a chef and as a consumer I need a guarantee that what I put on a plate is, to at least some extent, sustainable and ethical, and a certification helps me in that sense. Even though the organic regulations are criticized by both extremes in agriculture, with the industrialized side seeing it as too expensive and the idealist, beyond-organic side seeing it as too watered-down, there's no doubt that getting organic certification is still an easily understandable—and recognizable—stance for us to take.

That said, after we made the decision to go completely organic, we encountered problems. One of the most famous farmers in Denmark who grows the tastiest asparagus in the country was not certified and had no plans to get a certification. If we chose to go all the way on this, we would probably miss out on asparagus season, because it is close to impossible to source organic asparagus in Denmark. Our long-lasting friendship and collaboration with the Coffee Collective down the street would also be put at risk, because they didn't work with any organic certified coffee growers at the time. Apart from chicken and lamb, finding organic meat such as pork and grass-fed beef was quite difficult. I spent a lot of time on the phone in those months, trying to figure out what we would actually lose out on and what we would gain. The more I learned from questioning the practices of nonorganic producers, the more I was determined that certification was a necessary step for us to take.

Ultimately, going organic focused our cooking even further, making it more simple and direct. The white asparagus went off the menu, and we are still looking for an alternative, but until then, we will just enjoy all the other bountiful vegetables in spring. The Coffee Collective ended up going through the same agonizing and bureaucratic process as we did to achieve an organic importing license and found a fantastic organic Ethiopian coffee farmer for us.

After months and months of bureaucracy, we received our organic certification in the spring of 2013. Today I see it as one of my proudest moments. We chose overall ingredient quality over having the bragging rights of serving exotic cuts of veal, pig's head, or lamb tails. We were pulled through a process of questioning every single thing on our shelves, welcoming new and passionate producers that share our philosophy and saying good-bye to others that no longer live up to our standards. We started our own wine import business (see page 21) so that we can assure the same standards in the glass as on the plate. We have also had to become extremely organized to keep up with sourcing our ingredients from more than thirty-five suppliers. But all this has been worth it, as every single plate we dress, we can dress even more proudly than before.

Breaking Bread: The Cornerstone of an Ideal Meal

"We say that the bread should speak English—*sjoop, sjoop, sjoop,*" the French baker told me, mimicking the sound that dough slowly kneading in the machine makes when you add more water. I'm not sure *sjoop* qualifies as an English sound, but apart from that, I take everything this baker says seriously. I first met Alex Croquet during an event called Extravaganza Mediterranea in a hotel in Ravello, on Italy's Amalfi coast. Alex was there to make his incredible bread, and I was there to do a dinner on behalf of Noma. I was lucky that I speak reasonable French, because as you can tell, Alex couldn't speak a word of English. At the welcome dinner for the event, I was seated at the same table as this charismatic and passionate baker, who hails from Wattignies, Normandy. That conversation didn't really require much more French than the occasional nod because Alex was speed talking about his passion and his craft for the entire night. I just tried to keep up with the vast amount of information he threw at me.

I asked to see him mix his dough later that night, which is when I got the "*sjoop*" lesson. "Nothing but water, flour, and a pinch of salt," he told me. Alex uses only natural levain in his breads—instead of using commercial yeast he makes his own sourdough starter by harnessing wild yeasts that occur in the air, which allows his bread to develop much greater depth of flavor—and he kneads the dough slowly. When his breads come out of the oven the following day, his loaves are intensely flavored, almost bitter, with an open crumb and thin crust. When I first tasted his bread, back in 2008, it was a revelation. The simplicity of it—working with just three ingredients—was incredibly appealing. He relied on craft, sensibility, and experience to make his final product great.

Though our interaction was limited to that dinner discussion and little more, Alex has probably had the greatest impact on how I cook and, obviously, bake. At the time, I was not very involved in baking bread, but as soon as I quit Noma I understood that my own restaurant should celebrate this simple yet essential part of a meal. I liked the idea that once you reduced something to just flour, water, and salt, there would be no limit to how good a bread could be. Even if you source the most expensive flour you can find, bread will still not be a luxurious and expensive item on the menu. The luxury lies in the craft and technique you put into it. Yet the bread conveys a message to the diner. It can show how much care we put into the basics. I wanted to bake hearty rustic loaves that we would break in two by hand to reveal the perfect crumb. The bread had to be fantastic, because it would be the only item that everyone would taste. It would be the backbone of our menu.

When I stopped working at Noma, I immediately started baking bread at home using a small batch of sourdough starter (also known as levain) that a German friend had given me. I indeed had time on my hands, as it would be one and a half years until the restaurant opened. I was determined to make my own bread, so I started mixing up my own recipes based on my research and avidly fed the starter daily. I bought a ceramic baking stone to put in my small home oven, which I would crank up to its absolute max. I watched as my oven puffed out black smoke for long periods of time. I added only minimal amounts of commercial yeast to my dough and kneaded everything by hand. The process was fun but the bread was horrible: dense, thick-crusted, and way too sour. Yet I was relentless and kept trying to improve it. Maybe I wasn't kneading it enough, maybe it should have proofed longer, maybe the flour was not good. I had baskets to proof the bread in and I sometimes punched the wall in anger when the dough stuck to the basket, scaring my girlfriend and worrying the neighbors.

This was all before Relæ ever opened. Because construction on the main restaurant was delayed, we decided to open a small eatery across the street. We called it Manfreds and sold organic, vegetable-focused, rustic takeaway food. It eventually morphed into Manfreds og Vin, Relæ's noisy younger brother and soul mate. Manfreds was a venue for me to conduct my bread trials and experiments on a slightly bigger scale, this time with a kneading machine and a proper oven. The bread got lighter and improved a lot with each trial. I found a routine of kneading the dough the day before and keeping it cool until I was ready to bake it the following day. Still, it was not consistent, and I did not have the knowledge or experience to counteract the fluctuations in weather and climate. But I did my best, and the bread was tasty.

When Relæ finally opened, I was pretty satisfied with the results of my baking endeavors. We served the bread I baked, and the customers praised it as it was served, simply ripped in two with olive oil on the side. But I knew there were ways of improving it. At this point, the starter I was using was quite dry and sour since I was feeding it only once a day, which made a very rustic bread that was high in acidity. Sometimes it completely overproofed, making it flat and dense.

Alex had told me how he believed that tap water needed to be "revitalized" before being added to flour in order to contribute to a

dough's fermentation. Basically, the idea was that chemical remnants in tap water can arrest bacterial fermentation, preventing the bread from rising properly. He had built a complex system in which he would pump the water through a sort of fountain made of natural stone, making it, as he called it, "active," again, by removing some of those chemicals. Bread dough can be made from equal parts water and flour, and since I was making bread using Alex's "water, flour, salt—and nothing else" model, I wondered if sourcing the water might be as important as sourcing the flour. I hoped that the water filtration system the Coffee Collective had suggested we use for our coffee (see page 52) might help our bread too.

When it came to the flour, we decided on Per Grupe's wonderful Ølandshvede, or Øland wheat, after being introduced to it by Nicolai Holle of the acclaimed Meyers Bakery down the street. We opted for a mix of finer-ground wheat, stone-ground wheat, whole-grain wheat, and the Ølandshvede in varying ratios. We loved the flavor from this combination of flours, but the dough still had structural issues—it became so slack that it would occasionally fall apart completely. Luckily we had a young baker, Karen Man, staging with us (completing a short internship, in restaurant speak). Now the pastry chef at Oxheart in Houston, Texas, she introduced us to the practice of folding the bread throughout the bulk fermentation, which strengthened the gluten. The effects were immediate; the crumb became lighter and airier and we were able to use the flour mix we wanted. She also suggested using less starter, which reduced the amount of fermentation, lightened up the gluten structure, and reduced the acidity slightly.

One day an American baker named Chad Robertson came to eat at Relæ. He had booked the table online, and even after I had looked him up, I honestly wasn't too sure who the guy was. As he commented on the bread we were serving him, we started chatting and it turned out that he and chef Nick Balla were on a trip researching everything from Hungarian pickles to Nordic varieties of wheat and rye for their San Francisco restaurant Bar Tartine as well as Chad's Tartine Bakery. Just chatting a bit in between the dishes, we immediately clicked, and I mentioned that I was satisfied with our bread though I knew it could be so much better. Our chatting led to a few emails about bread and fermentation, and after he kindly sent me his cookbook *Tartine Bread*, we adopted some of his techniques to improve our bread. He returned to Copenhagen several more times, and I also had the opportunity to cook a meal at Bar Tartine and spend time with him and his team, sealing our friendship. Talking with Chad pushed our bread another step further; it was great to bounce ideas off someone with so much more experience. Most important, his technique of cautiously folding the bread throughout the bulk fermentation helped us strengthen our dough considerably.

I still made the bread daily at Relæ, baking the buns for the restaurant and the loaves for Manfreds in our small but effective hearth oven. That was until the oven, which we had imported specially from Germany to fit the small kitchen, broke down and left me desperate. Luckily our baker friends at Meyers left their bakery in the early afternoon and let us use it until we opened at about 5 p.m. As if Jægersborggade wasn't colorful enough, for a few months you would see a line of stagiaires, dishwashers, and whoever had an available hand follow me down the street, each of us carrying a tub of fermented dough. I would enjoy my Zen moment alone in the quiet bakery, shaping and baking dough just as the restaurant was reaching its peak of preopening frenzy. Eventually we expanded Manfreds, making it a sit-down restaurant and not just a takeaway spot, and we made space there for a proper baking oven. Now our cooks have to run around with bread only in the short distance between Relæ and Manfreds. As both Relæ and Manfreds grew, it was time to hire a dedicated bread baker. Carol Choi has taken our bread making a step further; her sensitivity toward the dough and our daily discussions about its state and well-being give me almost as much satisfaction as if I were putting my own hands in it every day. Since we stopped adding yeast a few years ago, monitoring the bread and its actual fermentation is essential. My work with charcuterie—in which you measure the pH value to monitor the fermentation process—gave me the idea to do the same thing with the bread. We eventually found that the initial bulk fermentation done at room temperature improved if it reached about 4.7 pH before being cooled, and that baking it as it reaches

about 3.9 to 4.0 pH after about 24 hours at refrigerator temperature gives the most open crumb and complex flavor. Omitting commercial yeast also made a huge difference in flavor. As Alex, the French bread savant, said at that dinner in Ravello when I first met him, "If you add [commercial] yeast to a dough, it is like inviting someone extremely rude and loud to your table. You miss out on all the other voices and can only hear its monotonous speech."

Ultimately our bread—the simplest dish on our menu, with just three ingredients—is the most essential. It is the dish that requires the most attention, and even gets a full chapter in this book. It is what brings me the most pleasure day in and day out.

Chapter 2

Ideas on a Plate

The essays in this chapter cover a wide range of subjects—including ingredients, practical ideas and techniques, and the theories and philosophy that inform our cooking every day at Relæ. I've grouped these essays into categories—such as "Liquids," "Animal," and "Inspirations"—which I hope will help readers understand my thought process that much better. Each of these categories corresponds to a colored tab on the right-hand side of the book.

Many of the essays in this chapter focus on my favorite products and producers, especially the ones we use in innovative ways. While our pantry is lined with seaweed from Iceland (page 110), olive oil from Sicily (page 59), anchovies from northern Spain (page 108), and Danish pear vinegar (page 58), we also find inspiration in things as simple as water (page 52).

Other essays in this chapter dissect the techniques I use to manipulate the produce we bring into the restaurant, whether it's vacuum-sealing cabbage for a quicker yet more consistent choucroute (pages 148–49) or just barely cooking slices of asparagus in butter emulsion to achieve a tender texture while maintaining the vegetable's essential flavor (pages 120–21).

When we develop new dishes at Relæ, our inspirations are almost subconscious, even though we consciously create each dish. Many of the essays in this chapter examine the underlying principles and inspirations—be they geographic, seasonal, or experiential—that guide my cooking. As a chef, an immigrant, and a traveler, I find inspiration in equal measures from around the world and just down the street.

Ideas
Liquids

Water
Wine
Fruit Vinegars
Extra-Virgin Olive Oil

Water

Look at every dish on the Relæ menu—really, on any restaurant menu—and you'll find that there's only one ingredient that they all have in common: water. Of course, most chefs don't think of water as a fundamental building block. Some don't think about it at all. But luckily for us at Relæ, one of the first alliances we made on Jægersborggade was with the young and vibrant team of the Coffee Collective—the best coffee roasters in Copenhagen, some say the world. Their geeky, uncompromising approach to their craft clicked with us, and they showed us how precise the work of a barista needs to be. But perhaps more important, they taught us the importance of selecting the highest-quality products, and for them, water was the most essential.

The Coffee Collective has an ambitious policy of offering coffee farmers much higher prices than even a fair-trade standard would dictate, in return for the highest-quality beans. That allows them to roast at lower temperatures and with lighter profiles. Their signature is all about letting the raw material shine through, whether its characteristics tend to fruity acidity or complex caramel notes.

But the most important raw material at their disposal isn't green beans from Kenya or Ethiopia—it's the water they ultimately infuse everything with. A cup of coffee is 99 percent water, so it's quite easy to imagine how big an impact good water, or conversely, low-quality water, can have on the final cup.

The Chicken Stock Test

Here is a simple way to measure the quality of two different waters: Make two batches of chicken stock with 1 kilogram chicken wings in 4 liters water, using tap water in one batch and filtered water in another. Simmer both batches for about 4 hours and strain through a fine-mesh strainer. You should already be able to taste the difference in purity, but this becomes even more pronounced if you then reduce each liquid by half. After tasting the end result, you'll never go back to tap water.

After understanding their philosophy and learning how to pull off the simple French press brew we'd decided on for the restaurant, my brain, which consists of 75 percent water by the way, was 100 percent certain that we needed the same approach in the kitchen. If these pristine coffees are worthless after infusing them for four minutes in subpar water, what was there to say about our stocks, which cook for four, six, eight hours and reduce to one-tenth of the original amount?

With coffee, calcium and chlorine residues can coat the mouth and completely obscure top notes, acidity, and freshness. It doesn't take a degree in chemistry to figure out that when reducing a stock, the same thing happens as the water evaporates, making it even tougher for all the flavors and aromas to come through.

After that game-changing realization, preparing stocks and marinades, blanching vegetables, and making infusions would never be the same. It's a paradox in high-end restaurants that we spend fortunes on salt crystals flown in from all over the world, which all consist of basically 99.9 percent sodium chloride and a few impurities, but we don't question what is flowing in through the taps, which make up 80 percent of the soup or bouillon on the menu. After a few demystifying tests (see "The Chicken Stock Test," at left), we managed to order the same water-filtering system as our coffee-savant friends, and it has thoroughly altered our kitchen. After all, what's the point of sourcing the greatest chicken for stock or the freshest green herbs for an infusion if you don't have worthy water to cook them in?

All dishes (pp.230–363)

Wine

We all know that the tannins, alcohol, and acidity of a carefully selected, complementary wine can turn a great meal into a fantastic meal. But as a cook, there's more to it than that, because studying wines, attending tastings, and trying to understand the complexity in the glass makes you better at what you do. The training you get by using your palate to venture blindfolded down a path where your eyes won't guide you is incredibly useful when you later have to season a sauce or a soup.

Using wine as an ingredient is to me the clearest representation of classic French cooking, well, next to adding butter in copious amounts. At Relæ and Manfreds, our cooking is often defined by its acidity, and our use of Reduced Wine (below) plays an important part in creating that perception. It's just that the way we use wine is not exactly in line with classic French techniques.

So many basic and classic sauces, braises, and other preparations call for the same flavor-enhancing first steps: sauté onions and maybe carrots and garlic, add wine, and reduce. Alcohol is crucial in braising as it completes the process of enhancing the meat's flavors and umami. A beef bourguignon wouldn't be the same without red wine, and a Piemontese *brasato* would be nothing without Barolo.

This is one of the first lessons you learn in cooking, or at least it was for me. But it wasn't until my days as sous chef at Noma that I learned

---

Reduced Wine

At the restaurant, we reduce liters and liters of white wine every week and keep it in squeeze bottles. In this case, the *mise en place* is quite easily transferred to the home kitchen. Whenever a dinner at home leaves me with some leftover wine in a bottle, I just pour it into a pot and leave it to reduce to one-quarter of the volume while I am doing the dishes. A small amount like that will be ready in only a few minutes, and after it is reduced, I just store it in a Mason jar in the fridge so I always have a bit of acidity *en place*. Use a dry red or white wine. Don't use a wine with residual sugars, such as an off-dry Riesling, as it will make the reduction far too sweet and unbalanced. For the same reason, be careful not to over-reduce the wine, as caramelization can be very disturbing flavorwise, giving the final dish an unwanted sweet note. The wine just needs to be cooked until the alcohol is gone, so the acidity is pointed and clear.

to deconstruct that method and make it slightly more flexible and multipurpose. If you just reduce the wine on its own, let the alcohol evaporate, and bring it down to about one-eighth of the original volume, you can comfortably add it as the very last thing to correct the acidity of a sauce or a stew. That way, you avoid having to estimate the exact amount of wine needed when you start out. The carrots you add to your beef bourguignon today might be sweeter than usual or the actual wine might be less acidic. Since the wine's alcohol needs to be cooked out first and you can't just compensate by adding more of it raw somewhere halfway through cooking, having it precooked and reduced makes it readily available for a crucial final touch.

Now, in the cases of stews like beef bourguignon or *brasato*, where the wine is actively a part of the cooking process, I wouldn't leave it out, but the vast majority of our meat sauces, on the other hand, are cooked in plain filtered water and then mixed with the right proportions of reduced wine before service. Reduced wine goes into the sauce in our *Pork from Hindsholm and Rye* (page 322) and in a fennel puree accompanying the *Fennel, Smoked Almond, and Parsley* (page 312).

Fruit Vinegars

Fruit vinegar is a staple of our kitchen pantry. Luckily we have a local vinegar expert in Andreas Harder, from the company Nordhavn Eddikebryggeri. Andreas has an Italian background very similar to mine, and his passion for Italian traditions launched him on a quest to make vinegars with local Danish apples but prepared in the traditional Italian *aceto balsamico* way. The result is one of the most complex and fascinating vinegars I've tasted, with some batches aging for more than 10 years.

After years of work, Andreas has moved out of a garagelike workshop and set himself up in a more professional facility. His portfolio has expanded into many other vinegars, such as black currant, cherry, and rose hip.

Our absolute favorite, and Andreas's biggest contribution to our cuisine, is pear vinegar. Somehow it is made for what we do, as its mature natural sweetness is in perfect balance with its acidity. It really sparks and supports any sauce, vinaigrette, or other preparation with inherently fruity qualities. The darker and more intense cherry and black currant vinegars are also very useful, especially during the colder winter months, when we work with deeper-flavored dishes such as braises or roasted red beets.

Extra-Virgin Olive Oil

One of the things I looked forward to most when I opened Relæ was getting away from the whipped and flavored butter that was being served along with bread in just about every other high-end restaurant in Copenhagen. I wanted to go back to the grassy, green extra-virgin olive oil of Italy, where my father and I were born. For me, having olive oil on the table serves as a simple answer to the recurring question, "Is this a Nordic restaurant?"

Besides serving it with our bread, our olive oil plays a significant role in many of our dishes, cold and warm, savory and sweet. Its pungency almost seems to cleanse your mouth, which is why I think our olive oil is well suited to serve throughout the meal. It doesn't coat the tongue as much as animal fat does, and it can reawaken the palate between dishes. Along with our bread, it is probably the flavor our diners are most often exposed to, so we had to choose an olive oil of sky-high quality.

The symbolic value of importing an oil directly from Sicily meant a great deal to me, and the research process was part of my personal rediscovery of the great food products of the Mediterranean island. One of my favorite olive oils is made from a local Sicilian variety, Tonda Iblea, whose

---

Storing Extra-Virgin Olive Oil

Olive oil is quite sensitive to light and warm temperatures, so you need to consider storage. All serious producers send out their oil either in metal cans or very dark glass to keep light away, which turns the oil rancid. In the restaurants, we store the bigger batches of oil in the wine room at a controlled temperature of about 16°C (60°F); the oil solidifies at temperatures not much colder than that. In the kitchen at Relæ, we keep it in squeeze bottles wrapped in aluminum foil, so that we have only the amount we will use up entirely during service. At Manfreds, which serves more diners, we keep it in larger bottles with a cooling element (like what you would use to chill wine) around them. The kitchen can get insanely hot there, and the oil will deteriorate in a half hour without those precautions.

In the home kitchen, the last thing you want to do is to keep oil next to the stove, where the heat will hit it daily. Store it in the fridge, or if you are too impatient to wait for it to liquefy at every use, store a small amount wherever you store your wine, in a cool and dark place.

main characteristics include green tomato, grass, and artichoke aromas. The olives are cultivated in the Monti Iblei, a mountain range in the south-central part of the island.

When producers of a high-quality oil came to visit us for the first time at Relæ, they cautiously suggested that they serve the oil with a much "whiter" bread than ours, that is, one with less flavor, at tastings. It's true that the olive oil we serve has such amazing qualities that it can stand on its own, but I believe that its firm and fruity backbone is exactly what makes it such a great partner to our hearty, naturally leavened breads.

Earlier, when I went to visit the Frantoi Cutrera mill, located in the beautiful hills behind the town of Chiaramonte Gulfi, the reasons for the high quality of their oil became clear. It was right before harvest, and stressed workers were jetting around the brand-new, state-of-the-art equipment, which really put my romantic ideas of a good old Sicilian grandpa operating the stone mill to rest. The mill's insistence on the laborious work of sorting away leaves, branches, and overmature or damaged fruit shows in the quality of the oil, which has a green freshness rarely experienced elsewhere, combined with a peppery spice. Often diners who are used to lower-quality, more commercially available brands find it hard to believe that we haven't mixed something else in the oil. "Herbs or basil?" they ask, when tasting it.

I believe olive oil of this quality is one of the truly great man-made wonders, but it is not suited for cooking at all—let me repeat, at all. In fact, I believe that olive oil's reputation suffers a bit because both consumers and producers consider it a cooking oil, a purpose for which I believe there are far superior oils. I think it's a shame to use something of this quality and price for cooking, which destroys its complexity and freshness. The closest I get to cooking with our oil is when I add it to a sauce in the very last second, toss a cooked vegetable in it, or let it hit a warm plate before serving. It isn't very easy to work with since its character at times can take over a dish as easily as it can lift its flavor, aroma, and acidity to a higher level. But when used well, in a small dose and carefully treated, it amplifies flavors, as we see in *White Asparagus and Anchovies* (page 272) or in the *Pickled Skate, Mussels, and Celery Root* (page 274).

Even though it carries a defined bitterness of its own, olive oil has an ability to mellow out other bitter ingredients, allowing improbable harmonies. It also lifts fruity and sweeter flavors, nudging them in a savory direction, almost like salt. We once did a great dessert consisting of a light parfait of our bread sprinkled with olive oil and crispy freeze-dried black currants. The fruitiness from the berries and olive oil really connected and created a zesty contrast to the mellow parfait.

Ideas
Animal

Lamb
Fat
Chicken
Hindsholm Pork
Butter
Buttermilk

Lamb

Our approach to sourcing great organic and beyond-organic products brings us out to almost every part of Denmark. Henriette Guld and her family rear lambs in Havervadgård in the farthest southwest corner of the country, very close to the German border, where the animals freely roam and graze the Danish West Coast. The salty winds and tides give their meat an incomparable iodine savoriness, with qualities similar to what the French call *pré-salé* lamb, making them without a doubt my favorite lamb.

We braise, poach, and roast the lamb, we serve it completely raw, and we make use of its roasted fats to season vegetables and as a garnish. In *Lamb, Shrimp, and Dill* (page 270) we serve the meat raw and seasoned with powdered dried fjord shrimp and some of the roasted lamb fat for a "cooked" flavor, while in *Lamb, Turnip, and Samphire* (page 324) we cook various cuts before serving them with juicy turnips and samphire, the coastal plant that echoes their mineral flavor.

The small, tender animals, which rarely reach much more than six months of life, don't usually need extensive cooking; even cuts like shoulder, neck, and legs are easily cooked sous vide in a few hours. I want our lamb pink and juicy, so we keep to low temperatures, which gives us time to tenderize the less lean parts of the leg.

How We Cook Lamb

Shoulder: Cook sous vide at 58°C (136°F) for 5 hours, then sauté in pan and glaze with sauce.

Shanks: Brine for a minimum of 24 hours in 3% Salt Brine (page 438), then braise traditionally in pots.

Legs: Cook sous vide at 58°C (136°F) for 3 to 4 hours, depending on the size.

Rump: Pan roast, fat side down. My favorite piece.

Loin and neck: Debone and cook sous vide at 58°C (136°F) for 1½ hours, fat on, then roast fat side down in the pan until caramelized and crispy.

Breast: Brine for 24 hours in a 7% Salt Brine (page 438), rinse, and cook sous vide for another 24 hours at 63°C (145°F). Brown in the pan before serving.

Offal: Most often, brine and turn into terrines and pâtés for Manfreds.

We normally receive about four lambs a week fresh from slaughter, dry-age them for about 7 days or so, and then break them down. We usually group the smaller cuts, such as the shanks, and then braise them for the Manfreds menu, and save the more prized breast for diners at Relæ, or spread out the remaining cuts in small amounts for dishes like the *Lamb, Turnip, and Samphire* (page 324).

Lamb, Shrimp, and Dill (p.270)
Lamb, Turnip, and Samphire (p.324)

Fat

Nutritionists have reportedly started to doubt whether animal fats deserve their status as evil villain of the human diet and greatest cause for cardiovascular and cholesterol-related diseases. I, on the other hand, have never doubted them and have always seen them as an eternal wellspring of flavor, texture, and aroma. Of course, it is unhealthful to indulge in saturated fats immoderately, but I always point to the French paradox. I consider life to be a means to enjoy as much great food as possible.

With our focus on vegetables, animal fat has a great role to play in the balancing act between flavor and lightness. It transmits flavor much more clearly than the meat does on its own, and since we tend to add more vegetables than meat to a plate at Relæ, the fats—roasted, rendered, or crispy—have a lot to contribute.

Our approach to animal welfare, organics, and quality products assures us that the animals we work with are pastured and have their own "healthful" and natural diet. We avoid grain-fed beef and pork and any livestock practices that try to push for faster growth, which inevitably reduces the development of essential omega-3 and omega-6 fatty acids. Pastured, grass-fed beef is ultimately a better source of fat for us, and the most simple and meaningful diet advice I can give is to eat healthfully by eating healthy animals.

A lot of people very wrongly consider tenderness to be the ultimate criterion for good meat, whereas I believe all the secrets are kept in the fat. When we first started to work with the incredibly high-quality

Hindsholm pork, I was struck by how clear the difference was from other organic pork. The Hindsholm pig's slower growth and older age meant its fat is much firmer to the touch, is pearly white, and has seemingly lower water content. When rendered, it turns into liquid fat almost immediately, whereas others bubble and foam for a long period of time before the water evaporates. Fat, very much like offal, is the best way to judge the true nature of an animal. If the fat tastes great, you can feel safe and appreciate what you are eating even more.

Chicken

On our very first menu, chicken was the main course. I had bumped into the producers of Sødam chicken during my research prior to opening the restaurant, and their beyond-organic approach had me convinced that their product needed to be displayed in our restaurant from the very first day. Putting the spotlight on Sødam chicken on our first menu and preparing it with the respect it deserved was a way to sum up our philosophy in one single dish. Because from the very beginning, I wanted Relæ to offer humble ingredients of high quality rather than an exclusive cut from an intensively reared animal.

For our very first meat course, we poached the thighs and breast so that they were only *just* cooked and served them with fava beans in a deep green lovage sauce. For an acidic touch, we added a few tart gooseberries on top, together with the chicken hearts cooked for just minutes. We even gathered all the excess skin, poached it, cooled it down while stacked under a heavy object to form a square, and then cut and baked it into crispy flakes we used to top the dish.

We wanted the dish to challenge the status quo, since chicken had become such a standardized commodity. When I was first researching fowl for the restaurant, I was disgusted by the quality of what was available. Somehow I am very picky about chicken, even more so than beef or lamb. The industrial chicken-rearing process is so intense and unnaturally sped up that most chickens are alive for only thirty-five days before slaughter.

Sødam chickens are always raised to at least seventy-five days old and can be up to four months old at slaughter. They spend plenty of time out and about, which means they actually have the chance to *move*, which adds flavor and structure to the meat. To avoid having to send their chicks to Germany for slaughter, which is often the case in Denmark, the Sødam company built its own slaughterhouse just a short drive from the coops. Once plucked, they air-chill the chickens rather than soaking them in water (the latter, which is the norm, causes the chickens to suck up moisture and makes the skin wet and tricky to get crispy). The air-drying keeps the skin natural, and roasting it brings out more flavor, as caramelization starts earlier.

The muscular legs and the wings are my favorite parts, as I've never been a big fan of chicken breast. When we served the mix of different cuts for that first dish, the structure of the wing and thigh meat surprised our guests, as so many are used to chicken being uniformly textured and bland. One of our favorite preparations is to poach the wings, remove the meat, and combine it with anchovies and thinly sliced white asparagus, as we do in *Chicken Wings, White Asparagus, and Anchovies* (page 328). Or we just serve the chicken wing meat hiding under a layer of slightly salted slices of zucchini and pickled zucchini flower.

The quality of the Sødam chickens and other well-produced chickens really puts a perspective on the brine-pumped industrial chickens that fill up supermarket aisles. During the first few months Relæ was open, one of the chefs ordered regular chicken breast for staff meals and I just couldn't make myself eat it. I couldn't live with us serving the best quality for our guests and going against everything I believed in when it came to our own dinner. To be reasonable about the pricing of our staff meals, I decided that we would have at least one vegetarian meal a week, which enabled us to pay for the organic Sødam chicken and made us all appreciate those days when we had a small portion of great chicken that much more. Somehow, Sødam chickens made us occasional vegetarians.

Chicken Wings, White Asparagus, and Anchovies (p.328)

Hindsholm Pork

On a sunny Sunday in June, we had the picnic of a lifetime when twenty of us—our cooks, waiters, sommeliers, and families—visited Poul and Carla of Hindsholm Pork, located on the island of Funen, about a 2-hour drive from the restaurant. We came to see what their pigs were all about and to spend the day together. As we strolled around the ranch, with its background of vast green fields and view of the Zealand coastline across the water, it wasn't difficult to imagine what the difference would be between conventionally reared specimens and the ones oinking on with their lives right there in front of us.

The first time we had roasted a piece of Hindsholm pork at Relæ, our already high expectations turned into sheer excitement. The pink flesh was speckled with firm white fat, which dispersed flavor, a nutty aroma, and a juicy bite. We had been looking for a new main course for the menu, and Poul's pork gave us a new platform to work with, allowing us to feature it roasted and simply covered with slices of Jerusalem artichoke. Its flavor is so deep and wholesome after aging for just 8 to 10 days that we can make it a centerpiece of a dish, simply garnishing it with supporting flavors. The Relæ menu is so focused on vegetables that we often let them take the lead, even in meat-based courses, but the quality of these pigs asks for dishes in which the meat can stand on its own.

Guanciale

The fatty and tasty jowl is my favorite cut of pork, and it is probably also the most easily cured piece of meat. The end product can turn a very good carbonara into an incredible carbonara, or it can just be used like a regular piece of good bacon, sautéed, roasted, and munched on. Remove the jowl from the head, rinse, and remove any wobbly pieces of gland. Weigh what's left, and measure out 3 percent of the trimmed jowl weight in salt. Pat the jowl dry and brush the meat and skin with the salt. Add toasted juniper berries and bay leaves for flavor at this point, if you like, vacuum-seal, and leave to cure for about 8 days in the fridge. Rinse off the excess salt and pat dry. Next, cure for at least 14 days in a well-ventilated room that stays between 14°C and 16°C (57°F and 61°F).

Poul has a patient and natural approach to everything surrounding his small herd of about two hundred. The hogs are predominantly Duroc, a heritage breed known for its juicy and flavorful meat, but they aren't purebreds, to avoid the diseases and asocial behavior often observed in purebreds. The piglets aren't weaned until they or the sow decide it's time, which is often not until 20 weeks. That's in contrast with Danish organic standards, which require the piglets get access to milk for only the first eight weeks, before they are moved onto a protein-rich diet that pushes their growth, and pushes it fast.

The animals at Poul's ranch work for their living, clearing out fields and tilling the soil, acre after acre, in their search for roots, plants, and the occasional fallen fruit from the abandoned pear, plum, and apple orchard on the property. Enjoying the outdoors year-round, with only small sheds to serve as shelter in the coldest months, their varying and natural feed combined with a high activity dictates their much slower growth. The pigs are ultimately ready for slaughter after spending at least a year roaming around the orchard like wild boars and enjoying the green grasses of the island of Funen. In return, the flavor of their meat is incomparable. The slower growth combined with the later weaning creates flavor-packed marbling and a more natural composition of fatty acids. A Hindsholm hog's butchered weight is between 120 and 135 kilograms, which a conventionally bred pig would reach in about half the time.

When I first met Poul, he told us how everyone kept telling him that what he and his wife wanted to do wasn't possible. That not feeding the pigs supplements and vitamins would cause them distress, and that the two of them would go bankrupt. But Poul was determined to create a better standard of life for his pigs, and the result is a better end product. At Relæ, we are glad that Poul decided to keep challenging convention.

Mussels, Seaweed, and Allumettes (p.264)
Pork from Hindsholm and Rye (p.322)

Butter

Before New Nordic cuisine redefined cooking in Scandinavia, most Southern Europeans, particularly members of my own Italian family, would simply define Danish gastronomy by saying, "They eat a lot of butter, right?"

When going south in the summer, I remember bringing salted butter to my Sicilian aunt, who simply couldn't get the same quality in her local supermarket. I later realized that the butter we used to bring her was far from Denmark's best. With time, I went from being an Italian immigrant who saw butter as the antagonist to the beautiful olive oil of my own country to someone who could really appreciate it. Mostly, I appreciate its versatility.

Cooking with butter is a gentle and intriguing process. You can't just sauté meat in it at high heat, because it will burn long before the meat reaches the desired temperature. The same goes for olive oil, by the way. But I'm not saying that butter does not benefit from heating, because that is actually when all the magic happens.

If you just throw a dollop of butter in a cold pan and start heating it, it will first melt, then slowly start to foam and bubble as the fats and milk solids separate and the water evaporates. Once the water is all but gone, the solids start caramelizing and develop more and more flavor until they burn. Brown butter, or beurre noisette, as the French call it (literally, "hazelnut butter," named for its nutty and toasted flavor), was a revelation to me when I first started at Noma. I was very familiar with the French method of slowly browning butter in a small saucepan, but at Noma, they took it a step further by cooking it in bigger batches, carefully controlling the browning, and straining it and then using it as a flavoring in a sauce or final addition to a dish.

You can take advantage of this process when cooking meats by first sautéing them at high heat in a suitable plant-based oil to caramelize the big, flat surfaces of the meat. Next, add butter to lower the overall temperature and slightly slow down the cooking. As the butter bubbles and foams and the solids caramelize, slowly and gently baste the meat with a spoon. Maillard reactions will happen all over the surface, creating more browning and deepening flavor. The process of sautéing a squab or a slab of beef brings most cooks a step closer to nirvana, despite the high risk that they will baste their left hand in sheer excitement.

Sometimes we take another cue from the French and simply warm and whip good-quality cultured butter into an acidic liquid to create a buttery sauce. In the *Fried Salsify and Bergamot* (page 316), we fold citrus skins into a beurre blanc and serve it over a silky salsify puree and crispy chunks of skin-on salsify, which has a slight bitterness that the sauce balances out. There are also plenty of times when butter plays more of a background role, delivering fatty deliciousness to a puree, such as the *Baked Potato Puree* (page 298), or the pressure-cooked sunflower seeds in *Sunflower Seeds, Kornly, and Pine* (page 296).

Buttermilk

Traditionally, buttermilk is a by-product of making butter: raw cream is left to sour and ferment with a small amount of previously made buttermilk acting as a starter. During fermentation, the milk and cream separate, and the cream is churned and solidified into butter, while the remaining milky liquid becomes a new batch of buttermilk. Since it was a by-product, buttermilk was normally a food of the poor. Long gone are the days when buttermilk was produced this way, as microbial technology has advanced and the larger dairy companies have developed much more profitable ways of making buttermilk, by simply adding a culture to milk.

In Denmark, buttermilk is used especially in the traditional *koldskål*, a refreshing dish served in the summer that has a number of variations, most traditionally buttermilk flavored with sugar, lemon, and a touch of vanilla. It is often poured over sweet Danish strawberries when they reach their peak in summer, fulfilling seasonal demands for thirst-quenching desserts. I always look forward to the first *koldskål* of the year sprinkled with *kammerjunker*—small biscuits seasoned with cardamom. We make a killer version at Manfreds all through the warm months.

We don't do much *koldskål* at Relæ these days, but buttermilk has been a staple in our kitchen since the very beginning. Modern buttermilk is made by culturing skimmed milk with isolated bacteria, giving the flavor a buttery richness and tart freshness I am a big fan of. This complex combination of creamy richness and lactic acid suits many of our cold dishes, savory as well as sweet.

The combination of buttermilk with horseradish is seen a lot in New Nordic cuisine, and freezing it into a granité or adding it to a vinaigrette always gives interesting results. While yogurt gives more body and structure, it often leaves a dry aftertaste, whereas buttermilk seems to have a much more direct acidity and tartness that attacks the tip of the tongue and makes the mouth water. In *Cooked Onions, Buttermilk, and Nasturtium* (page 256), the buttermilk's acidity brings out the textural crunch of slightly cooked spring onions, and it's one of my absolute favorites.

Celery Root Taco (p.232)
Unripe Strawberries, Cress, and Buttermilk (p.246)
Cooked Onions, Buttermilk, and Nasturtium (p.256)
Baked Potato Puree (p.298)
Mandarin, Buttermilk, and Egg Yolk (p.344)

Ideas
Land

Jerusalem Artichokes
Carrots
Horseradish
Celery Root
Herbs
Cresses
Citrus
Unripe Strawberries
Elderflower
Crab Apple
Nuts
Seeds
Olives

Jerusalem Artichokes

The Jerusalem artichoke is our steady companion throughout the cold winter months. We don't use them as often in August and September, which is the beginning of their season, even though the freshly dug varieties are very crisp. We prefer to save them for the darker months since they keep extraordinarily well.

I enjoy using them raw, especially cut in small cubes, because they display a great snap and crunch that's almost like a raw potato but without any mealiness. With cooking, the inside turns velvety and creamy, and when we cook them and mix them with the skin, the flavor is intensified greatly.

But it's actually the Jerusalem artichoke's mild—almost bland—flavor that makes it work so well in the kitchen: it delivers texture while letting other flavors shine through. Anything burnt or charred works well as a contrast, and anything bitter or acidic provides a great punch, such as lemons and other citrus skin, bitter almond flavors, mustards, bitter greens, and even ground coffee, like in *Jerusalem Artichoke, Quinoa, and Coffee* (page 294).

To me, a trio of Jerusalem artichokes with brown butter and the acidic and zingy local sea buckthorn berries is an emblematic flavor combination of Nordic cuisine, and a combination you see often in Danish restaurants. We like to play on that theme by swapping the fatty brown butter, which accentuates the toasty qualities in the tuber, with another fat or even a nut puree, and the sea buckthorn berries with the similarly flavored passion fruit. The Jerusalem artichoke's natural sweetness when cooked has also made it one of our favorite experimental platforms for dessert, such as in the *Jerusalem Artichoke, Malt, and Bread* (page 350), with Jerusalem artichoke ice cream garnished with the crystallized skins, and malt oil adding that welcome bitterness. The same flavor combinations work well in a sweet version, underscoring once again its versatility in the kitchen.

Carrots

To me, carrots are another iconic Nordic vegetable, because they're basically what we have all through the winter. There are plenty of other root vegetables out there, and some might be a bit more exotic or at least sound more intriguing, but the orange root has always been the base of our vegetable-focused cooking. We often build an entire dish around a single carrot. One of the first dishes on the menu in 2010 was a whole roasted carrot, basted and buttered in a pan and served with *söl*, the Icelandic seaweed, and a black currant sauce.

The carrot's rounded sweetness might be its main attribute, yet controlling that sweetness is also presents its biggest challenge. It can turn out overly sweet and hence can be difficult to pair with other foods in a savory context. This is why we so often cook it quite brutally, either roasting it for a very long time or drying it, adding a bitterness that suits and constrains the sweetness very well. Looking for all its secretly hidden textures, we have cut it in every conceivable way. We've even gone as far as using the skins: in *Nordlys, Carrots, and Orange Zest* (page 340), we cook thin slices of the unpeeled root until crisp to serve with a runny cheese. We can pair carrots' sweetness with something fruity and acidic that also has a slight bitterness, such as black currants and sea buckthorns, but berries that lack that bitter edge, like raspberries or strawberries, will not work at all.

Texture is also important to consider when working with something this sweet. For me, a puree of carrots is one of the most difficult things to pull off; no matter what, the cooked sweetness combined with a lean and homogenous texture makes you think of baby food. The only way you can overcome that is by adding bitterness and alcohol to it, as we have done in *Carrot, Elderflower, and Sesame* (page 304), in which dehydrated carrots add bitterness and we make a sauce with Chenin Blanc. The alcohol opens up the flavors and distracts the palate from the baby mash feeling—well, unless your mom treated you to something like that as a kid.

Horseradish

Heat and spice have never been a part of the traditional everyday cooking of Scandinavia or even the newer wave of Nordic restaurants. That is, with the exception of horseradish. Though considered a pale, distant cousin to Japan's beloved wasabi, this white root is packed with plenty of heat and has a huge culinary value in our kitchen. Horseradish is traditionally just scraped with a knife, almost as if whittling a wooden stick to a point, and even though you could use a box grater or even a sturdy juicer, the old way is still the most efficient. The root varies a lot in heat. At times its strength is noticeable even as you prepare it, giving you red and runny eyes long before you taste it for strength.

Used with caution, horseradish can give an interesting spark to many dishes, but mostly cold ones. It does not cope well with higher temperatures, when its fragrance and peppery aromas completely lose out to its bitterness, which becomes overwhelming with heat. We tend to sprinkle it as an accent on cold dishes, such as over a few slices of cod in *Cod, Kohlrabi, and Skins* (page 278). Even in a frozen preparation, such as a snow, granité, or even sorbet, the bitter spice comes out very clear and bright, perfect for when you want minerality and freshness to start a meal.

As a usual companion to boiled meats or cold cuts on Danish traditional smørrebrød, horseradish is traditionally served alone or with chopped onions or pickles. I find its peppery spice also works very well with all types of fermented dairy, including buttermilk, cream, and yogurt. In *Oysters, Cabbage, and Capers* (page 262), the horseradish-spiked yogurt is a foundation for raw oysters with lightly pickled cabbage.

Oysters, Cabbage, and Capers (p.262)
Cod, Kohlrabi, and Skins (p.278)
Turnips, Chervil, and Horseradish (p.284)
Charred Cucumber and Fermented Juice (p.306)

Horseradish Cream
Scrape a few spoonfuls of horseradish into about half a liter of whipping cream and add lemon juice to taste. Leave at room temperature to sour and thicken for about an hour. Use in or to accompany anything that needs a kick, such as salads, cooked meats, or cold cuts.

Celery Root

I am big fan of this bulby and aromatic root vegetable. While most root vegetables tend to have a simple and at times flat flavor profile, celery root is often sweet and juicy when cooked, and slightly fibrous yet aromatic when raw. Its versatile shape and characteristic flavor makes it useful in a number of ways.

I remember when variations of salt-baked celery root were as iconic as foraged elderberries when the Nordic wave was taking over the world. At its peak, I don't think you could find a restaurant in Copenhagen, whether fine dining, bistro, or café, that didn't serve hay-baked celery root, salt-baked celery root, or celery root baked with burnt ashes. It reminds me a bit of American chef Daniel Patterson's speech at the first MAD Symposium in 2011—which René Redzepi organized to bring chefs together from around the world—about how beet and goat cheese had taken over California cuisine. Well, if Patterson can have mixed emotions about beets dominating California cuisine while still creating one of the most beautiful beet dishes I've ever seen, the Beet Rose, I have a similar relationship with celery root. Even though I normally steer clear of highly trending phenomena, my love for celery root has steadily grown and I just can't stop cooking it.

Baked Celery Root

To do a traditional salt crust for a celery root, mix flour and salt in equal parts and add half a part of water (i.e., half of the weight of the flour), to bind it together. You will need about 500 g of dough per bulb. Spread the dough to about 1 cm thickness and wrap it around a cleaned, unpeeled celery root. Bake at 220°C (425°F) for 1 to 2 hours, depending on what texture you are looking for. Before adding the salted dough, you can add all the flavoring you like to the celery root. The infamous and very decorative burnt hay or even better garlic scapes, lemon zest, or spices will penetrate the vegetable during cooking. You can just wrap whatever you want around the bulb before wrapping the dough around them. If you aren't planning to serve the celery root in its crust, there is a less romantic but just as effective alternative. Scrub the celery root with plenty of coarse salt, a few splashes of water, and whatever flavoring you like and wrap it tightly with aluminum foil. Bake it the same way as in the salt crust.

At Relæ, we salt it, ferment it, dry it, and juice it both raw and cooked. We even turned it into a soft taco shell at one point and realized that its slightly caramelized crisp and dried slices are great paired with goat cheese and black olives.

When raw, celery root's flavor brings a few almost zesty high notes that complement its sweetness while keeping it fresh and appetizing. Its sweetness is far more pronounced once cooked, when those high notes tend to mellow out. Texturally, its meatiness is unique when either baked or cooked soft, which has made it a staple of our vegetarian dishes on both sides of Jægersborggade. Celery root is often found on everyday dishes on the menu at Manfreds, as well as in the signature eggs Benedict, our vegetarian version of the classic, in which thin slices of baked celery root take the place of cooked ham.

Celery Root Taco (p.232)
Pickled Skate, Mussels, and Celery Root (p.274)

Herbs

When I first opened Relæ, I wanted some distance from the foraging movement, which all of the New Nordic chefs seemed to be so caught up in. Foraging just wasn't that interesting to me, but that doesn't mean that I don't love herbs; on the contrary. Wild or farmed, free-range or greenhouse raised, these beautiful leaves—with their green freshness and incredible aromas—are integral to light, fresh, and vegetable-oriented cooking.

In the beginning, I wanted to go against the trend of picking herbs into tiny and perfect leaves to use them as superficial ornaments and to instead focus on their flavor. It's true that herbs are fragile and volatile in flavor; if overcooked, they become flat and broken down (though in exchange, they add freshness and aroma to whatever sauce or liquid they're cooked in, such as the sauce for *Cauliflower, Veal Sweetbread, and Basil*, page 326).

We blanch parsley, chervil, and lovage to make intensely flavored purees, which we often add to sauces to lighten up their meaty structure or seafood flavor. In the *Pickled Skate, Mussels, and Celery Root* (page 274), we fold the juices of the steamed mussels into a parsley puree to dress the dish.

I feel like too many restaurants fall back on scattering herbs across the plate—creating a wilderness of greenery—when they've run out of other ideas. I wanted to do the opposite. We reverse the traditional role of herbs by pulling them away from the surface and "hiding" them underneath the components they season. With *White Onions, Crayfish, and Fennel* (page 280), we season the creamy interior hiding underneath the onions with finely chopped fennel tops. In *Raw Beef, Anchovies, and Ramsons* (page 268), the garlicky ramson leaves—also known as wild garlic in the United States—contrast the irony and bloody raw meat.

Since opening Relæ, I have loosened up, allowing for the odd picked sprig on a plate. I also allow for the occasional foraged "weed" like oxalis (wood sorrel) to grace our dishes, and I tend to look at these greens in a similar category as herbs. But I still prefer to chop or blanch herbs to solidify their flavor and turn them into sauces or purees. That said, with dishes like *Herb Bouquet* (page 230), our "bouquet" of fresh edible herbs, even I'll admit that a bunch of freshly picked herbs can have a great impact on the palate, and the eye.

Cresses

Most greens and herbs are packed with bitterness and aromatics, but cresses also have the more rare quality of spice. Along with horseradish, cress is probably the closest you come to spiciness or heat in Nordic cuisine, and the top notes they contribute add life and complexity to just about everything. Because of their complex flavor and also their leafy, juicy texture, most cresses can play the role of both a leafy green and a flavoring herb.

Cresses include not only the common watercress, but also a wide array of land cresses, all with their distinct flavor profiles. I prefer wild watercress, which is bigger and naturally sturdy. I am not too fond of the small, farmed sprouts and cresses that have become incredibly popular the last few years.

Watercress is probably the most widely used wild herb in the Scandinavian countries, and it grows copiously around rivers and streams through the warmer months. It is also cultivated, mostly in pots and hothouses, but those versions can't compare to wild watercress. The thick-stemmed plant has a refreshing spice and a pleasant bitterness. Until they grow too woody and fibrous, I like to serve the succulent stems either raw or just slightly cooked. In *Unripe Strawberries, Cress, and Buttermilk* (page 246), we make a puree from both stems and leaves, giving a fresh bitterness to the dish.

Many cooks are familiar with the edible flowers of nasturtium, another type of cress, but I also enjoy cooking with the round green leaves, which have a slight sweetness along with bitterness and spice. Not succulent enough to work in purees, however, the leaves don't do well with cooking and must be kept raw. In the *Sheep's Milk Yogurt, Radishes, and Nasturtium* (page 248), we plate small nasturtium leaves with the light yogurt mousse and crunchy radishes.

With its tiny green leaves, pot cress is the most approachable and easygoing type of cress, as it is only slightly bitter but has a distinctive flavor recognizable to most Danes. Almost all urban Danish children have tried to grow cress in small pots on a sunny windowsill. Others worth mentioning would be roset cress (*Cardamine hirsuta*), also called hairy bitter cress, though as the name implies, it's a bit too bitter to use on its own; and different types of mustard, which mostly end up being a bit too bitter to find a proper spot on the menu.

Citrus

Before our move to Denmark, my father ran a wholesale business selling lemons from our part of Sicily to the rest of Italy. The packing facility was close to our home, and the scent of fragrant lemons is one my first memories, along with the image of the kind and friendly faces of my father's crew. This is why I often connect the distinct and appetizing smell of freshly squeezed lemons with summer vacations back on that Mediterranean island, after we had emigrated to Denmark.

In the restaurant, our cooking is known for its high level of acidity. When I'm looking for a drier style of acidity, I most often opt for reduced white wine, and when a dish has a more fruity body, I reach for a fruity vinegar of some sort. But when I'm seeking raw freshness and top notes, nothing beats citrus juice.

I've learned, though, that lemon juice rarely survives cooking, and its flavor is always short-lived; it will fade out or, at least, lose everything but its acidity if I add it too early.

On the other hand, the flesh, pith, and zest of all kinds of citrus are quite interesting when cooked. We blanch halved and juiced lemons to soften their bitterness and then puree the pith and skin with the fresh juice. The puree has a velvety texture from the cooked pith, a lingering bitterness

---

Lemon in a Humidifier

To add a final and evenly spread-out freshness and acidity to a dish, we fill spray bottles or handheld humidifiers with lemon juice. When serving, we give a cold dish a spray or two with it, always a certain number of times to maintain consistent acidity levels. Still, the acidity we need for a dish can vary from hour to hour, for example, when a sauce has been on the stove for a while, or the kitchen gets hotter as the night progresses, and preparations change flavor. That's why senior members of the kitchen and sommelier staff regularly taste the dishes during service just to verify these small details as well as others.

from the zest, and a fresh acidity from the raw juice. Alternatively, a few gratings of lemon zest always guarantees freshness on any dish, adding perfume without acidity.

When venturing beyond the common lemon, bergamot has become one of my absolute favorites, with its intense bitterness and aroma, which balances and accents the bitterness of salsify in a beurre blanc–style sauce on the *Fried Salsify and Bergamot* (page 316). Mandarins and bitter orange also often find their places on the menus of both Manfreds and Relæ, such as in *Mandarin, Buttermilk, and Egg Yolk* (page 344), where it shows up both in a light mandarin curd and a granité.

Unripe Strawberries

Danish strawberries are downright incredible. We have some fantastic producers and a cool climate letting them slowly develop sweetness and aroma until perfectly ripe.

The now almost extinct Dybdahl is the most revered variety for its flavor, but its low yield and extremely short shelf life have made it difficult to come by commercially. My personal favorite is the Polka, which mixes natural sweetness and a deep ruby color with a nice tang. It's especially useful when not quite ripe. In fact, we often use strawberries when they are green or unripe. *Green* is technically not the correct term since what we want are berries that are picked when ripe enough to have fruit and aroma but that haven't yet developed their distinct and comforting sweetness, making them extremely versatile in the savory kitchen. When the berry is actually green, it is woody and dry, expelling no juice or liquid when bitten into. But when the color of the flesh slowly turns toward white with the occasional green spot, right before a slightly red blush starts appearing on the inside, the strawberry is packed with live, acidic, and fresh juice.

It never crossed my mind to use these berries before working at Noma, but since the great escalation of New Nordic cuisine, they have become very common in Scandinavia. To take them a step further and really bring out their tangy qualities, we have tried all sorts of things, but nothing has compared to the revelation of simply warming them.

By heating them slowly and in a closed environment to avoid dehydration, unripe strawberries turn into small grenades of juicy, fruity acidity ready to explode in your mouth. Pairing them with bitterness or green, peppery notes has a fantastic effect and releases that natural, clear, but balanced fruit they carry, such as in the *Unripe Strawberries, Cress, and Buttermilk* (page 246), where the warm berries are placed on top of buttermilk snow in a plate lined with a cress puree.

Unripe Strawberries, Cress, and Buttermilk (p.246)
New Potatoes, Warm Berries, and Arugula (p.286)

Elderflower

Elderflower is easy prey, even for the most distracted foragers. In Copenhagen, it grows in every park, and a drive outside the city during the June blooming season will show why it is used so often in Nordic cooking to add a floral note. The most traditional thing to do with it is to make a tasty cordial that every Danish kid loves, an infusion of the flowers with sugar, lemon juice, and water. This drink often appears on the nonalcoholic juice pairing at Relæ, and we sell it by the glass throughout the year at Manfreds.

But what I find most interesting about elderflower is how it has gastronomical value in many different stages of its life. When blooming, we use the flowers in pickles or to flavor fresh strawberries. As its tiny petals fall off, we salt and pickle the green berries, maintaining the floral aroma in a sharper and more pronounced way. When completely mature, the red berries can go into a sweeter and more rounded cordial, or into compotes and preserves. However, avoid eating the berries raw, as they are actually toxic. That was something I discovered when trying out a dish with onions and raw elderberries with one of the cooks in the kitchen. After many trials, which resulted in dizzy heads and upset stomachs, we concluded that the berries worked out much better cooked.

In the end, what we use most are the vinegar-pickled flowers, stem and all. Their flavor stands out so clearly this way, making them a great floral addition to any dish imaginable. The pickle's lack of sugar also makes the flowers more versatile in the savory kitchen.

Pickled Elderflower

These flowers are as easy to pickle as they are to find. Simply pick the bouquets off the shrubs and soak them in water to remove any insects or debris. Pack them in canning jars and fill the jars with white vinegar that isn't too dominant or sharp flavored. By using straight vinegar, you don't even have to can them, though you may want to if you plan to keep them all the way until the next season.

Crab Apple

The first time we met him, Lars Jacobsen walked into Relæ with a few samples of vegetables that apparently no one else wanted. He asked if we were interested in seeing what he had brought, and we gave our standard response: "Of course, we're interested!" It turned out that Lars had been working on some interesting experiments for many years in his search for unusual and forgotten vegetables. We connected straightaway.

Throughout the years Lars has fed our menu with all sorts of vegetables and herbs: celtuce, purslane, sorrel, Chinese chives, oka (New Zealand yam), fava beans, oxalis (wood sorrel), and elephant garlic. And one fruit makes an appearance on our menu just as often: his crab apples.

Lars does not work on a conventional farm. He works for a nonprofit project called Offside, whose goal is to create employment for people with learning disabilities. The organization has a small patch of land in Vadsby, about 35 minutes from the restaurant, where he brings a vanful of people three or four times a week to weed, water, and otherwise tend to vegetables. A lot of the produce is brought back to the project's kitchen and café on Nørrebro, which is quite close to the restaurant. Yet their field provides them with much greater volume than they can consume in the café.

The single acre they are in charge of cultivating was home to a great number of crab apple trees when they took over the place. They are all of mixed varieties that none of us have figured out, but they provide an array of colors, acidity levels, and flavors that have made them a regular ingredient on our menu. Crab apples are most often too sour, bitter, and mealy to eat raw so we usually cook or preserve them. They contain a great amount of pectin, which make them work really well in gels and compotes and to dry as leathers. We normally cook them with skin, pit, and everything to preserve their tannins, since we usually use them in the savory kitchen. For the same reason, we don't add loads of sugar, so they can more seamlessly integrate into our cooking. As a low-sugar sweet to serve with coffee, we make several different crab apple leathers, rip them up, and put them back together into a mosaic.

Lars is also an expert on alternative ways of growing greens, especially in pots. His experience and our curiosity led us to plan a rooftop garden that would be close to the restaurant. Unfortunately, our shared dream hasn't yet become a reality. But in the meantime, Lars keeps us satisfied with the myriad crab apples and unusual plant varieties he continues to bring to our doorstep.

Beet, Crab Apple, and Söl (p.254)
Coffee Table (p.362)

Nuts

Nuts are magical. Since I make such a conscious effort to reduce the restaurant's use of animal proteins and fats, nuts are an essential source of fat and creaminess in our cooking at Relæ. Like olive oil, almonds, hazelnuts, and pistachios all have heartfelt symbolic value for me, reminding me of my Italian roots and keeping my cooking from going totally Nordic. One of my clearest childhood memories sits in a cone of hazelnut-flavored *nocciola* gelato, and giving up beautiful flavors like that would be like giving up a part of my own heritage. I fell in love again with pistachios as an adult visiting a producer in the Sicilian town of Bronte, who explained why the volcanic soil of Etna makes the best pistachios conceivable. The image of those live green trees against the black, volcanic landscape has always stuck in my mind, and importing them to Denmark to serve them in my restaurant gives me incredible satisfaction.

Not all nuts have made it through the testing phase. After experimenting for days on a dish with cooked pine nuts, which meant I was eating them over and over again, I came away with a disturbing feeling. I eventually discovered that I'm allergic, and whether that was provoked by the repetitive tastings I will never know, but my allergy is slowly expanding to other nuts. Even though pine nuts never made it onto the menu, I hardheadedly continue tasting and experimenting with other nuts while keeping antihistamines nearby.

Manipulating nuts is interesting because they are so versatile. We roast and pressure-cook dried nuts, mimicking the texture of a fresh nut or a new potato cooked al dente. We turn nuts into milks and purees and thicken sauces with them. We often smoke them before using them for any of those purposes, turning them, as my staff likes to point out, into our own type of bacon.

Seeds

Rich in fiber and offering up a range of great flavors and textures, seeds often work their way onto all parts of our menu. Sunflower seeds and pumpkin seeds show up most often, and both mustard and nigella seeds—which admittedly are more often seen as spices than energy-holding seeds—season our snacks. We try to use similar approaches with seeds that we do with nuts, such as making purees and milks with them as well as pressure-cooking and roasting them.

Sunflower seeds have grown to be my favorite, and they are probably one of the most underrated items in the pantry. Sunflower seed puree has a smooth texture and a subtle nutty flavor. When the seeds are pressure-cooked, the texture of the individual seeds is incredible, almost like a risotto, such as in the *Sunflower Seeds, Kornly, and Pine* (page 296), in which the tender seeds are suspended in a light sauce made from the pureed seeds.

Pumpkin seeds play a recurring role as the Nordic counterpart to pistachios, and when roasted and blended into a puree, they make a great base for savory emulsions or cakes and ice creams, as in *Hokkaido Pumpkin and Mandarin* (page 354). They are also a great alternative for customers with nut allergies, which is a recurring challenge because of our extensive use of nuts in the kitchen. With pumpkin and sunflower seeds, we can fix up most dishes to a satisfying compromise.

Olives

Black and green olives are another Mediterranean addition to our not-so-Nordic menu. We use black taggiasche olives from Italy most often. Initially, we made a sauce by simply blending the pitted black olives with a small amount of water and later added chicken or another meat glaze, making an intense, dark, and very savory puree to serve with cooked and julienned celery root and sea lettuce. We use a similar technique with savory green olives, such as Tonda Iblea or the Spanish manzanilla, but get a very different outcome. Because the green olives are less mature in flavor, the sauce comes out more briny and aromatic but has less depth of flavor and goes very well with pork.

Now, we dry the olives more often than not. After pitting them, we dry them in a dehydrator until they are very brittle and crunchy, at 50°C (122°F) for about a day. This condenses and intensifies the salty flavors, and the pleasant crunch makes them work really well with a creamy puree, such as one made from baked potato, celery root, or cauliflower. We also pair the dried black olives with grated salted egg yolk in the *Romaine, Egg Yolk, and Nettles* (page 308). The dried olives work well in a delicate risotto, and even a freshly stretched mozzarella would marry very well with these olives.

We could blend the dried olives into a powder, but the incredibly high fat content would make the powder moist, and the olives would lose their crunch. The beauty of chewing into them is the release of those fatty acids suspended in a brittle and crisp structure, and that's why I prefer them slightly chunky and crisp. Our olives have almost become like a spice to us.

Baked Potato Puree (p.298)
Romaine, Egg Yolk, and Nettles (p.308)

Olive Sauce

This is a velvety and creamy olive-green sauce that's very well suited to a lightly grilled chicken thigh or something along those lines. Add a handful of pitted green olives to a blender. Add a spoonful of warm chicken, veal, or pork glaze and an equal amount of warm water. Blend until smooth and pass through a fine-mesh strainer. Depending on the water content of the olives, you might need to add a bit more water. Season with lemon juice or Reduced White Wine (page 439) and perhaps some good extra-virgin olive oil.

Ideas
Sea

Mussels
Coastal Fish
Mackerel
Sea Lettuce
Anchovy
Söl
Kelp

Mussels

Until I met Erling from the seafood company Villerslev Skaldyr,
I didn't realize that farmed mussels could be certified organic, and I
naively assumed that the animals would just grow without much human
interaction. Even though that's true, to some extent, whoever tends
to them faces a few obvious problems that can be resolved either by
complying with nature or by putting profits first. Erling is one of those
people who never doubts which path to take. His constant consideration
for the environment—he avoids all chemicals when farming and uses
biodegradable fuels on his boat—shines through in the impressive quality
of the mussels he brings to us. His small family-owned business, situated
in the most northern part of Jutland, is the only certified organic mussel
producer in Denmark.

Plump, juicy, and tasty, these blue mussels are far superior to any others
I've tried and have become an inspiration and a staple in our kitchen. We
often call on their natural sweetness and umami when making sauces or
flavoring emulsions. After steaming, we season their natural juices with
Reduced Wine (page 54) or lemon juice, creating the base for many sauces,
vinaigrettes, cold juices, and seasonings.

We have also built quite a few dishes with the very briefly cooked and
extremely juicy and plump bodies as a main component. In the *Mussels,
Seaweed, and Allumettes* (page 264) we chill blanched mussels in a cold
mussel stock made with wine, then serve them with fried matchstick
potatoes and a cold seaweed bouillon made of more mussel stock pureed
with blanched fresh seaweed.

Sometimes we follow a technique I learned at elBulli, where they blanched
the local rock mussels in seawater until they just peeked out from
underneath the shell and then cut them out while still warm. This gives

an incredible texture and a much more briny and fresh flavor profile than steaming. When cooked this way, the mussels close in on an oysterlike quality, whereas steaming them, which takes longer, tones down the briny element and allows a deep sweetness to almost take over. I remember the wild mussels from elBulli's coastal town of Roses to be small and almost bitter but packed with flavor, whereas the local varieties Erling provides have much more body and a more gentle flavor and sweetness.

Coastal Fish

For a moment I was about to lose it. I was at the point where I didn't want to have fish on the menu anymore. With the exception of some small batches of mackerel, the quality of fish coming from the local fishmongers around Copenhagen was not up to par. Danes eat surprisingly small amounts of fish per capita, and most traditional dishes involve preserved fish, such as pickled herring and smoked mackerel. That could partly explain the low demand for freshness, or maybe it's the clumsy logistics that always seem to add a few too many days to distribution.

After once again complaining about freshness to one of my fishmongers, he blurted out in an annoyed voice, "Hey! I can get you cod but I can't guarantee it any better than this!"

What a sad state we are in, I thought. How can we have the longest coastline conceivable, fish all around us, and great fishing traditions, yet such a low criteria for fresh fish in this country?

Then I happened to stumble upon a new website that puts small fishermen in direct contact with private customers. You would subscribe to a boat landing on a harbor close to you and an automatic text message would give you information on the catch of the day and its arrival time at the harbor. These boats would go out at about 3 a.m. and return to shore at about noon, delivering incredibly fresh fish before rigor mortis set in. I went as a private customer first and picked up the freshest cod that had ever entered our kitchens. It was a total game changer; my private scouting visit turned into a professional relationship with Max Christensen, a young and passionate fisherman landing his daily catch in a small town just north of the city. Now, we bypass the automated text messages and speak daily about my orders of 20 to 30 kilograms of cod carefully selected from his average catch of 500 to 600 kilograms.

Meeting Max and learning about his work was truly inspiring, and in the kitchen, we soon started creating dishes to showcase his stunning cod. The first dish with soft-cooked leeks and a light chicken broth entered the menu with a bang. By working with him, we do have to compromise a bit on variety, though, since cod is certainly his specialty with an occasional round of mackerel, plaice (a type of flatfish), sole, and turbot to change it up when cod season is over. Then, in the spring, he supplies us with fantastic lumpfish and lumpfish roe. Our four-course menu fortunately never requires we have more than a single type of fish at a time, if any, so we can live with less variation because we are getting higher quality, something that would have been completely impossible for us to do with an à la carte menu.

Max doesn't do any deliveries, so we have to drive up to the harbor ourselves, which makes buying at a high volume crucial for us. This is another time in which Manfreds comes into play, adding to the synergy of basing two restaurants on the same core philosophy. We break down the cod and divide it into several parts. For the menu at Relæ, we reserve the plump pieces high on the back, which come out incredibly firm and creamy if slightly salted, or juicy and translucent if poached. We cut up the thinner pieces close to the tail to use in a tartare at Manfreds. We poach the fat belly and either serve it with the back piece at Relæ or on its own at Manfreds. We turn the smaller bits such as the tongue and cheeks into small fun stuff for Table 0—our version of a chef's table (see page 17)—and the bones and carcasses are often turned into a fish soup for the staff. With careful planning, we have found a way to beat the logistical challenges and get the freshest fish possible, even from Copenhagen's surprisingly limited fisheries.

Pickled Mackerel, Cauliflower, and Lemon (p.276)
Cod, Kohlrabi, and Skins (p.278)

Mackerel

It is always hard to pinpoint your favorite fish, herb, or cut of meat, but if that were hypothetically doable, my top candidate when it comes to marine life would be mackerel. I am a great fan of fatty and oily fish, and mackerel combines the qualities I so appreciate with a texture of great complexity, offering up many possibilities in the kitchen.

As with other very oily fish, in Denmark, mackerel is traditionally smoked and even canned. The smoked version is often served on rye as smørrebrød, the Danish open-faced sandwich. The high fat content of a fish is always considered key to successfully smoking it, but I think the fat is equally useful for lightly curing, salting, or pickling a fish. Mackerel's tasty fatty acids come through very well even when served raw, or semi-raw in the case of the *Pickled Mackerel, Cauliflower, and Lemon* (page 276), but their tendency to turn rancid quickly demands that the fish be uncompromisingly fresh.

My inspiration for the Relæ's menu was the Catalan escabèche method, which calls for halfway cooking and then marinating fish in a vinegar-based pickling liquid. The fatty flesh of the mackerel seemed to be very well suited for both the slight cooking and the addition of tart acidity. To start, we remove the fillets from the bone while leaving the skin on, and then salt them and spread them out on a baking sheet to cure for about 30 minutes at room temperature. For the pickling liquid, we mix one part red wine vinegar or sherry vinegar to three parts water and heat it to 40°C (104°F) on the stove. When warm, we pour the liquid over the fillets, completely immersing them. After covering and refrigerating the escabèche for a few hours, we pull the fish from the brine. Just before serving, we pull the pickled mackerel out from the fridge to come to room temperature. We cut the mackerel in various ways, depending on how we would like to serve it, but no matter how we cut it, the texture is sure to be velvety and addictive.

Pickled Mackerel, Cauliflower, and Lemon (p.276)

Sea Lettuce

The potential of seaweed to become part of a meal at all levels seems fully appreciated only in Asian cultures, with the Japanese as obvious leaders in the field. In Denmark, the lack of a market for locally harvested seaweed makes it difficult to obtain. Even though the long shores of this tiny country are as generous as any other European coast, consumer interest, as we all know, dictates commercial value. Hopefully the New Nordic revolution that has reintroduced a passion for wild herbs and local produce among Danes will also succeed in creating an interest in local seaweed.

Sea lettuce, a lighter green seaweed that has ruffled edges that make it look a lot like lettuce, is incredibly versatile, with an almost dry and slightly hard texture that you find only in marine plants but with thin leaves that aren't difficult to tenderize. Sea lettuce can add marine salinity and umami to any type of meat or fish, whether served cold or warm. By sautéing it in a pan and slightly caramelizing it, a perfume spreads from the pan and it gains a fragile crispness that we once combined with our *pré-salé* lamb from Havervadgård with great success. You can elevate a dish by sprinkling dried and crispy bits of this marine terroir on foods like poached eggs or cooked potatoes. It works particularly well with mild-flavored, soft-textured raw meat or fish such as beef, veal, cod, or even mussels, as in *Mussels, Seaweed, and Allumettes* (page 264).

For me, sea lettuce brings complexity in a very simple and rewarding way, which is why it has become a recurring ingredient on both our regular and vegetarian menus. It even adds brine and minerality to our nonalcoholic juice pairings, in which we pair it with cucumber or apple.

Anchovy

No wonder Mr. Anchovy isn't the most popular guy around. Too often overly salty, manhandled, and kept in rancid, low-quality olive oil, he can be an acquired taste. My own first memories of anchovies are of nothing but disgust. They made a well-camouflaged appearance on the traditional Sicilian focaccia, hiding beneath tomatoes, mozzarella, and escarole. As a kid munching on those slices, I remember hitting these very salty, gritty weird bits that I couldn't spit out fast enough.

Most anchovies are processed mechanically, which rips up the meat, mixes it all up with the intestines, impurities, and bones, and creates the dirty flavor and rough texture I hated as a child. But my feelings toward anchovies took a 180-degree turn after I became acquainted with high-quality anchovies while working in Spain, where the North Coast and Bay of Biscay deliver the best in the world.

At their best, anchovies taste clean, ripe, and rich, but that takes careful work from the moment they are brought ashore. At elBulli, an anchovy dish on the menu turned us into Basque fish-factory workers. First we carefully cleaned and salted the fish. Later, we soaked them in water, then meticulously pulled the tiny bones out of each firm fillet by hand.

At both Relæ and Manfreds we use anchovies avidly. We source them from northern Spain, where the quality is just as good as I remember from my days staging at elBulli, but the picking out of bones is done there by old ladies with experienced hands and acute eyes. These anchovies give flavor and seasoning to vegetables and sauces, and it has almost become our signature to serve different types of meat with them. Raw beef or lamb, not to mention cooked chicken, work incredibly well with anchovy, as anyone who has had a proper Caesar salad knows.

I avoid buying anchovies soaked in oil, since the oil is rarely of good quality. The salted ones we use are quite versatile for many different preparations, such as the mayonnaise-like "Anchovy Emulsion" (page 386) we make from anchovy fillets, oil, and vinegar that is passed through a strainer. The emulsion comes out perfectly shiny and creamy and is a great accompaniment to raw meats or roasted vegetables; we dress several of our dishes—*White Asparagus and Anchovies* (page 272) and *Raw Beef, Anchovies, and Ramsons* (page 268)—with it. By now baked Jerusalem artichokes with anchovy emulsion has become a Manfreds classic—and who knows, you might do a great Caesar salad based on it too.

Söl

I should really call this seaweed dulse, but it entered our kitchen with its Icelandic name, *söl*, and it has stayed like that. When we present a dish with it at the table, it might sound a bit exotic to explain that it is an Icelandic seaweed, but this beautiful dark red, long-leaved seaweed is actually found throughout the far reaches of the Northern Hemisphere. Ireland, Alaska, and parts of Canada, in addition to Iceland, have traditions for harvesting and drying this surprisingly high-protein marine snack.

We receive *söl* from Eyjolfur Fridgeirsson, who harvests and dries it in Iceland. I only recently tried it freshly harvested and soaked in seawater, and it was subtle and bland, demonstrating how much Eyjolfur's processing brings out some of its outstanding qualities and flavor profiles.

His dried *söl* is chewy and intensely flavored, with marine, iodine, and a deep and fruity tobacco-like flavor as well as a deep umami-enhancing ability. We have used it in many more ways than show up in this book, in everything from starters to desserts. Pairing its tobacco, dried fruit, and umami with sweet and earthy components, such as beets or carrots, is a sure winner, and those same qualities are very well suited to the pastry kitchen.

As shown in the small *söl* tart (see *Coffee Table,* page 362) that we have served as a mignardise at the restaurant, slightly caramelized and buttery flavors work incredibly well with it. But even going in a completely different direction can work out very well, as we have braised veal shanks and served them with powdered *söl* as well as pureed the seaweed and mixed it into a sauce to serve with beef. I can clearly imagine how the tobacco-like qualities could contribute to the deep flavors of a Mexican stew as well. We also pair the dried powder with baked and tempura-fried

Jerusalem artichokes, where the marine flavor from the seaweed combines with the chewy texture of the Jerusalem artichoke skins to create the sensation of biting into soft-shell crab tempura.

If we aren't using it as a powder, we normally soak the *söl* in lukewarm water for a few minutes before it is ready to be untangled and put on a plate, cooked to make a puree, or just added to another preparation. If we want to use it in more of a dried form, we have to first soak it to remove any traces of small dried shrimp, stones, or grit, then rinse and dry it again before use.

Kelp

Eyjolfur Fridgeirsson, our Icelandic *söl* connection with the seemingly unpronounceable name, forages different kinds of seaweed as well as some other local delicacies, like wild berries. Once he visited us in Denmark and brought along a few bags of several types of seaweed, including bags of dried dark green kelp. It may as well have been produce from another planet. Whenever we encounter a new variety of carrot or potato, we have a general idea of how to attack it—there are rarely surprises lurking in unknown spuds. But when it comes to seaweed, each variety is so different. Unlike *söl* or sea lettuce, which can be soaked in water and eaten as is, and which react well to heating or even sautéing, kelp is just so hard and tough that we had no idea how to handle it.

We thought the kelp might work on our juice menu, so some of the cooks started infusing it into all sorts of things—milk, other juices, and water. The results were all over the map.

In the end, the best outcome came from infusing the kelp directly into apple juice. The kelp-infused apple juice had a saline body and was well suited to match the savory dishes *Oysters, Cabbage, and Capers* (page 262) and *Pickled Skate, Mussels, and Celery Root* (page 274). But what we got even more ideas out of were milk infusions, which inspired us to make the *Milk, Kelp, and Caramel* (page 346), managing to move this exciting ingredient to a dessert made with ice cream infused with kelp and caramel, and triggering many more experiments involving seaweed.

After we got over our initial hesitation, we ended up cooking, toasting, and drying kelp, but its incredibly sturdy texture has made us believe that infusions are probably the best way to extract its qualities. Its saline umami depth is incomparable.

Enoki, Kelp, and Seaweed (p.310)
Milk, Kelp, and Caramel (p.346)

Ideas
Manipulations

Fermentation

During my entire apprenticeship—which took place at Le Petit Bofinger in Paris and Røgeriet north of Copenhagen—no one ever taught me about fermentation. This is in spite of the fact that fermentation plays a huge role in my cooking (and, well, everyone's cooking). It's pretty ridiculous that these ancient techniques are so stigmatized—I suppose people hear the words "bacterial growth" and get frightened.

Thankfully, there is a bit of a fermentation frenzy spreading through the high-end restaurants of the Western world right now. There are several food labs—like Momofuku and René Redzepi's Nordic Food Lab— experimenting with fermentation at entirely new levels. My hope is that cooking schools will follow suit and start teaching their students about the world of yeasts, bacteria, and fermentation as part of the curriculum. (This is not currently part of any schooling program that I know of.)

Ever since we began exploring fermentation at Relæ and Manfreds, it felt like opening up a treasure chest filled with new flavors, new tools, and new cooking dimensions. So many of my personal favorite foods are directly connected to a fermentation of some sort, be it bread, charcuterie, cheeses, wine, even the yogurt I eat for breakfast.

I love to think of fermentation as just another way of cooking a vegetable. The point is not whether a carrot is blanched or boiled or pickled, it's about whether it is tender or crunchy. Fermentation should be a means to enhance produce, to "fortify" it with more of its own flavor, or at least another level of it. To reach that level we need bacteria, and we need to know how to control it.

We mostly do very basic fermentations with our vegetables by submerging them in a salt solution, at times adding a splash of whey to favor the growth of lactic bacteria, one of the most common starter cultures in fermentation. The goal is to create the right environment for the right bacteria, which then triggers the development of umami and acidity. We have put lettuce, various mushrooms, gherkins, cucumbers, roots, fruits, and greens to the test with varying results—but the learning process has been great no matter the outcome. We are still not experts, but this is a path we will keep pursuing to add more and more depth to our cuisine. I'm close to developing an addiction to drinking the flavorful brines that are the tasty by-product of most fermentations (cucumber is a particular favorite). It's yet another reason for us to keep experimenting with this fascinating technique.

Pickling Fruits and Vegetables

Like many other restaurants—and home cooks, for that matter—at Relæ, we have taken to pickling fruits and vegetables to save the season and get us through the darker winter months. These processes range from very quick—such as when we pass sea lettuce through a vinegar brine for seconds, just long enough for the flavors to freshen up—to many days or months long. Most often, we pickle vegetables in a brine consisting mostly of vinegar, at times thinned out with water, in vacuum-sealed bags. The added osmotic pressure from the vacuum seal speeds up the pickling process, breaking down the vegetable's texture and impregnating it with vinegary flavor in a matter of minutes. This technique is very useful for thinly sliced carrots or celery root, for example, or thin watercress stems and green leaves like ramsons and nasturtiums or even rose hips.

To get through winter, we have started to preserve a few things in vinegar in jars and then keep them in a cool basement. Because we can still get a variety of root vegetables and a few herbs throughout the winter from farms, we stick to preserving what can act as an added flavor, spice, or interesting element to dishes, such as pine shoots, ramps, unripe strawberries, and elderflowers, as well as capers made of rose hips, elderberries, and ramson and nasturtium buds. We also put away the crunchy watercress stems that are so abundant in spring, and pickled mushrooms, crab apples, and other fruits are great to have in stock when the snow and frost hit.

Pickling Fish

In Danish tradition, several types of fish are pickled, smoked, and salted; in fact, Danes are more likely to eat pickled fish than fresh fish. The best-known preparation is pickled herring, served on rye for the classic smørrebrød. The herring is salted and then put in a brine made of more or less equal amounts of water, vinegar, and sugar, resulting in a very sweet flavor that I am not too fond of.

I am more inspired by the Spanish way of pickling fish, such as boquerones—small anchovies in a vinegar brine—or the pickled mussels and shellfish in the Catalan escabèche. I got introduced to escabèche during my time in elBulli through brilliant staff meals, as well as by eating in the local tapas bars and during various trips to Barcelona. I love how escabèche adds a briny acidity to a fatty fish, often with sherry vinegar, and that whole concept sparked the first inspiration for the *Pickled Mackerel, Cauliflower, and Lemon* (page 276) in this book. For me, this style of pickling solved a quandary: how to serve a fatty fish cold, or almost raw. The slight change of texture caused by the acidity and the partial cooking makes the fish melt on the tongue, and the fattiness is constrained by the vinegar, keeping the flavors alive.

Even Denmark's time-honored pickled herring could benefit from this slightly modernized pickling technique. In other words, lose the sugar and shorten the brining time. Try salting a raw herring only slightly, then pickling it in water and vinegar for no more than an hour or so. The fish will remain fresh, briny, and, most important, not sweet.

Pickled Skate, Mussels, and Celery Root (p.274)
Pickled Mackerel, Cauliflower, and Lemon (p.276)

Cooking in Butter Emulsion

Let's just be clear, I sure didn't invent this. Poaching vegetables in a butter emulsion or "beurre monté" is a classic French approach, but it is so essential to our cooking I decided it was worth a mention.

Liquid fats retain heat for much longer than water-based liquids, such as stocks and juices. Whenever we have something that needs even slightly elaborate and therefore time-consuming plating, cooking it in a butter emulsion helps maintain the food's temperature for a longer time. However, when spooned directly over the surface of a vegetable, most liquid fats will just slip right off. This is why we emulsify butter into water, creating a thick, warm liquid that can coat any type of food and keep it warm, moist, and appetizing until eaten.

We use butter emulsions mostly for vegetables since the temperature of the emulsion stays around 75° to 90°C (165° to 194°F). Even though the temperature is quite high, the emulsion keeps the cooking quite gentle, since the the fat coats the greens and helps prevent overcooking. If a vegetable might require a longer cooking time, we might blanch or cook it first another way, portion it to the exact amount we need for a serving, and then give it a quick reheat in the butter emulsion. The main adjustment we have made is to reduce the amount of butter we use and increase the amount of water by adding xanthan gum to stabilize the emulsion.

The usual setup on the Relæ garnish station is to have two pots and a strainer for every preparation. The first is a large pot that we fill with the butter emulsion, which we always keep very close to the boiling point. The generous amount keeps the temperature from dropping if we need to add a lot of vegetables at the same time. We keep the other pot empty and covered with the strainer. After we add the desired portion of vegetables to the warm butter emulsion, we can quickly pour the contents of the first pot through the strainer into the empty pot. The excess butter stays in the second pot for the next use, and then we can season the cooked vegetables in the strainer. After plating, we move the strainer to the now-empty pot and repeat the procedure again and again all through the night.

Cooking Salads

As soon you become successful treating something a certain way or you are taught to do it that way—a sirloin should be sliced into steaks and grilled, broccoli florets should be blanched—too many of us stop wondering if there is another technique hiding in there, some gem waiting to be discovered. There is no question that romaine lettuce, with its bitterness and crispness, tastes great dressed with olive oil and vinegar or even lightly tossed in the ubiquitous Caesar dressing. Really good indeed. But I love trying to see things from a different angle. I wanted to cook lettuce just because I hadn't done it before, and I had every reason to believe that it would turn out perfectly delicious.

After trying a lot of different cooking techniques, we ended up vaccuum-sealing the lettuce with butter and then poaching it sous vide, and found that those crisp, juicy stems that keep the leaves together become even juicier once carefully cooked. The lettuce head's very juicy, soft tips and crisper core combine with a subtle and grassy bitterness, making it an ingredient that very often returns to our menu. For *Romaine, Egg Yolk, and Nettles* (page 308), we halve the poached lettuce heads and cover them in grated salted egg yolk to counter any bitterness, along with crunchy dried olives and a sauce deepened with nettle puree. We also add the creamy poached lettuce to a dish with braised beef and pistachio puree (page 332) offering a wonderfully juicy texture to what is essentially a dish of braised meat.

So many times in our kitchen, we find something even greater hiding beneath what already seems fantastic. It reminds me of my time at Noma, when I had to find a use for the stringy and slightly tough inner muscles that open and close the shells on razor clams. When I brined them and quickly tossed them on a burning hot *plancha*, they came out tender and tasty and were actually more appetizing than the much leaner main muscle. The experience taught me to look for the unexpected in all ingredients, which was a defining moment for how I eventually came to cook at Relæ.

Precision Cooking

Many chefs have abandoned so-called molecular gastronomy in favor of immersing themselves in laborious study of ancient cooking methods such as pickling and bread baking (see "Evolving a Technique: Making-Old School New School," page 172). Yet I think it is important to pick up the remaining pieces of the "techno-molecular" era and use them to become a better craftsman with a broader toolbox, and this is where "precision cooking" comes into play.

We cook a lot of our meats sous vide, both at Relæ and Manfreds, partly because we also do a lot of nose-to-tail cooking that requires several types of cuts to be cooked and combined in the same finished dish. When serving dishes like the *Lamb, Turnip, and Samphire* (page 324), we often slice up shoulder, leg, breast, and loin alike, and they all must be juicy and pink. Yet those different cuts ask for vastly different cooking approaches; the shoulder needs a longer cooking than the loin and the leg needs a lower temperature than the shoulder or loin for it to come out tender yet still pink and moist.

We could take a traditional approach and roast the legs in the oven, and even the shoulder, but that combination of tender and pink wouldn't be within our reach in either case. This is a problem we solve by carefully separating the pieces, cooking each cut sous vide, individually, at its appropriate temperature and time span, and then roasting them all to add caramelization just before serving. It gives our diners a consistently high quality throughout the night and it's a respectful way of preparing our incredible organic lamb. We also use the same technique for pork and beef.

But I do not believe that cooking sous vide is as simple as bagging up meats and forgetting about them. When I first learned the method, it felt as though everything could be dumped in an immersion circulator at 58°C (136°F) and come out perfectly cooked. But with experience, I started understanding that even though cooking in vacuum bags seals in the juices, it's not unheard of to end up with dry or off-flavored meat, and in the worst case, a spreadable meat puree. And even though we've mastered sous vide cooking, there are some dishes that just taste best when cooked the traditional way. We roast mallard duck in the pan and finish in the oven exactly as you would in a French restaurant 20 years ago.

Ultimately, our goal at Relæ is to understand the meat we cook by experimenting with all sorts of techniques—some require machinery and bags; others do not. At times, you find a new dimension or texture by braising a cut of pork you would normally roast, or by cooking a thigh just a few degrees lower than the last time chicken was on the menu.

Barely Cooking

For the sake of texture and flavor, at times, I like to keep certain elements somewhat raw yet slightly warmed on the plate. This includes anything from meat to numerous types of vegetables, because when cooking any type of food, protein or plant, its flavor changes as the texture changes.

The whole al dente approach to cooking vegetables is welcome after all the overcooking of past decades, but it is too narrow to apply to all foods as a general rule. It all really comes down to what context the cooked element is subsequently put in. Sometimes cooking an ingredient until it is very soft is what you need, and at other times, a dish calls for raw flavors and crunch. For example, raw asparagus's distinct green and grassy notes slowly fade into sweeter notes with cooking. In some cases, that is what you look for, but if you need a fresher flavor, you must reduce cooking to an absolute minimum. To maintain the raw asparagus flavor in a warm dish, we thinly slice the green stalks and cook them for just a second in a boiling butter emulsion, which also keeps them warmer longer than if blanched in water. Or we pour a warm chicken stock on top of asparagus slices so that it just warms through.

In some cases, we might want a vegetable to display several layers of its flavors and textures in the same dish. We can cook broccoli florets until just tender while turning the fibrous stalk into a soft-textured puree. Or maybe we will cut up the stalk into smaller pieces and cook it for just an instant to maintain the crunch and flavor as if it were raw but so that it reaches the same temperature as the rest of the dish. At times, we will even just arrange a few slices of cucumber, kohlrabi, or green strawberries on top of our warming oven to slowly warm them through, just to soften the texture a bit.

When it comes to meat, we have found ways to serve raw meat with more "cooked" flavors at a slightly warm temperature. In dishes like *Lamb, Shrimp, and Dill* (page 270), we roast lamb bones or scraps, combine the fat with vegetable oil, cook it a bit more, and then brush the resulting deeply flavored fat onto the raw slices of meat just before serving. As you bite into it, the initial flavors speak of cooked meat but the texture stays intriguingly raw, giving the dish unexpected complexity.

Stocks

In cooking school, I was taught to always use veal stock when cooking veal, beef stock when serving beef, and so on. To some extent I agree, but it very much depends on the expression you want from the dish. Because our cooking tends toward lighter flavor profiles, I often find that veal and beef stock, especially when reduced to a glaze, are way too powerful. They become so reductive that in a way it feels as if all of the flavors from the original ingredients have been absorbed into a sort of vortex, out of reach of the palate. Pork stock can be light enough in flavor, but it doesn't reduce well if not degreased extremely well.

Chicken stock is even lighter, and that's why we base all of our stocks, with very few exceptions, on chicken. Its mild flavor and balanced mouthfeel make it exceptional for giving body to a dish or sauce. Once reduced into a glaze, it has more of a roasted flavor than an actual chicken flavor, making it quite a universal tool. We don't add any vegetables to our stocks, because they can always be added to the final sauce if needed. I feel that vegetables sweeten stock unnecessarily and muddle flavors in the long cooking process.

When we cook up a dish of sweetbreads or veal tongue, we add some veal stock to the sauce for flavor, but we lighten it up with chicken stock to keep it balanced and clean. Pork is mostly accompanied by the juice of its roasted bones, which adds flavor to a base of chicken broth. In general, we keep all of our sauces very light and just barely reduced.

Multipurpose Chicken Stock

For optimal mouthfeel, use equal parts chicken carcasses and chicken wings, but any chicken part will do. At home, I always cook up all the bones and scraps from a roast chicken, which easily makes for a tasty bouillon. Add the wings and bones to a large pot and fill with water. You must at least have four times the amount of water to wings and bones. At both Relæ and Manfreds, we use filtered water, which is crucial for a clearer taste from the final product. Bring the water slowly to a boil, and skim off the impurities thoroughly as soon as it has boiled. Turn down the heat to a slow simmer. Let simmer for about 8 hours, while carefully skimming off the fat flowing to the top on a regular basis. Strain the stock and reduce it to about a fifth of its original volume and cool down.

Sauce can be a double-edged sword, as it must underline flavors and bind together the dish but not take it over entirely.

We don't prepare fish stocks all that often, because we most often serve fish raw or lightly pickled, and a stock has rarely fit into those dishes, except *Cod, Kohlrabi and Skins* (page 278), in which a splash of lightly reduced cod stock adds to the gelatinous qualities of the dish. In fish-based dishes, we more often use mussel stock, which gives a briny marine element to any fish. Fish dishes that use mussel stock often come out cleaner and more precise in flavor than those that do without.

<u>Nut Milks</u>

Probably healthier but just as rich, creamy nut milks can battle it out with any velouté or cream sauce out there as the base for a sauce. Their strikingly opulent and nutty flavor is often highlighted on our menu.

I first saw what nut milks could do during my time at elBulli. The Catalans are unique in recognizing nuts as a truly important gastronomical tool beyond their obvious uses in desserts and pastry, and you see almonds and hazelnuts all over traditional Catalan dishes. elBulli took the local use of nuts in savory dishes a few steps further. The sweet and nutty perfume of almond milk still brings me back to my days in Spain.

In *Rhubarb Compote, Almond, and Vinegar* (page 348), we use almond milk as a counterpoint to the high acidity of rhubarb compote and vinegar sorbet, which is also garnished with a few toasted almonds. We go even further in *Fennel, Smoked Almond, and Parsley* (page 312) when we smoke the almonds before turning them into a milk to go with lightly brined fennel shoots.

You can easily make nut milks by soaking blanched and peeled almonds, hazelnuts, cashews, macadamia nuts—you name it—in equal parts of nuts to water. Walnuts can be soaked skin-on if blanched a few times to remove their excess bitterness.

After soaking them for at least a few hours or ideally 24, blend the nuts to a fine paste and press it through a superbag strainer with brute force. This requires a good amount of physical effort, but the milk that comes out is of incredible quality. This nut milk can be served ice-cold, turned into a granité if you freeze and grate it, or just barely heated for a warm dish.

We have slightly modified this basic nut milk technique over time, since the labor is extremely demanding if you make it by hand. We purchased a small stainless steel fruit press that does all the work for us over the course of a few hours. It gives us a better yield and probably a better quality, considering the reduced manhandling of the very delicate puree.

Since the fatty acids of nuts turn rancid very fast, freshness is key with this preparation. When we have nut milks on the menu, we need several liters per night, but the amount needed for a handful of diners can easily be pressed by hand.

Our smoked nut milks, which have a bacony aroma combined with a high fat content, probably have one of the most comforting flavor profiles ever. They really help us keep our vegetarian cooking complex and flavorful while still freeing us from heavy sauces.

Hiding on the Plate

During my time at elBulli, I was as amazed by the beauty of some dishes as I was perplexed by others that seemed to be put together by a four-year-old. I knew that nothing there was made by accident, and that what might look like unfinished mise en place would probably punch you in the face with its flavors and techniques. I realized that a casual approach to plating transmits a very important message to the diner, that the qualities of the food do not reside in its surface, but deep underneath, in its flavors and textures, and in the ideas behind it.

I knew when I opened Relæ that the initial concept would need to be better and sharper than any other restaurants in Copenhagen but also cut to the bone because of our limited space and staffing. With just a handful of cooks preparing food for about seventy guests per night, I knew we couldn't serve a perfect piece of meat lying next to a tiny bouquet of picked chervil stems and punched-out disks of truffle. Why? First of all, I never want to trim off pieces of meat just for cosmetic reasons—I want to be able to serve irregularly shaped cuts and even mix up fattier pieces of pork with less fatty pieces on the plate. At first, when we served chicken, we would use breast, leg, and wings as well as hearts and a bit of liver, but plating it became a disaster: the dish tasted great but looked so messy.

Our nose-to-tail approach was the first reason why we decided to "hide" an element of a dish underneath another component. That chicken dish, for example, would have looked much sharper if we had placed some of the chicken parts underneath the small pieces of cabbage that were also part of the dish. Today, we think about our plating approach on much more than just an aesthetic level.

The cooking we do is vegetable-driven, even if guests consider meat the primary component of a dish. When we serve *Lamb, Turnip, and Samphire* (page 324) or *Chicken Wings, White Asparagus, and Anchovies* (page 328), I watch for our guests' stunned reactions when they look down at the plate and all they see is vegetables. "*That* is chicken?" Many guests can't even wait for an explanation of the dish before they start untangling slices of white asparagus to find out where that chicken went. *Sheep's Milk Yogurt, Radishes, and Nasturtium* (page 248) looks like a tiny armadillo made of nasturtium leaves and stems; guests may feel as though they need to force their way through armor before getting to the core of the dish to experience the creamy mousse and spicy radishes. I love playing with people's expectations like this.

Sometimes our "hiding" approach serves a practical purpose. With our desserts, for example, we "hide" components by arranging them in layers, which helps us control how the guest enjoys the dish. If a dish is so complicated that you don't know how to eat it—a highly composed plate with a quenelle of sorbet here, a crumble there, and square of sponge cake in the other corner—it is very hard to predict how a diner will approach it. That's why I like to present a dessert more like a layer cake, where we get to decide exactly how much granité or crumble is in every mouthful.

Consistency is another reason to take this path, because the dish can be executed quite quickly during service. Whoever makes it just has to layer one component on top of another and doesn't have to spend time arranging different shapes and forms and sauces. All the dishes come out differently, depending on who is plating them, but going for this simplified, monochromatic way of doing things leaves much less room for error.

"Hiding" components of a dish has almost become a signature of ours, and it really symbolizes our philosophy of cooking and hospitality: not everything may be as it seems, and there is probably something hiding underneath the surface.

Ideas
Textures

Contrasting Temperatures

One of the most eye-opening experiences for me at Heston Blumenthal's restaurant the Fat Duck was tasting his famous Hot and Iced Tea, a drink with two different temperatures in the same glass.

Contrasting hot and cold temperatures is a common technique in desserts, and to a lesser extent, starters. At Relæ, our dessert style skews toward savory, and we try to limit the number of ingredients we use for each one. For this reason, texture and temperature are how we play with the complexity of our desserts; most of them juxtapose comforting warmth and ice-cold freshness, as well as crunchy and soft textures. Also, the temperature contrast makes the generally low sugar levels we use less obvious to diners who have a sweet tooth.

To put a spoon through a frozen granité surrounding a fragrant, slightly warmer mousse, as in the *Chanterelles, Apples, and Granité* (page 342), results in a few instants of crunchiness before all the ingredients mix on the palate and release their flavors. When combining a frozen buttermilk sorbet with a warm and tangy rhubarb compote, as we do with *Rhubarb Compote, Almond, and Vinegar* (page 348), those assertive contrasts create a playful way to finish off the meal.

To avoid complications when mixing hot and cold, we often "insulate" the cold element by topping it with a thin layer of gel, such as the milk gel we lightly set with agar in the rhubarb dish. This helps keep hot and cold elements from losing their boundaries for the few crucial minutes until the dessert is on the table. When the diner spoons into the dish, the "insulation" is broken and the temperature contrasts stay clear and purposeful.

Unripe Strawberries, Cress, and Buttermilk (p.246)
Lumpfish Roe, Daikon, and Almonds (p.260)
Baked Potato Puree (p.298)
Chanterelles, Apple, and Granité (p.342)
Mandarin, Buttermilk, and Egg Yolk (p.344)
Rhubarb Compote, Almond, and Vinegar (p.348)
Sheep's Milk Yogurt, Beets, and Black Currant (p.352)
Corn, Bread Crumbs, and Marjoram (p.356)

Crunch!

A good textural contrast is a great way to add complexity, especially if a dish's flavors are mostly in harmony. Everyone loves munching on something crackling and crunchy—breakfast cereals being a prime example—but there are other ways to add crunch to a dish beyond dehydrating and puffing grains. A dehydrated vegetable, toasted nuts, or crispy dried olives can add textural dimension while also keeping flavors focused.

In general, everything crunchy must be dried, toasted, or dehydrated to such an extent that any aromas beyond toasty and slightly bitter seem to be sacrificed. Therefore, pairing these crunchy elements with foods that have creamy, soft, and comforting textures and a pleasing and mellow flavor profile is a sure winner, as we do with the *Baked Potato Puree* (page 298) with buttermilk powder and crunchy black olives.

Freeze-dried products are an exception to the rule of crunchy foods that have lost their top notes and aromas. The freeze-drying process is so gentle that both the aroma and acidity of berries and other fruit are actually intensified. We are in the process of experimenting with a small freeze dryer with Copenhagen University to venture further into the world of crunchiness.

Chewy

The word *chewy* almost always has a negative connotation: "the meat was chewy" is probably the most often heard complaint about food worldwide. I reject the notion that the quality of meat should be judged only by its tenderness, but that's another story entirely. Regardless, I believe that chewy can actually be a very positive thing. There's something wonderful and primal about having to masticate my way through my food; I think of how our ancestors must have chewed through the raw meat of caught prey. The challenge, then, is to find the right amount of chewiness—not so much that eating feels laborious, but enough to create a pleasant surprise.

Most dried fruits have the chew we want. Dried apricots, figs, and dates need a little pull when first bitten into. A bread with a strong and solidified gluten network has a nice chew to it, and many types of charcuterie call for just enough work by the teeth to be dangerously addictive. But in all cases, chewy must be combined with an appropriate amount of tenderness. A bread with a long and properly executed fermentation brings you softness straight after that chew, and the high amount of fat in cured meats will melt on your tongue when you're chewing through a *saucisson sec* or a salame.

We have tried to bring out those same chewy qualities, mostly when working with vegetables. Drying and rehydrating most often seals the deal, and starting with a dry cooking method for a long period can also bring

---

Chewy Jerusalem Artichokes

We sometimes reheat these in butter in order to tenderize them a bit further and use them as a garnish, but they are at their best when served whole, slightly warmed, and sprinkled with brown butter and salt as a snack.

Scrub Jerusalem artichokes meticulously until all of the dirt has been removed, without ruining the skin. Put them on racks with enough room around them for good circulation and bake them in a well-ventilated convection oven at 190°C (375°F) for 2 to 2½ hours, or until quite dry on the outside but not yet completely petrified on the inside. Without a convection oven, the cooking time might take twice as long. Keep turning and flipping the chokes every 20 to 30 minutes, so they cook evenly, and it's a good idea to open the oven a few times, to release excess steam. The moisture coming from within the Jerusalem artichokes will soften the dry skin, making them chewy as they cool down.

a good amount of chew. We slightly char a slice of baked celery root, which gives it a chew that makes it reminiscent of a tortilla, from which we make a "taco" for our snack menu. We warm dried citrus in brown butter, which gives us a chew that's packed with acidity and bitterness, and we use it to liven up a potato puree. Even just salting or curing the more juice-packed vegetables, such as cucumber and kohlrabi, gives a pleasantly juicy and chewy texture.

Often with vegetables, the skin is where we find the fibers strong enough to give us the desired chew after prolonged cooking. Carrot skins and parsnip skins have been on the menu, such as the dehydrated carrot skins that contrast with soft-ripened cheese in the *Nordlys, Carrots, and Orange Zest* (page 340). Jerusalem artichokes are particularly suited for turning vegetable skins into a chewy and caramelized casing for the tender and sweet interior. First in snacks and later in many dishes, the baked Jerusalem artichokes deliver the perfect chew, as always, balanced with tenderness.

Leathery

Leathery, very much like chewy, seems to be an acquired taste. When asked, most people seem to associate the word *leathery* with pet treats—hardly something you'd want to encounter at a restaurant. But I maintain that leathery textures can add an elegant dimension to a dish—which is why we use several types of seaweed in our restaurant. The various sea lettuces and dulse display that mouthfeel at its best—think of a traditional miso soup with bits of green seaweed adding a delicate contrast to the soft tofu. Yes, kelp might be too tough to eat on its own, but it can be shaved finely into what the Japanese call *tororo kombu*. However, that is where some people, especially Westerners, tend to slam the brakes, finding a texture that might be unknown to their palate and thus anything but comforting.

Though they have nothing else in common with seaweed, you find a similar leathery mouthfeel in dried fruit purees or fruit leathers. Fruit leathers are made of pureed fruit spread out in a thin layer and dried slowly until the pectin gels to the point of giving it that flexibility and pullback that makes it so interesting to chew on. Pectin is a complex carbohydrate that's naturally found in stone fruit, citrus, and other types of fruit that acts as a thickening agent in jams and gels.

The textural common ground between fruit leather and seaweed made me want to experiment with combining them in a dish, despite their very different flavors. In *Beet, Crab Apple, and Söl* (page 254), we dried several varieties of crab apples and apples into leathers, ripped them into small pieces, and combined them in a varied palette of colors, all with different acidities and aromas. We added very little sugar to the leathers, which allowed us to use them in a savory dish combined with similar-size pieces of dulse, which provided a tobacco-like depth of flavor. We then bound everything together with a vinaigrette made of apple juice blended with soaked and softened dulse. The end result, I'm pleased to report, was very far removed from anything resembling a pet treat.

Dehydrating/Rehydrating

One winter, we found ourselves caught up in an irresistible drive to dehydrate just about everything. It wasn't just the expected herbs. We dried shrimp, fish roe, and cured and uncured meats. We even tested dehydrating everything at different levels, trying, for example, to see if we would have any use for half-dried celery root. Dried shrimp, partly inspired by how it's used in Thai cooking, became an important part of our pantry and so did the various fruit leathers, while the process of drying most aromatic herbs seemed to confirm that, in some cases, fresh is best.

Drying foods was historically done for preserving purposes, but if you look at the drying process as a long cooking method at a low temperature, you can achieve interesting results in both texture and flavor. No matter how gentle the drying, the manipulated food's texture completely changes, and the flavors are intensified at the same pace. One thing we discovered was that if we peeled and dried a zucchini at 50°C (125°F) for 5 to 6 hours, we got a very interesting texture. The outside layer turned leathery and dry, but the inside would be less affected and even turn very juicy once placed in a boiling butter emulsion for a few minutes. This experiment turned into *Dried Zucchini and Bitter Leaves* (page 314).

Root vegetables, which are quite fibrous, are best when rehydrated again after drying, as they turn leathery and chewy yet juicy. One of the easiest applications of rehydrating is dehydrated raw carrots, which we cook in boiling water for about a minute until tenderized. The same goes for turnips, parsnips, and parsley roots. We just cut the turnips in smaller bits, while cutting carrots in longer and thinner slices. Beets, at least when kept whole, have to be cooked before dehydrating, which helps break down the structure and shortens the dehydrating process but also favors an intensely sweet and chewy, almost candylike texture.

The texture of rehydrated root vegetables in addition to their appearance has similarities to rustic pasta, and their spongy characteristics make them well suited for similar preparations, such as tossed with butter or with herbs and olive oil, or in the case of *Turnips, Chervil, and Horseradish* (page 284), with a creamy butter sauce.

Vegetable Skins

As a part of our determination to make use of the entirety of things, including all the cuts of an animal and even every part of a vegetable, we have spent a lot of time making good use of the skins and peels of several roots and tubers. The skins are nearly always packed with flavors, and one of the main physical activities of a cook at Relæ, and even more so at Manfreds, is leaning over a sink for the agonizing scrubbing of carrots or other root vegetables for hours at a time.

Even though serving a vegetable so close to its natural state might look very rustic, I see it as a much more refined way of doing things because scrubbing is not easy—at all. It takes so much more time than just peeling, and it is part of the extra effort we put into our cooking to maximize flavor.

At times, you may be looking for a sweeter carrot flavor with less bitterness, so the carrots need to be peeled, but you also might want to focus on that outer layer, separating it from the sweeter interior flesh to use it for a dish on its own. The *Jerusalem Artichoke, Malt, and Bread* (page 350) is all about the crispy and crystallized Jerusalem artichoke skins obtained by first baking the root vegetable until soft, scooping out the inside, and then "crystallizing" the skins by soaking them in sugar syrup and baking them until crispy and dry.

Potato skins are incredibly nutty and flavorful once baked, and we use them to infuse the milk that we add to the *Baked Potato Puree* (page 298), making for the comforting feel of the dish. Even salsify skins found a use in our kitchen. We fry the roots whole, so the skin makes a sort of shell in which the vegetable could steam, then scrape off the more bitter, outer layer of skin and fry them again. The bitterness the skin brings to the *Fried Salsify and Bergamot* (page 316) creates such a complexity that it has become one of my favorite dishes in this book.

Ideally, we would never discard the skin of any vegetable or root, but in reality our desire to use the skins is borne out of a continuous seeking of flavor and texture, not so much out of necessity. It is just another lesson learned about how to look for flavor in all the layers of the produce at hand.

Salting and Brining Vegetables

Even more often than with meat, we brine or dry-salt vegetables to retain moisture, manipulate texture, and control cooking. With a whole roasted chicken, you don't get the satisfying impact of the salt solution until the chicken is cooked, but with vegetables, brining and dry-salting is more like a cooking technique than just a precooking preparation. With brining, the food is immersed in a salt-water solution, while dry-salting calls for covering an ingredient with salt for a certain amount of time until it is effectively brined. Either way, the vegetable's structure and texture are broken down to such an extent that they don't necessarily require more cooking.

With juice-retaining vegetables such as button mushrooms, cucumbers, and firmer fruits such as apples and pears, brining changes their texture so that they seem slightly cooked but their flavor is still raw. All of the nutrients are retained and we are able to keep a certain bite and juicy crunch. Brining also helps alter the texture of more fibrous vegetables, like cabbage and kohlrabi, that normally require a bit of hard work to chew on raw. We also dry-salt some vegetables, such as in the *Cod, Kohlrabi, and Skins* (page 278), where we dry-salt thin slices of kohlrabi for 15 minutes to garnish the cod, which is also dry-brined overnight, naturally.

For the *Potato, Seaweed, and Pecorino* (page 288), we brine our potato "noodles"—thinly shaved slices of potato—then cook them. This helps rid them of excessively mealy starch, prevents them from oxidizing and turning brown, and allows us to cook them less than we would normally, thus keeping an interesting and pleasant crunch.

The question for most vegetables is whether to dry-salt or brine them. It very much depends on the goal of the preparation. If something needs a slight manipulation of texture, using 1.5 percent of sprinkled salt (i.e., salt in a quanity that is 1.5 percent the total weight of the food) can do wonders. If the preparation is done with the intention of washing out a vegetable's bitterness or starch or even precooking it, use a brine with 3 percent salinity (i.e., 3 percent as much salt as water by weight). Then seal in vacuum bags, because the pressure speeds up the process of dry-salting or brining considerably. Without a vacuum sealer, you can get decent results by brining the vegetable in a container with plenty of room for the brine for two or three times as long, but in the end, the brine won't penetrate as evenly as with vacuum-sealed bags. In fact, if cut into thin slices, most of these ingredients need only a few minutes in the brine to completely change texture. We brine most ingredients for a few hours or until the following day, but you can usually judge when the brine has penetrated the vegetable, as it is often visible to the eye.

Salting and Brining Meats and Fish

My exploration of brining meats started off when I was trying to get a better understanding of sous vide cooking. I often found that the meats that required longer cooking ended up dry and mealy. They understandably lost moisture from cooking for as many as 24 or 48 hours—some countermeasures naturally had to be taken if the meat really needed those long hours of cooking to break down.

During my days as a sous chef at Noma, I needed to find a suitable cooking method for veal tongue, which has a very particular texture. I prebrined the meat in a 7 percent solution before cooking it sous vide at a series of different temperatures. But the biggest revelation for me came when I vacuum-sealed the tongues with brine in plastic, instead of putting them in huge buckets of brine. Even in the bags, they would get evenly brined, making the process smoother and faster and taking up less of our valuable kitchen space.

At Relæ, we continue to bag up much of the meat we brine. The brining technique makes use of osmosis, which is sped up considerably with the pressure from a vacuum seal, which extracts all the air from the bag in a matter of seconds. In that closed environment, we are able to brine medium to large cuts of meat, such as roasts or whole chickens, in 48 hours, and smaller cuts, such as chicken wings and fish, in 12 to 24 hours. But even more important, the meat ends up very evenly brined, because the liquid always covers all parts of the meat at all times without the need for big tubs, large volumes of brine, or repetitive checking and turning of the cuts that are brining.

When poaching chicken wings or thighs, we use a lighter brine of just about 3 percent to cook sous vide for 2 to 3 hours at 65°C (122°F). The thighs are seasoned, and the texture is still firm and just tenderized to the point that the muscles are easily pulled apart. Sweetbreads and veal hearts as well as chicken hearts all gain from brining, allowing us to cook the chicken hearts for only 10 minutes at 58°C (136°F), just until tenderized, moist, and tasty.

Even when braising traditionally in the oven, we go for a light brine of 3 percent for veal cheeks, short ribs, beef neck, shoulder, and similar parts. It seems to help the cuts better withstand cooking without falling apart, and they end up very precisely seasoned.

Fish also benefits greatly from brining because the salt gradually breaks down some of the muscular tissue while allowing us a shorter cooking time, with a much juicier result. Prior to cooking, we brine skate, which softens its rather tough tissue without damaging the flesh. After cooking, it pulls apart into transparent, tender, and appetizing pieces.

With roasts and a few other traditional cooking methods, we opt for a light dry-salting of the meat or fish. While a heavier salting or brining would give pork neck characteristics a bit too similar to cooked ham, we rub 1.5 percent salt all over the surface before poaching it for just 2½ hours at 55°C (131°F) and then finishing it in the pan. In this case, dry-salting rather than brining gives us a more caramelized, roasted, and deep flavor.

Juiciness, the Natural Sauce

It took us a long time to crack the code of cooking squid. Squid often ends up tough, or worse, dry and rubbery. So we were in a state of nirvana when we finally nailed perfectly juicy squid. The key was to slice it thinly and cook it for just a few moments in loads of brown butter—nothing more.

Juiciness is the ne plus ultra of cooking. It is why we cook food in the first place. Whether you're braising, blanching, roasting, or grilling an ingredient, the goal is always a juicy steak, a juicy pork neck, a juicy cauliflower floret, or a juicy piece of poached fish. Whenever we experiment with temperatures, times, and cooking liquids, it is always while aiming for that ultimate state of juiciness. That's because the amount of retained juice in a dish is crucial to the diner's experience. For a pleasant and enjoyable bite, you need just the right amount of liquid to exude from the cooked item as you chew it.

The rules of the juiciness game are a little different for vegetables then they are for meat. Some vegetables are just ripe with the potential of becoming more appetizing and juicy. At times, salting or marinating them will break down their cells more forgivingly than any type of cooking would do. Even just cutting them up in a different way can give you juices that are ready to explode. In *Cucumber, Caraway, and Lemon Balm* (page 250), we just grate the cucumber so that its pulp retains most of its juices, which are ready to release at the first bite. By cooking turnips whole for the *Lamb, Turnip, and Samphire* (page 324), they stay extremely juicy; and we also salt and bake celery root, and then grate it for a juicy base for slivers of skate in *Pickled Skate, Mussels, and Celery Root* (page 274).

We were also surprised to see that freezing then thawing sliced pumpkin, as we do in *Hokkaido Pumpkin and Mandarin* (page 354), removes the mealy sensation of biting into raw pumpkin and makes it incredibly juicy. But just slightly cooking newly harvested onions and peeling the layers apart, such as in *Cooked Onions, Buttermilk, and Nasturtium* (page 256), is probably the best example of how juicy vegetables can get. That's also why we so often cut up our vegetables in thin slices or small pieces—so that we can control exactly when and how that juice is released, giving a natural sauce to everything we serve.

Ideas
Flavor

Butter and Bitter
Charred and Grilled
Toasted and Nutty
A Touch of Umami
Meat with Seafood
Minerality

Butter and Bitter

Bitterness gets a bad rap. Admittedly, we humans are preprogrammed to fear bitter flavors—biologically speaking, bitterness often signifies poison. That said, now that we aren't cave dwellers who risk death every time we eat something unfamiliar, I think "bitter" merits reexamination.

I've found that bitterness is that magic touch that keeps flavors tight and orderly, mouthful after mouthful. It prevents sweetness from taking over, it constrains opulence, and it gives a direction for the other flavors to follow. Because we want so many of our dishes to be precise, tight, and to the point, bitterness very often completes the palate. But bitterness always needs to be attenuated by other components. Acidity is crucial, as is one certain ingredient we use whenever we need to mellow out the bitter in a dish: butter.

If some rather bitter components dominate a dish, we often use butter—melted, as a sauce, slightly toasted and burnt, or even just folded into other elements of a dish—to bridge the bitterness as well as the acidity we add to counter that bitterness. When we prepare skin-on vegetables, such as Jerusalem artichokes or salsify, the skin skews the dish toward a more bitter direction. We often pair these preparations with even more bitterness and a high acidity, in most cases citrus, which has both bitter and acidic qualities. But in addition to the fragrant lemon puree we use to lift the Jerusalem artichoke, we also add a healthy dose of brown butter, which bridges the flavors of the citrus and the vegetables.

When we combine bitter sesame with the sweetness of carrots in *Carrot, Elderflower, and Sesame* (page 304), we add a good amount of pickled elderflower for acidic balance and flavor. But if the carrots were not cooked in a coating of butter emulsion, the result might end up being too sharp and aggressive.

The fat in the butter does most of the work in these cases, and we often switch out butter with other fats, such as roasted lamb or beef fat, or even creamy nut milks with an elevated fat content.

Charred and Grilled

We have gotten pretty good at mastering bitterness, but when deliberately burning or charring some foods, you achieve a particularly dry and aggressive bitterness that can be used in many ways.

A grilled steak would be nothing without the charred marks on its surface, bitter on their own yet flavoring the meat brilliantly. We riff on that idea and bring it to the plate in very different ways. While purposefully burning meat might be going a bit over the top, doing that with vegetables— which are packed with carbohydrates and sweetness to back up the bitter notes—opens up many possibilities. We char onions for sauces and purees, deliberately cooking them way too long. We grill raw Jerusalem artichokes until the skin turns crisp and completely burnt, acting as a sort of seasoning for the incredibly sweet and concentrated soft flesh inside.

We have flame-torched dried cabbages into burnt leaves to contrast with raw beef, almost creating the sensation of having a steak when you're actually eating raw meat. In that case, we almost deconstruct that steak by pulling the two contrasting elements even further apart, making the grill marks even more charred and the meat even more bloody and tender.

Toasted and Nutty

Toasty and nutty is probably the most comforting of all flavor profiles. When you inhale the addictive perfume of toasting nuts, newly baked brioche, or slices of rye bread frying in butter, you instinctively understand that something very tasty is on the way. Toasty and nutty comes from a controlled Maillard reaction that transforms simple and complex carbohydrates into absolute deliciousness. It's the combination of a tiny amount of bitterness with a controlled sweetness that turns it into this mouthwatering package.

Many of the other flavor profiles we work with can be far more aggressive. Bitterness and acidity give a great punch to a dish, and the combination of charred and fatty foods create an amazing balance, but all these flavors and components are turned up to the max. Toasted and nutty is a more gentle and friendly flavor that gets along with the palate from the first bite.

In the *Baked Potato Puree* (page 298), we do everything possible to accentuate the nutty notes naturally found in the cooked potatoes by infusing the puree's milk with baked potato skins, which give it a caramel color and flavor. We then add several types of dried citrus, such as mandarin or blood orange, for contrast. We also might go in another direction, such as underlining the nutty notes of Jerusalem artichokes with something bitter like coffee, a combination that has found solid ground on our menu with dishes like *Jerusalem Artichokes, Coffee, and Passion* (page 360).

A Touch of Umami

Umami is the most elegant and least assertive of the five basic flavors, and it's the most difficult to single out and master. But even if, just like a bass line, it is rarely noticed by the majority of people, all food will, like music, lack depth and richness if deprived of it.

Since we keep our cooking mostly light, refreshing, and high in acidity at Relæ, we rarely play to the most obvious comforting notes, like aged steaks, braised beef, or reduced sauces. That makes getting enough umami and depth onto the menu a challenge.

As with many other kitchen skills and techniques, it turns out that a young Western cook like me can find all the help he needs when it comes to umami by just looking east. *Enoki, Kelp, and Seaweed* (page 310), a dish of steamed enoki mushrooms in a mushroom-kelp broth, has ended up being very Japanese both in expression and flavor. We lightly cook kelp at 60°C (140°F) for an hour and season the liquid with two kinds of mushroom juice, one made from salting sliced fresh mushrooms and collecting their extracted liquid and a fermented mushroom juice we make from brined mushrooms (which we call our "mushroom soy sauce"). Our broth has a depth of flavor very reminiscent of dashi, but with a sort of Relæ touch to it—deep and fulfilling yet without any meat or fish involved whatsoever.

Fermenting is a versatile tool for adding umami to vegetables. A seemingly light dish like the *Lettuce, Smoked Almond, and Olive Oil* (page 290) is full of umami because we ferment baby lettuce hearts with lactic acid bacteria from whey. A light tang is a bonus of this fermentation process.

We regularly use seaweed in our vegetable and vegetarian dishes for a sense of meatiness. We also find that prolonged roasting or grilling of some root vegetables, like carrots, intensifies their flavor and helps make their natural glutamates—the amino acid and protein component that transmits flavor in meat and vegetables—shine through. The caramelization and Maillard reaction of this extensive cooking process brings out the sweet and savory notes of the vegetable.

We have also become very fond of salting and drying egg yolks to give an extra touch of umami to a vegetable dish. We completely cover the yolks in salt for about a day, rinse them, and then dry them for 4 to 8 hours. We grate them over the *Celery Root Taco* (page 232), and have even used them flattened into thin sheets to wrap up bits of baked Hokkaido pumpkin.

In general, many of the foods that add umami are dried, such as dried anchovy and shrimp, dried egg yolks, dried mushrooms, and dried seaweeds. Our *Milk, Kelp, and Caramel* (page 346)—a kelp-infused milk ice—is the most intense mouthful of glutamate that I have ever experienced, especially in a dessert. Kelp has the highest amount of glutamate of the seaweeds, and it comes through clearly, even with a short infusion with the milk. I remember when I would help send out the dessert from the pastry station and taste it over and over again. By the end of service, I always got this buzzing sensation in my mouth; I was basically high on glutamate. Even though overdosing on a kelp-infused ice cream felt like a bad idea, it was so addictive I couldn't stop eating it.

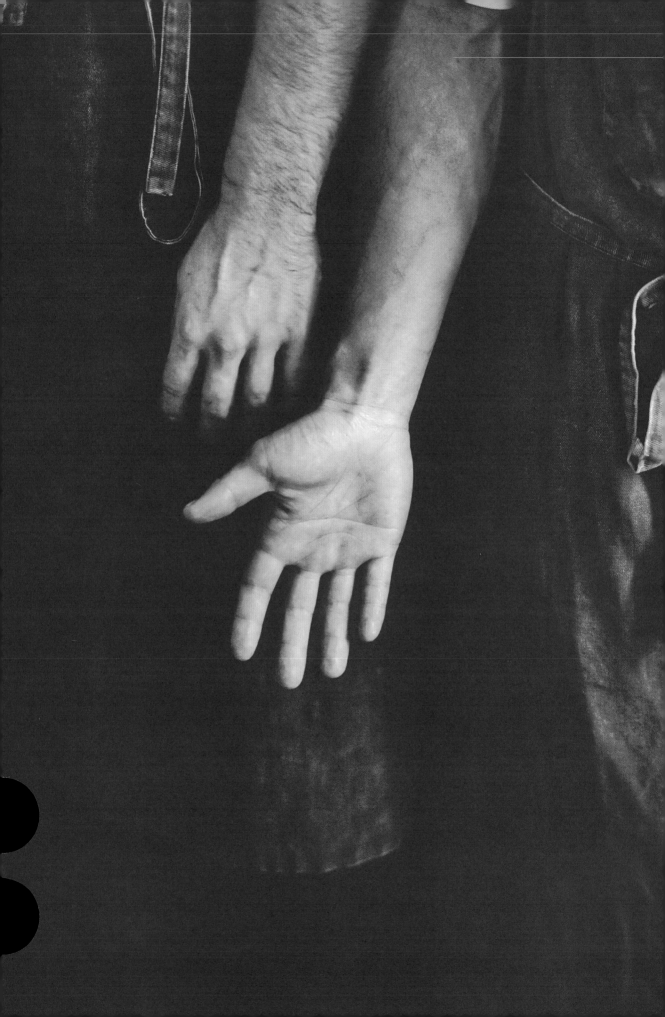

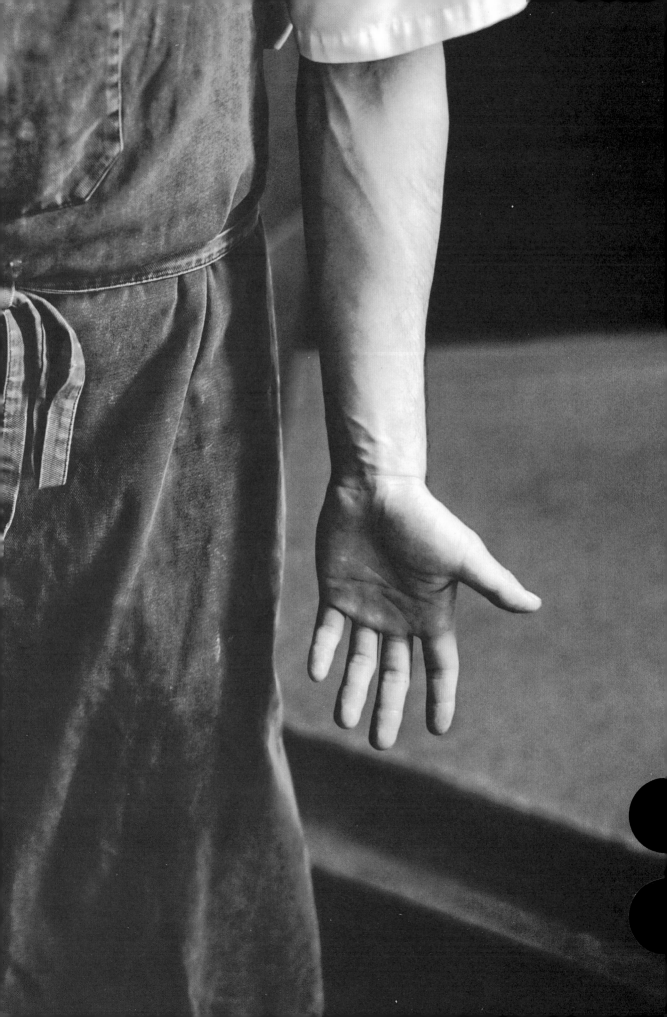

Meat with Seafood

When a Greek friend and very talented pastry chef came in for his first meal with us at Relæ, he sat at the counter and asked in his thick accent, "Tell me, Christian, why do like to put meat with fish so much?" After a defensive moment wondering what he really meant, I realized that we had served him mussels in his beef tartare and anchovies on his chicken. For a few days after that, I began to really consider his question.

Why do we like to pair meat with seafood so much? Well, the brine and punch that mussels, oysters, anchovies, and sea urchins deliver have the effect of placing a big Marshall amplifier straight on the plate with the umami knob turned all the way up. These briny marine notes lift up the natural flavors of meat, whether it's pork, lamb, beef, or chicken.

The saltiest of the bunch, anchovies, act almost like a seasoning, and blander types of meat like chicken really benefit from its salinity. If we serve chicken with anchovy without explaining what the dish contains, most people won't be able to pinpoint the anchovy. And while the salty, marine touch of anchovy is a sure winner with white chicken meat, we found that with poached cod, it has a less fortunate effect, making the cod taste fishy and less clean.

An oyster blended or slightly cut up can play a supporting role to raw beef or even cooked chicken, adding an elegant and velvety quality. When just barely cooked, mussels have an almost oysterlike elegance and briny flavor, and their soft and pleasant texture makes them a perfect match with raw beef, such as in my Greek friend's tartare.

Dried mullet roe, called bottarga, makes a great seasoning for everything meaty; actually one of the first dishes on the Relæ menu based on this idea was a combination of chicken, bottarga, and baby corn. And inspired by the Thai predilection for drying and fermenting fish, we have made dried fjord shrimp a staple of our cuisine, as it adds complexity to just about anything, including sprinkling it as a powder over raw lamb in the *Lamb, Shrimp, and Dill* (page 270).

Seaweed can give the same salinity that fish does. In fact, people often confuse seaweed with something fishy, which makes it versatile for pairing with main course meats, as we have done with a dish combining roast lamb, bitter greens, and pan-fried sea lettuce.

Minerality

The great whites of Burgundy and the legendary bubbles from Champagne all have one thing in common: a chalky terroir that brings out their minerality. I am very fond of these kinds of tight, fresh, and crisp wines, and when I compose a new dish I will sometimes look for that same crispness, or a salty dimension that evokes minerality, as a style to frame it around. I want these dishes—which often include sea plants or seafood—to be "dry," with no sweetness whatsoever, so that the shellfish's minerality has room to come out and shine.

In *Oysters, Cabbage, and Capers* (page 262), we add pickled cabbage, which underlines the saltiness of the shellfish and gives a crisp crunch that suits those flavors very well. The caper puree is slightly metallic, which also increases the minerality of the dish, which overall has the cleanliness and purity of a very minerally Aligoté.

Lambs from Havervadgård (see page 64), which we use exclusively in our restaurant, are marsh lambs that roam the coast of Jutland, eating sea plants right off the beach. I'm convinced that their seaside pasture helps season the meat; it almost tastes as if a tiny bit of salt has been sprinkled on it. Even though the meat's saltiness is very subtle, it makes us instantly want to bring in seaweed, samphire, or cooked turnips to pair it with, as we do in as we do in *Lamb, Turnip, and Samphire* (page 324), where the light and briny flavors connect with the minerality in the lamb.

With minerality comes a clean-flavored dish, so I would not use mayonnaise or a heavily reduced sauce in a dish that goes in this direction. Instead, we often use yogurt or buttermilk in combination with mineral flavors, as the dry aftertaste and lingering acidity of these acidified dairy products suits them very well. Our most recent experiments in vegetable fermentation, such as with celery root, daikon, and radish, brought yet another flavor to add to the mineral components found in roe, oysters, mussels, squid, and skate. For example, the briny and umami-rich outcome of fermenting daikon gives us a perfect companion to lumpfish roe in *Lumpfish Roe, Daikon, and Almonds* (page 260).

It sometimes helps me to perceive a dish as a glass of wine, even more so when I need to find an actual wine to complement it well. So I suggest that when cooking ingredients in which you can perceive a natural minerality—even if it's subtle—enhance that quality by avoiding any type of muddling sweetness or cloying richness. Instead, combine it with other components of similar minerality and a lively and dry acidity.

Ideas
Theory

Building onto a Dish

Creativity is at the core of our work at Relæ. If we have created something meaningful, we call that a success—whether we just thought out of the box, or if we went further, working around limitations or traditions to create something that is truly ours. With the opening of the restaurant, we gave ourselves total liberty to cook the food we wanted to cook. We could easily have been lost in too many choices, but, luckily, our physical and financial limitations reduced our options. We didn't have an unlimited budget or the staff to support the most intricate preparations, and we also didn't have anyone telling us what was right or wrong. We were on our own, searching for the right path.

Surprisingly enough, it was not a very difficult task. I already had a very clear idea of what I liked and what I didn't like, as well as which ingredients I wanted to cook with. Slowly we started creating techniques suited for exactly our purposes, pushing the ingredients we could afford to the next level. The six months we took to test out dishes and work on the creative side of the restaurant was worth it.

We took that time to define preparations, ideas, and approaches. How did we want to cook chicken? Would the breast be best roasted or poached? What about the stocks: would we make it with half bones and half wings, vegetables or no vegetables? We questioned everything and always asked ourselves if we could do better. This was a different restaurant than Noma or elBulli. We needed to form and shape everything to fit into our little box.

The first year as we went through the four seasons, we felt obliged to start from scratch whenever a particular vegetable's (say, asparagus) season began, and then again when it suddenly ended. We felt pressure to create something new with produce we didn't really have the time to dig into.

Now that we've had the chance to define our basic ideas, we have a more patient approach to creating new dishes. Today we can look back at piles of notes that tell us how we got the best out of a fleeting ingredient, such as pine shoots, last year. Remembering what a great match Jerusalem artichokes and coffee was in *Jerusalem Artichokes, Coffee, and Passion* (page 360), we decided to use that winning combination once again in *Jerusalem Artichoke, Quinoa, and Coffee* (page 294).

Now we've slowed down our creative rhythm from frenetic to slightly more deliberate, and overall, the kitchen is more prepared and mature. Initially, because we wanted our cuisine to be original, if we heard about another restaurant making something similar to ours, we would cut it straight off the menu. That was a very demanding criterion for a new restaurant. Because we are now established, we can be less dogmatic, having created our own foundation to build on, one dish at a time.

Evolving a Technique: Making Old-School New-School

In the international chef community, there has been a return to the wholesome values of "natural" cooking lately, with chefs dismissing immersion circulators and sous vide bags in favor of live fire and smoldering coals. At industry conferences, slick executive chefs who once bragged about the nine types of hydrocolloids they use to make frozen olive oil cubes have turned into bearded foragers who name-drop the close-to-extinction heritage breeds of beef they've been dry-aging for the last nine months.

Shifting the focus back to age-old cooking methods is, in my option, a change for the better—most importantly because it erases the boundaries between the home kitchen and the avant-garde professional kitchen. Great cooking comes from great ingredients, not great machinery. But, as always, I am wary of counterreactions to trends, because all they do is create new trends.

Perhaps the most important lesson I've learned over the years is that great chefs cook exactly what they like to cook, without paying attention to which trends are influencing gastronomy at the moment. It seems like the public's attention span is getting shorter and shorter, so trying to keep up with the demands of the industry, foodies, bloggers, and social media is basically impossible. But even if you do, trend chasing will never give a chef the satisfaction of actually creating something genuine.

The culinary zeitgeist naturally has an influence on how you approach your ingredients and dress your plates. Now that every bright idea conceived anywhere around the world can surface in a matter of minutes through Twitter, Tumblr, or Instagram, it often seems as if what you do has not only

been done before, but also already been copied. Because I want Relæ to speak its own language and stand out from the rest, at times, I just sink into a sort of bubble and don't look at what anyone else is doing.

But you can't stay in a bubble forever. When looking for inspiration, I often find it more interesting to look back to trends and techniques that have already passed. Not long ago, absolutely everything was going into a siphon bottle and being charged with carbon dioxide to make foam, the *espuma* first made famous by Ferran Adrià at elBulli. Nowadays foams are considered passé—but hey, siphons are still extremely useful. I make an airy yogurt mousse for the *Sheep's Milk Yogurt, Radishes, and Nasturtium* (page 248). It covers lightly cooked radishes like a cloud and is a texture I can obtain only from the siphon.

And there is always room to find new ways to tweak old-school techniques that have reemerged as culinary trends, like choucroute. In *Oysters, Cabbage, and Capers* (page 262), we brine the cabbage in sous vide bags for only two to three days, so that it maintains a firm texture but has extra umami. Using a slice of celery root as a tortilla in the *Celery Root Taco* (page 232) is another update on an age-old technique. I don't expect to see roadside taco trucks swapping masa for celery root slices anytime soon, but for us, it was an interesting deviation from what is traditionally done.

At Relæ, we find it's most valuable to really look at a trend or even an age-old cooking method and figure out which techniques are hiding underneath. Once when I was grinding semifrozen meat for charcuterie— you want the meat to be close to freezing since the friction of the grinder really heats up the muscle—I noticed that the meat came out much fluffier and separated than when I grind it at room temperature. So I decided to grind semifrozen beef for tartare, and the results were great: if carefully dressed, the fluffy texture of the meat prevents the tartare from becoming a sort of protein puree, as it often does when prepared the traditional way.

The texture was so interesting that we put it on Manfreds' very first menu with watercress, rye bread, and mustard cream. It is now the signature dish of Relæ's little brother and has anchored the menu since Day One. It's another example of how there is almost always a way to evolve a technique—whether it's old or new.

Snacks: Starting a Meal on the Right Note

As meals at the leading restaurants around the world have stretched longer, with chefs adding more and more dishes to the menu, the amuse-bouche has taken on an increasingly important function. elBulli was probably the first restaurant to offer multiple snacks before embarking on the actual menu, and I can see why. Similar to desserts, the small snacks, as we call them, give chefs permission to go a bit wilder than they can with the more composed dishes that come later in the meal. Plus, the first few items are often what diners remember most and provide a clear idea of what to expect from the meal shortly to follow.

In order to reduce the price of our menu, we took a different track. Instead of offering a snack as part of the fixed menu, we wanted to let the guests skip it if they were on a budget, as younger couples and students visiting our restaurant often are.

So we started offering the option of ordering a snack. Because there is only one, it's always vegetarian to suit both our omnivorous and vegetarian guests and because of our general focus on vegetables.

The pizza-inspired *Kornly Cracker* (page 240), for example, is a thin puffy cracker that's covered with salted mushrooms, fresh sliced mushrooms, and Danish Kornly cheese. For our *Grilled Corn* (page 236), we remove the silk from baby corn, add marjoram leaves, then rewrap the miniature ears in their husks and grill them.

The only other rule for snacks is that they must be eaten by hand. For me, asking someone to pick something up and eat it with their hands signals that they should relax, get comfortable, and have fun. There is something so truly primal about putting your hands in your food that most people find it natural—at least as soon as they feel they are allowed to do so. It's also a great icebreaker for a first date and can help diners loosen up. When guests hold on to the *Celery Root Taco* (page 232), it helps us take the pretentiousness out of the meal.

At Noma, René served a legendary beef tartare for the guests to enjoy with their hands, where the raw meat is covered in tiny leaves of wood sorrel. It was a great surprise for so many people; it pushed boundaries for some diners and was also a bit too much for a few. In a fine dining restaurant at the time, eating with your hands was unheard of, though most diners clearly had fun. Relæ is a much more casual restaurant, and we want the guest to feel completely free to enjoy their meal however they want to. The tabletop's drawer is filled with cutlery, but it's up to them to decide whether to use a spoon, fork, or their hands.

Challenging the Guest:
Why You Shouldn't Always Let People Choose What They Want

We once had a dish on the menu that we simply named "Veal." When the thin slices of red meat arrived with baked Jerusalem artichokes and a black pepper sauce, most people assumed we were serving them veal loin or another rather innocent cut. Then we explained that the pink and juicy meat in front of them was poached veal hearts, which resulted in some interesting facial expressions.

Yet the beauty of this was that only a small percentage of diners ever showed a negative reaction to this "trick" of ours. We were surprised at how many thanked us for serving them a food that they might otherwise never have tried, or maybe even have had some difficulties with because of a childhood experience that scarred them. If we had written "Veal Hearts" on the menu, I am quite confident that we wouldn't have been able to fill up the restaurant.

I always want the wording on the menu to be very loose and not give away too much, to leave room for surprise and to raise more questions than it gives answers. Whenever we have the opportunity to use a less familiar word, we do—I like leaving people to wonder what kelp, enoki, or *söl* is until the dish is served.

I think Relæ is obliged to keep people guessing, to challenge the usual conventions. Of course, the food should be tasty; that is always the first priority. But it should do something more than just taste good. It can be as simple as cooking chicken sous vide until still slightly pink, which triggers a range of reactions from our guests but keeps the flesh incredibly juicy and delicious. A guest told me recently, "What you do is not for everybody, but it is fantastic," and she is right, as it is definitely not for everybody—at least it's not for the ones who come in with closed minds.

Sometimes we challenge the guest by playing with the structure of the menu. Because Relæ focuses on vegetables, we make the second dish on the menu (which is a vegetable dish) the most filling, which means we can serve a smaller portion of meat for the third dish—even though that's the dish most guests expect to be the "main." The second dish is also the same on both the vegetarian and omnivorous menu and therefore has to be vegetarian. Most guests don't want their main course to be vegetarian, but once they are pushed in that direction, they really seem to enjoy it.

We have probably pushed preconceived notions the furthest with our desserts by serving vegetables, mushrooms, and even seaweeds as the last course. On the written menu, we don't point out that the last dish is a dessert. When the dessert is called *Chanterelles, Apple, and Granité* (page 342), it's not surprising how often our guests point out that they still haven't gotten the last course. That's when we make clear they are having mushrooms for dessert.

Vegetarian: An Inspiration in Cooking

A step into full-on vegetarianism would be a radical move for many, myself included. But I have a great respect for those who take that extra step, if it is motivated by a feeling of ethical responsibility. It's a step I have been tempted to take myself numerous times, and I actually believe that life as a vegetarian would be a whole lot simpler. It turns out that being critical about the meat that you eat can be a much more complex matter than simply being able to just say no. Instead I subscribe to part-time vegetarianism, leaving room for indulging in meat when it is at its best, and avoiding it when of dubious provenance.

I really do love meat. Not in the macho steak and fries kind of way—which is actually low on my list of favorites—but I appreciate many other types of meat greatly, when they are of a certain quality. And the more I learn about quality meat, the more opinions I form about the ethics behind raising it. That means I'm putting meat on the plate less and less often, because good meat is expensive. I would prefer to be a vegetarian all through the week in order to enjoy a beautiful pastured roast chicken on Sunday, rather than stacking up on cheap animal proteins day after day.

In the last few years, more and more chefs are executing vegetarian meals at the highest level, but the gastronomic idealist still doesn't have that much to choose from. From the beginning at Relæ, we have always offered an omnivorous and a vegetarian four-course menu. I love being able to serve a menu based on high-quality ingredients and creativity to vegetarians who normally have limited options for a great gastronomical experience. A beautiful plate of *Beet, Crab Apple, and Söl* (page 254) followed by steaming *Potato, Seaweed, and Pecorino* (page 288), a fragrant *Romaine, Egg Yolk, and Nettles* (page 308), and *Milk, Kelp, and Caramel* (page 346) is a treat to many vegetarians, who are often left to eat the garnishes in fancy restaurants.

I like the challenge of vegetarian cooking, which demands that we focus even further on vegetables, because we can't add any umami from animals. Our desire to limit animal proteins has forced us into many hours of work researching how to best use nuts, seaweeds, and grains. We've also introduced more fermentation in our kitchen, which gives a complexity and depth to vegetables. Because we decided to always make the second course a vegetable dish for both menus, each guest to Relæ receives at least one vegetarian course, regardless of their ideals.

Vegetables over Meat: The Right Proportions of a Dish

Since the first day we lit the gas-fired stove at Relæ, our ambition to deliver high-end gastronomy at affordable prices caused us to reprioritize many things. One of the biggest outcomes of this was to push away cost-heavy proteins, such as meats and fish, leaving room for roots, greens, and brassicas to take the main stage.

Without compromising on quality, we wanted to approach our produce in a very humble and respectful way. I was born in Sicily, where the postwar life of poverty somehow feels much more recent than in well-fed Scandinavia, and Sicilian home cooking is a great inspiration. Red meat is rarely eaten, and when served, it is often hammered out to paper-thin slices and breaded heavily before cooking. Even the veggies are stuffed or coated in bread crumbs, and whenever there is leftover sauce, it is used to flavor a pasta dish the following day.

We may avoid an excessive use of bread crumbs at Relæ, but we follow a similar path by keeping the amounts of proteins low while making sure the quality and ethics of the ingredients are high. Even when the point of departure for a dish is a specific cut of braised meat, lamb, or chicken, we end up pushing the dish toward a vegetal focus. Even for meat dishes, our creative inspiration is most often sparked by a vegetable and the given flavor and texture it has to offer. *White Asparagus and Anchovies* (page 272) is asparagus accompanied by an anchovy sauce, and *Lamb, Turnip, and Samphire* (page 324) is a plate of small pieces of lamb that are completely covered in cooked turnips.

I also enjoy cooking vegetables with the slightest hint of meat. You can use the roasting pan from a rabbit to cook carrots, or use a small amount of scraps from a salted ham to bring great flavor and umami to boiled potatoes.

Technically, this kind of cooking makes our cuisine lighter, more healthful, and yes, more affordable. Flavors and most certainly textures are much more varied when the focus is on vegetables. When considering meat as an addition to flavor and umami instead of the main element, the variations and directions you can go with a dish are numerous. In reality, our focus on vegetables forces us to work more creatively, but it also pays back by giving us a larger repertoire of flavor profiles and textures to work with.

Intertwining Flavors: The Few Times You Get It Just Right

A fellow chef apprentice during cooking school was showing off when he drizzled a bit of béarnaise sauce over a dollop of chocolate mousse. "You don't know until you try it," he said with a smirk. I probably could have predicted that his experiment wouldn't be entirely successful, but I had to agree that at times it's worth giving it a shot and putting random stuff in your mouth.

As a chef, your palate is your most important tool, and honing it, challenging it, and adjusting it is crucial for your further development as a cook and a taster. I taste such a mishmash of flavors during a day at work that it is a wonder that I don't suffer more gastrointestinal disturbances. At times tasting just once isn't enough for me. I can find myself repeatedly chewing on something and really trying to decode it, just like playing a favorite piece of music over and over again.

I look for balance, contrasts, and harmonies among flavors. What inspires me to try something new? Sometimes it's just intuition—a gut feeling that brined celery root and sea lettuce will combine perfectly, or that black tea and lamb fat might pair together well. Often it might be pure luck, such as when we were discussing a new lamb dish while I was drinking black tea. My mind connected the flavors and sparked a new idea. I figured that the fatty and aromatic richness that permeates great lamb could benefit from the tannic and reductive qualities of fragrant black tea. We ended up flavoring the cooking juice of a Havervadgård lamb with black tea oil.

The idea behind a dish might sound intriguing, but if it does not charm the palate, there is no dish. It is important to experiment, but it's also crucial to do many test runs on your own palate first. I ate numerous variations of sliced lamb with black tea sauce before that dish came to its final version.

At the moment, we are working on a snack based on a small buckwheat pancake folded around a vegetable filling. We have filled those tiny pancakes with baked Jerusalem artichokes, with sliced and brined

Jerusalem artichokes, with yogurt, without yogurt, with *söl* as a powder and with *söl* in soaked pieces, with slices of *mashua* (a root vegetable with a spicy kick), and even with fermented celery root—all with mixed success. The *mashua* paired the best with the buckwheat so far, and even if we still need another component with more body to actually fill up the pancake, at least we have found the two best-matched flavors.

We munch through a great number of flavor and aroma combinations throughout the year, and some of them seem to stay on our menu, becoming our own little classics. They are the ones that have defined our cuisine. Below are a small selection of some of the most interesting, and at times surprising, intertwining flavors that we remember the most.

Lamb–black tea	*Smoked almond–fennel*
Lamb–dried shrimp	*Pecorino–sea lettuce*
Jerusalem artichokes–ground coffee	*Kornly cheese–pine*
Oysters–capers	*Sesame–elderflower*
Lettuce–pistachio	*Veal hearts–black pepper*
Mussels–bergamot	*Nordlys cheese–dried carrot*
White asparagus–anchovy	*Mandarin–buttermilk*
Raw beef–ramson leaves	*Chanterelles–apple*
Red beets–söl	*Caraway–lemon balm*
Carrots-söl	*Kelp-caramel*
Smoked almond–cauliflower	*Corn-marjoram*

Savory Desserts:
Why You Might Find Yourself Having Vegetables for Dessert

Not too long ago a Danish magazine was going on about how they hated how the new young Nordic chefs always put vegetables in their desserts. And it's true that ever since the New Nordic wave picked up, chocolate and nougatine are often replaced by carrots and sea buckthorn as the final note of the meal.

I don't agree with the magazine's criticism, though, as I believe that dessert can be the perfect playground for gastronomical adventures. Let's face it, you rarely need dessert. After a several-hours-long tasting menu or even just a couple of courses at a bistro, your digestive system isn't exactly screaming for sugars and saturated fat.

So why not cap off dinner in a lighter and fresher way? At Relæ, a heavy and sugary finale would clash with the acidity levels and freshness of the previous dishes. We rarely use sugar during any part of the meal, and since our menu has only four courses, it's extremely important to properly integrate the final course: dessert. In this context, it makes perfect sense to highlight the natural sugars found in so many vegetables.

Jerusalem artichokes, or sunchokes, are one of the most versatile vegetables that can be used in dessert. After baking, their insides come out creamy and sweet, and the outer skins can serve as a crisp component in desserts like *Jerusalem Artichokes, Coffee, and Passion* (page 360). We use Hokkaido pumpkins' sweet notes to create the base for *Hokkaido Pumpkin and Mandarin* (page 354), in which we also candy and crisp up some of the slices, taking place of traditional tuiles or nougatine so often seen in French-style desserts. We also dry and rehydrate corn, resulting in a texture and flavor profile so intriguing that it works wonders paired with bread crumbs and the fragrant marjoram in *Corn, Bread Crumbs, and Marjoram* (page 356). This combination would have also worked in a savory context, but the meringue adds just enough sweetness to make everything fall into place.

The key to using unexpected ingredients in desserts is isolating and enhancing their dessertlike qualities and tipping the balance just slightly toward the sweeter side. Natural sugars, acidity, freshness, and toasty or caramelized notes are what we tend to look for in a dessert. You can look for those qualities in more obvious ingredients and preparations—berries, chocolates, custards, and caramels—or you can look for them in unexpected places. Baked Jerusalem artichokes result in a nutty, caramelized exterior and a custardy interior. The deep and fruity notes of a dried and rehydrated beet can be as intense as a cherry compote.

On the savory side of the kitchen, it's rare that you find something entirely new to work with, such as an heirloom variety of celtuce or a spice we didn't know existed. But when you play with the idea of using vegetables as dessert, the adventures are there for the taking.

It's not that we don't notice that diners often raise their eyebrows when presented with seaweed, mushrooms, or potatoes in their desserts. But if the execution is perfect and the flavors and balance work out as intended, then they rarely complain. By now, only the most conservative eaters consider the occasional Jerusalem artichoke in their dessert to be crossing the line.

Nose-to-Tail Cooking: A Choice the Chef Has to Make

What is a nose-to-tail restaurant? The term *nose to tail*—made famous by the great book *The Whole Beast: Nose to Tail Eating* by Fergus Henderson, the chef-owner of St. John in London—has been used so often that many chefs have forgotten its real meaning.

The concept of using the entire beast, from one extremity to the other, is nothing new. Pork has gained its sacred status in numerous cultures for its versatility and because every square inch is perfectly delicious. But it seems to me that the Italian saying *Del maiale non si butta niente* ("Nothing is thrown away from the pig") could be applied to any animal raised for its meat.

So is nose-to-tail cooking all about cooking livers and kidneys, or is it more about cooking everything you get from the animal? At Relæ, we cook for an average of seventy guests per day, most of whom order the omnivorous menu and are served meat during just one course. If I wanted to serve chicken livers as the main component of that dish, I would need a serious amount of livers from a great number of chickens. And if I am cooking only the chicken livers, am I then cooking nose-to-tail or not-nose-nor-tail-but-just-the-livers?

Our commitment to source only organically certified meat as well as to have an affordable menu lets us work only with whole animals, since specific cuts from small producers make the per-kilogram price skyrocket. That means no picking up the phone and calling in for 30 kilograms of tongues or kidneys. In any case, those amounts are not readily available from smaller producers.

Here's where I should stress that our nose-to-tail, whole-animal approach is made possible only because we have two restaurants. Relæ would be absolutely nothing without Manfreds. When we had *Wild Duck, Elderberries, and White Onions* (page 330) on the menu at Relæ, we would confit the small thighs and serve them as an extra at Manfreds. When we served raw slices of lamb dressed with dried shrimp for *Lamb, Shrimp, and Dill* (page 270), on one side of the street, the braising cuts like shanks, necks, and breasts would be the theme of the dish of the day on the other.

Our two-restaurant version of nose-to-tail cooking provides the occasional opportunity to brine and sear lamb heart to top a few leaves of dressed kale at Manfreds or Table 0 (see page 17). And we use the same philosophy with fish and game: when we serve thinly sliced squid at Relæ, we always poach the squid tentacles and use it for a dish at Manfreds.

I'm struck by a great paradox hiding in all this. I wanted more vegetables and less meat on the menu, and as a result, we ended up using a higher quality of meat. Nose-to-tail cooking requires organizing the logistics so you can choose the highest-quality meats based on the way they are raised and not on the specific cut you might need. It's truly the choice a chef and restaurateur needs to make.

Leaf-to-Stem Cooking: The Synergy Between Two Kitchens in One

Leaf-to-stem cooking is perhaps an inevitable offshoot of the nose-to-tail movement—both are ways to show respect toward nature and the integrity of ingredients. Nowadays chefs have stopped looking for exotic fruits and ingredients from around the world, looking instead at their local produce in a new light and finding novel ways of preparing them. The New Nordic restaurants serve the outer leaves of a cauliflower instead of the florets and the roots of lettuce rather than the leaves. Their kitchens also experiment with berries and fruits in their less-ripe stages.

I remember how Michel Bras, one of the greatest French chefs and an inspiration to so many of us, once said that his favorite part of the apple is the tiny seeds. He enjoyed their slightly almondy and bitter taste and didn't understand why anybody would want to avoid eating them. He appreciated eating an apple to the point of eating those small, bitter finishing notes, which was a way of showing respect to the fruit and the tree. In the same vein, my aunt in Sicily always kept the inside stem of romaine lettuce to herself as she cleaned it for a salad. She would eat them as a treat, saying that nobody else liked them anyway. Those are the secrets kept by people who really value the produce they work with.

Now, when this becomes a tendency in professional kitchens, how do you bring those small treats and rarities to all your guests' plates? You simply can't, if avoiding food waste is a priority for you. If you want to make a dish with a spoonful of apple seeds, how are you going to use the apples? If lettuce heart is going on the menu and the ratio of heart to leaves on a head of romaine is one to ten, where will all those leaves go—to the staff meal?

That's why we often try to use the entire vegetable in one dish. In *Pickled Mackerel, Cauliflower, and Lemon* (page 276), we cook the cauliflower florets until soft and serve it as a cold puree with the tangy, fatty fish and crunchy slices of cauliflower stem. In that dish, we also use lemon zest after pressure-cooking juiced lemons (reserving the juice for another use). In *Lettuce, Smoked Almond, and Olive Oil* (page 290), we brine and ferment lettuce hearts, warm them in almond milk, then present them in a dish covered with thinly sliced outer lettuce leaves.

Again, Manfreds helps us ensure that nothing goes to waste. If we need a certain size of potatoes at Relæ, we sort out the big ones and turn them into a beautiful crushed potato dish at Manfreds. When we serve roast pork with thinly sliced Jerusalem artichokes and a ramson sauce at Relæ, we turn the excess artichoke bits into several types of purees and chop up the ramson stems to garnish a meat dish at Manfreds. We will probably never have apple seeds or other hard-won rarities on the menu at Relæ, but because Manfreds has Relæ's back, we have the liberty to experiment with produce without being wasteful.

Acidity

For years, I was completely ignorant of the importance of acidity to a successful dining experience. Acidity makes the mouth water and sparks the appetite. It properly balances other flavors and keeps things interesting and enjoyable rather than repetitive. Tart, acidic, and sour flavors stimulate the tongue's other taste buds and can really sharpen any flavor perceptions that follow. Learning how to control that mechanism—to harness acidity to make other flavors more vibrant—has been a fundamental part of my cooking for many years, and I owe that to the person who woke up my palate: René Redzepi.

When I first became a sous chef at Noma, I set about calibrating my palate to René's so that I could convey his ideas to the rest of the staff. In the beginning, he seemed very peculiar and precise about what he liked and disliked flavorwise. Until then, most of my mentors taught me to reduce sauces or season food heavily, to the point that the overall flavor profile became reductive and aggressive, like a brawling boxer who lacks technique or speed. René taught me to hold back on the salt and turn up the acidity, opening up a whole new spectrum of flavors. At first, I was surprised when he didn't want to cook a seemingly tasteless sauce even further to intensify its flavor. Instead, he would add a touch of vinegar, reduced wine, or beer, which magically unlocked the sauce's aroma and balanced it with just the right amount of acidity.

Our commitment to matching food with wine at Relæ sharpens our senses, since our cooks constantly taste the selected wines while developing the dishes they go with. And that's especially true when it comes to acidity, as you can't allow wine and food to argue—there must always be balance. Too much acidity in the food can clash with the wine, and not enough acidity leaves the two unconnected.

The ingredients in our acidic arsenal range from lemon juice, fruit vinegars, and reduced white and red wines to tart berries like sea buckthorn, elderberries, and lingonberries. While some dishes simply have a more pronounced overall acidity, such as the *Grilled Jerusalem*

Artichokes (page 234) with its tangy lemon skin puree, almost all of our dishes have at least some acidity as a backbone. In most meat dishes, we add a light, acidic sauce seasoned with good amounts of reduced wine, such as in *Lamb, Turnip, and Samphire* (page 324) or *Wild Duck, Elderberries, and White Onions* (page 330). In our desserts, where we have to control fats and sweetness rather than umami, the level of acidity very often reaches high levels. From the first sip of wine to that last bite of dessert, the guest experiences our constant play with acidity at every point in the meal.

Creativity Is in All of Us: Integrating the Staff into the Process

My original idea for the creative process at Relæ was much simpler than what it became. I wanted the dishes to be clean, naked, and true, and I imagined making them up on the spot. Say lumpfish roe comes in at the peak of the season; we would just morph whatever else was on the menu into a dish with the crisp pink roe. Since the dishes would have only a few components, I didn't think it would be that difficult to incorporate new ingredients. With time, I realized that "simple" is much more complicated than I thought.

We all tasted our first dishes again and again, looking for balance, complexity, and a clear voice in the food. It quickly became obvious that no roe would just show up on our menu on any given day—any dish using it would have to be tested and retested many times. And all the testing, plus tastings for the wine pairings, was time- and space-consuming. When we originally designed Relæ, the intention was to have a maximum of three or four cooks catering to forty guests. Instead, both numbers doubled, and we really had to squeeze into the kitchen.

When we had to work on new dishes, it was right in the center of the kitchen. We have a very open layout where purveyors, other staffers, and all sorts of distractions could walk straight in, all day long. It wasn't a very effective way to develop new ideas, as we were taking up space and disturbing the other cooks, who were scrambling to get ready for service.

It stressed me out to never feel as if there was room for this fundamental part of our cooking. As head chef/restaurateur/problem solver/decision maker, I was running around leaving a trail of dirty pots, pans, and unfinished plates with experimental flavor combinations, which would sometimes get swept away if I stayed on the phone too long.

Then, in 2012, we had the opportunity to add a small creative workshop to the Manfreds kitchen. The space is no more than about 25 square meters, but it's a single room focused entirely on creativity and development. It suits us perfectly. The downside is that even though the studio is only fifteen steps away from the Manfreds kitchen, it is still out of view of many of our skilled cooks, who no longer have a direct opportunity to be involved in the creative work.

As a solution, we involve all of our cooks in our brainstorming sessions. During a session for the juice menu, our cook Margaretha Jungling was trying out kelp in all kinds of ways. Kelp became *söl*, and then *söl* juice sparked the idea of making a *söl* mousse for dessert; somehow that *söl* mousse turned into the kelp ice cream in the *Milk, Kelp, and Caramel* (page 346), one of the dishes that I am the most proud of.

The collective work and discussion that involves as many clever individuals as possible is what sparks true creativity. Feeling ownership of ideas in any way is the true killer of evolution. Even though we haven't found the perfect system yet, involving as many members of our staff as possible in the creation of dishes is our key to becoming a better restaurant every day.

Where Is the Cheese Trolley?

When Relæ opened, we were certain that the three-star cheese trolley, with its landscape of mature cheeses spotted with ashes, bits of hay, and red-washed mold, would neither fit our philosophy nor our physical space. So then, what were we supposed to do about the cheese course?

We set up a menu of four courses, with an entree, two warm dishes, and a dessert. This highly reductive approach of cutting down to just four courses was basic to our philosophy. The simplest way to achieve that was to reduce the guest's choices in as many situations as possible. So if he wanted cheese, we decided we would choose it for him. We didn't want to complicate things by making an actual cheese dish, so we picked one cheese we felt a strong affinity to and just rolled with that. We didn't even garnish it; it was just a naked slice.

The first cheese we picked was Pecorino Roncione, a quite mature and hard Italian sheep's milk cheese that served as a reference to my homeland. Presenting an Italian cheese in Copenhagen was an unusual choice in those days, when Danish cheese producers like Arla Unika and Grand Fromage had successfully reintroduced Danish cheeses to the better restaurants, making a great impact on fine dining's cheese platter. But I didn't care—Relæ is not a Nordic restaurant and the mature and deep-flavored cheese was one of my favorites. After all, we used olive oil instead of grapeseed oil, so we could put a nice Italian pecorino on the menu too.

It worked out well to begin with. I realized that many people considered our cuisine more challenging than I perceived it myself, and I appreciated that with the cheese course, our guests could have a second to regroup with something comforting and well-known. It gave them a small cliff to grab on to before returning to the wild current that would soon drag them into a sea of desserts made with vegetables, vinegar, and seaweed.

But we slowly started to change our approach. It turned out that we enjoyed the challenge of making a dish that could count as a cheese course and still satisfy our more adventurous customers. We soon swapped the pecorino with a fresh Swedish cheese from Hagelstads Gårdmejeri, a goat cheese made from unpasteurized milk. We played around with the cheese and changed it up a bit. We whipped it up, and Anders Hansen, the sommelier back then, really pushed for the addition of some chopped fresh herbs for a wine pairing he had in mind. The variations kept surfacing, and we eventually settled on serving the whipped goat cheese with parsley puree.

We went even further with an Époisses-style cheese called Nordlys from Arla Unika. We matched up its funky and fruity qualities by serving it with sweet carrot crisps in the *Nordlys, Carrots, and Orange Zest* (page 340), giving the cheese a small twist in both flavor and texture. We have also served a blue cheese by cutting it up into small pieces, freezing it, and then blending it while still frozen into a coarse powder. We sprinkled that powder onto a plate dressed with a few chopped herbs and left it to come to room temperature before serving. The lightness of the powder's texture mellowed out the characteristic aggressiveness of blue cheese to the extent that many diners who previously hated blue cheese were raving about it. There is no doubt in my mind that a simple and creative way to serve interesting cheese is worth a million cheese trolleys, any day.

Whipped Goat Cheese and Parsley (p.338)
Nordlys, Carrots, and Orange Zest (p.340)

Ideas
Inspirations

Italy
Denmark
France
elBulli
Thailand
Spring
Summer
Fall
Winter

Italy

I was born in Italy in a small town on the Sicilian east coast called Roccalumera, where my father is from. When he and my mother, who is Norwegian, decided to live somewhere else, we moved to Denmark, a small, cold place that's far from the windy Sicilian beaches. During our first year in Denmark, when I turned eight, Italy was in the 1990 World Cup semifinals, and my fellow Sicilian Totò Schillaci scored in Italy's last match against Argentina. The goal unfortunately wasn't enough; Argentina won the game and left me on my knees crying in front of the TV. I was a new immigrant and a patriot, and since that young age, my Italian roots have been a big part of my persona. In addition to my loyal soccer allegiances, my connection to the home country was defined by my longing for the food of my family.

The aroma of boiling tomatoes, which I remember from when my family preserved them in summer to last us through the winter, is still clear in my mind after more than 20 years abroad. So is the fragrance of wild oregano and fennel growing in the mountains, after warming in the sun during the hottest summer months.

As a kid, I was very focused on food, and proud as I was of my upbringing, I believed Italian cooking was the only true cuisine. How could anyone deny the greatness of stuffed eggplant, *maccheroni*, and coffee granita served with brioche and whipped cream for breakfast? Mortadella was no doubt way cooler than Danish *leverpostej*. Taking pride in the great traditions of my own food culture had a fundamental impact on my choice to make a living as a cook. When we moved to Denmark, my father followed the path of countless Italian immigrants before him and took a job as a server in an Italian restaurant. As both my parents were working night shifts during our first years in Denmark, I occasionally had to tag along with my dad and hang out in the restaurant. When I wasn't busy eating tiramisù, I was in awe of the *pizzaiolo*'s skills as he flattened out the pies. I would watch the cooks for hours; the simple but powerful craft of the *pizzaiolo* still inspires me.

I may have been a bit narrow-minded when I was a kid, but as I matured, I realized that Italian food is no better than Chinese food, and that traditional foods from all over the world have much to offer as long as they are cooked with care. Still, I feel a special kind of satisfaction when I put a dish on the menu in which I can clearly see my Italian heritage. Not everyone sees it—and I have deliberately stayed away from pasta to avoid the restaurant being perceived as Italian—but you can find it in many of our dishes at Relæ. There might not be actual pasta on our menu, but perhaps something with a similar texture, such as "pappardelle" made of rutabaga or "maltagliati" made of dried and rehydrated turnips, such as in *Turnips, Chervil, and Horseradish* (page 284). The *Sunflower Seeds, Kornly, and Pine* (page 296) sounds nothing like a risotto, but that's essentially what you end up with when you cook sunflower seeds first in a pressure cooker and then warm them gently in a sunflower seed puree and top them with grated cheese. These dishes speak their own language—and it sure isn't Danish.

When we opened Relæ, the New Nordic frenzy was at its peak, but because of my heritage, it didn't make sense to me to use only ingredients from the Nordic region. After all, I myself am not a "local product." I had no doubt that we would accompany our bread with olive oil instead of butter, and that we would use lemons, olives, and anchovies on our menu. My cooking dared to find its own way.

If you had asked me what I would do when I was a young teenager, I probably would have sworn that I would open an Italian restaurant one day. When I actually opened Relæ, I didn't want it to be Italian, Danish, Nordic, or French. I wanted it to be completely its own. However, I recently had a great Italian chef eating in my restaurant, and he picked up on way more of those Italian ideas that anyone else prior to him. After the dinner he said, "Christian, we had a meal that was Italian to the bone!" It's an observation that still makes me incredibly proud.

Turnips, Chervil, and Horseradish (p.284)
Potato, Seaweed, and Pecorino (p.288)
Sunflower Seeds, Kornly, and Pine (p.296)

Denmark

"To be, or not to be Danish?" That was the question I constantly asked while growing up as an Italian immigrant in Denmark. As a young teenager, I wouldn't have any of it; I was as Italian as could be and I felt different from all the other people around me. A big part of my distance from "Danish-ness" was about not wanting to share traditions and, more important, traditional foods. Eating duck for Christmas seemed ridiculous. I hated *risengrød*, a rice porridge cooked in milk and sweetened with cinnamon and sugar, and eating the traditional Danish liver pâté, *leverpostej*, would take place only in my worst nightmares.

To this day, you will hardly ever find me munching on *leverpostej*, but now I actually love a good duck roast, even at Christmas. And I have stopped questioning whether I have turned Danish or not. Maybe I've just grown up. I have a family of my own now, so my future with them takes up more mental space than my past. Only time will tell how our family traditions will consolidate, but I appreciate creating our own weird mix of Italian, Danish, and Norwegian customs with whatever else feels right for us.

After my initial year cooking in Paris, I apprenticed in a Danish restaurant and was naturally forced to consider Danish cooking a lot more than ever before. I worked at Røgeriet (which means "the Smoker"), a restaurant located in an old smokehouse in the harbor of Rungsted. The cuisine was modern, which at the time didn't mean local or regional but rather borrowing inspiration from all sorts of cultures. Spanish cuisine and the tapas style of serving had a great buzz back then, but the chef also kept some traditional Danish techniques and dishes to respect the history of the location. That made the menu eclectic yet varied; it was a good place for a young apprentice eager to learn everything about cooking.

The lunch menu in particular was more focused on Danish food, with traditional dishes like the open-faced sandwich, smørrebrød, plus various versions of the flatfish plaice and sole meunière served with potatoes and melted butter. We served Danish tartare with horseradish and egg yolk, several types of pickled herring, and of course, smoked mackerel and salmon on rye bread, plus a number of traditional pickles and garnishes.

Lunch quickly became my responsibility, and I had the chance to start appreciating traditional Danish cooking from a professional point of view. Until then, the grains and seeds in rye bread had seemed more wholesome than tasty to me, but at Røgeriet, I grew to love the freshly baked bread's aroma and flavor. It has been a part of my cooking ever since and has even become an important staple in my own home. I learned to appreciate pickling and smoking fish, which gave way to how we smoke various vegetables at Relæ, such as with the *Smoked Beet "Fish" and Elderflower* (page 252).

At Røgeriet, the always-changing dish of the day helped me become better acquainted with lesser-known classics like *lam i dild og rejer*, braised lamb topped with generous amounts of tiny picked fjord shrimp and chopped dill, a flavor combination that would later become the inspiration for *Lamb, Shrimp, and Dill* (page 270).

Years later, I believe it was my international experience and my determination that secured me the job as sous chef at Noma, but my initial years at Røgeriet were also an asset. My early experiences cooking classic Danish cuisine allowed me to connect with Noma's broader goal of reevaluating and modernizing those old techniques. I knew there was something to that, something I wanted to be a part of and that still serves as an inspiration to this day.

France

My very first professional cooking experience was in Paris. I was 18 years old, I had finished my first year of hospitality school, and I knew absolutely nothing about gastronomy, other than that if I wanted to start cooking, I should do it in Paris.

Le Petit Bofinger was not a great restaurant per se, but it was a perfect place to apprentice and take my first steps in cooking. It served simple bistro classics and the place was extremely busy. On my first day, I put on my silly-looking chef's hat and started to learn how to make steak tartare, *salade au chèvre chaud*, and crème brûlée. I was taught to run a station and get my mise en place done, and I eventually took responsibility for both the starters and desserts. Just as important, I got to live in Paris for a year and breathe in the gastronomy of that city. A handful of years later I returned to Paname, as the Parisians call their town, to stage at the Taillevent, a classic three-star French restaurant. The cuisine there was of a much higher level, and detail and precision in the kitchen had a great impact on my future cooking.

As an inspiration, French cooking is something we look toward when we seek comfort and tasty wholesomeness. The French classics taught us to focus on great flavor and not too much bull. Turning vegetables—the technique of paring vegetable pieces into highly specific shapes—might seem completely stupid today, but in the classic French kitchen it was used to cook them evenly. I can recognize that sort of pragmatism in my own cooking. In a few of the dishes in this book, there are clear inspirations from France. For example, the *Mussels, Seaweed, and Allumettes* (page 264), which pairs cold, lightly cooked local mussels with blanched and fried shoestring potatoes, is an almost unrecognizable salute to *moules frites*. Yet the most important French influences are in the small details found in just about every corner of the kitchen at Relæ, from how we chop shallots to the way we warm up our vegetables in a beurre monté or base our sauces on stocks and beurre blancs.

I still consider French cooking to be the foundation of every restaurant where I have worked, no matter what its dogma or concept. Whenever someone starts whisking butter in a sauce, folding egg whites into a mousse, or reducing a stock into a glaze, they owe it to the great masters of traditional French cooking. The fact that France has had a hard time keeping the world's culinary attention during the last few years does not change that.

elBulli

Working at elBulli changed my gastronomical philosophy, just as the restaurant changed the philosophy of the entire culinary world. My arrival there as one of many stagiares in 2006 is as clear in my mind as if it were yesterday. Sitting on our suitcases in the sun, waiting for the first day of our new adventure to begin, we were all in awe as we watched Ferran Adrià walk down to the back entrance, just like that. We had come from all over the world to see the Spanish demigod of gastronomy in real life. We would be living the dream of working with him every day.

Life as a stagiare—a short-term intern—in Roses, Catalonia, had varying benefits. Some, like myself, made the best out of it, and it changed their lives, while others didn't see the genius in pushing seeds out of zucchini cooked to mush, day after day. Personally, everything about the place made me curious for more, as the kitchen's approach seemed entirely different from anything I had ever experienced.

Ferran's impact on gastronomy is partially due to his fresh approach, one that is not bound to traditions and that questions everything while also continuing to study and learn the basics. That became clear as I stood there quietly prepping and looking around at the binders and binders full of information, reports, and technical studies. This kitchen did not have a sous chef plating while shouting at the guy cooking the meat; it had creative head chefs and teams researching produce, gelling agents, hydrocolloids, and thickeners. Precision scales and brining percentage charts took the place of the touchy-feely kind of cooking I knew about. And a bit of shouting did go on from time to time.

When a task was particularly laborious or tedious, the elBulli approach was to do it as a team—line up ten to twelve stagiares around a table to sort peas into four different grades, or to meticulously peel walnuts with the tip of knife. That cooperative vibe stayed with me, as does elBulli's scientific-creative method. It really opened up my mind to the understanding that there is another way of doing just about anything.

The cooking also stimulated me in a much more intellectual way than ever before. I thought creativity was just based on instincts. I envisioned chefs daydreaming of new dishes and drawing their ideas in colorful Moleskine notebooks. The guys at elBulli didn't doodle much; they took proper notes, made conclusions, archived, and moved on. I was impressed by the depth of the work behind all of those gels, foams, and other weird stuff. But I was so immersed in it that by the end of my stage, I had had more than enough of it. It was like visiting another planet, fascinating and mysterious but not a place to settle down. I wanted to go back to my old reality, maybe not to the shouting sous chef, but to the guys cooking meats and reducing stocks for a good long while, to properly understand what I had learned while at elBulli.

Inspiration is something you can find in the deeper layers of the work of others, but it doesn't come until you carefully study the work to learn why it is so great. While the occasional hydrocolloid does hit our precision scale at Relæ, the influence of elBulli is more about the often scientific way we work with and test our ingredients; in the way we treat our staff, by having laborious tasks approached by many; and in how we free our minds. Also, my fascination with unusual textures probably started when I was trying to understand what was so great about those damn zucchini seeds.

Today we have our own *taller*, a food lab where we focus on developing our cuisine. Today food labs are widely spread all over the world of high-end gastronomy, though I don't believe many chefs would have seen the potential of a lab if it wasn't for Ferran forging that link between creative gastronomy, industry, and science.

Thailand

There are only a handful of cultural and regional inspirations I write about in this book, and of them all, Thai cooking remains the least familiar to me. That does not make it any less inspiring, because even my limited knowledge of it triggers my curiosity. I have been to Thailand only a few times—so far only to Bangkok and the southern part of the country—and not all of my travels there have offered me gastronomical revelations. But even when I found myself in the most touristy parts of Phuket with my family, we managed to find a street vendor cooking something truly great. In fact, those experiences have been some of my greatest eating experiences.

My travels to Thailand were clear inspirations for three dishes in this book and a few others that didn't make the cut. When my girlfriend and I were lurking around in Bangkok's Chinatown, we found ourselves in a huge marketplace selling dried fish, dried squid in a million sizes and types, and dried shrimp. The smell in there was incredible. Back at Relæ, when we were creating *Lamb, Shrimp, and Dill* (page 270), that experience—as well as unripe papaya salads with small dried shrimp flavoring the dressing—had a tremendous influence. The *Squid, Mussels, and Seaweed* (page 266) was as inspired as much from pad thai as it was from an Italian pasta dish. The refreshing lime flavor so characteristic of the Thai dish is a great contrast to the texture of its noodles, and that juxtaposition inspired me to season the squid with generous amounts of lemon. The rice bowl–style dish *Cauliflower, Veal Sweetbreads, and Basil* (page 326) leaves no doubt about its pseudo-Thai upbringing, as the texture of the minced cauliflower, glistening like a bowl of rice, served with a highly acidic sauce fragrant with basil, brings me all the way back to Southeast Asia.

What attracts me most about Thai cooking is its spontaneity and its freshness. The fast cooking on hot surfaces and the high acidity mixed with fresh, herbal, and fragrant flavors and crunchy textures is a true inspiration to my cooking.

Spring

Contrary to what most chefs will tell you, I think it's hardest to cook in spring. Winter is easy. Everybody can accept warm and comforting dishes based on sweet and rustic root vegetables in the dead of winter; the seasonality of the food we serve during the cold months is up to par with what the guests might have an appetite for and what we feel like cooking. But spring is when the problems start.

As soon as the very first few rays of sun appear, everybody jumps straight into a state of anticipation and demands that winter be over. During the always disappointing month of April, the Danes expect warmer temperatures and sunshine, and the sheer sight of green shoots on trees sparks the appetite for lighter, greener, and fresher food on the plate. At this point of the year, the last thing you want to cook is carrots and chokes, but the reality is that close to nothing, damn close to nothing at all, is ready to give a green injection of inspiration before the month of May. April is a bitch. And that is a fact.

We first received our organic certification in the spring of 2013 after a very long and cold winter. Our general focus on vegetables and our new no-compromise policy of buying only organic made their clear impact when it became impossible for us to make the menu actually feel spring until a few weeks into May. Even though I consider *Baked Potato Puree* (page 298) with buttermilk a brilliant dish, serving it when people are wearing T-shirts just doesn't feel quite right.

We had already, rich from experience, been quite productive about pickling, drying, and preserving through the previous year's summer and fall to keep a broad repertoire and to give an extra dimension to the wintry vegetables available. But these elements—capers, dried citrus, salted berries and fruits, and vinegars—are usually only an extra flavoring component and don't have the body or volume to play the main role in a dish. It actually made me reconsider whether our cuisine is ready to turn slightly more toward meats and fish in the colder months and loosen up on the vegetables until, well, they grow back.

But then things changed, as they always do. The first actual and useful signs of spring are when the ramsons start to shoot. They grow just about everywhere wild, and I can follow the development closely from my kitchen window at home as I see them grow in my backyard. While still very small, they are very aggressive and garlicky, but by the end of April, they are normally full grown and ready to be put into a sauce or puree or to cover the raw beef in *Raw Beef, Anchovies, and Ramsons* (page 268).

More or less in the same time frame, wild chervil, sweet cicely, rhubarb, and of course, the king of spring, asparagus, start showing up. Next comes the small new radishes, and in May, we gladly receive new potatoes, green strawberries, peas, greens, and lettuces. Spring is at its best just before it hands over the relay baton to summer. That's when you really feel it in your body, everything is growing, the temperatures are higher, the light is brighter, and the Danes start taking back the streets from winter's snowy darkness. Everybody starts cooking the first vegetables as the sunlight shines through the kitchen windows, making us all happy and, most important, inspired.

Summer

Copenhagen shows off its best side by far during the summer months. In a Northern European country that's considered, even by locals, to be rainy, gray, and wet most of the year, summer reminds us how beautiful our city can be. As the Danes take over parks, benches, and outdoor cafés, sucking in all the sun before summer slips away again, the farmers start seriously harvesting all the good stuff. New onions are sweet and crunchy, unripe and tart green strawberries are followed by deep red and mature ones. New potatoes reach a reasonable size and develop flavor in June.

Summer is also the time, for three years before we opened the restaurant, that we made the tradition of bringing our growing staff to the annual Roskilde Festival, an event that mixes gastronomy with rock music, beer, and sleeping in tents. We would cook organic and vegetarian food like a hearty vegetarian pea soup, since peas are at their best in the end of June or beginning of July. June is also when elderflower perfumes the city, and the elderflower plants are ready to deliver their green berries for us to salt and preserve as capers at some point in July. Then, as we step into August, sweet corn is readily available, both tiny ears with their anise flavor as well as big, sweet, and juicy ones.

For the first three years of operation, we closed the restaurant down for the whole month of July, following suit with all the high-end establishments of the city. It suited me and the rest of the staff very well, as we were able to unplug for a good period and cut up the year into two easily digestible bits. But since winter is so long and spring never really lives up to our expectations of bountiful, lush produce, summer always strikes us fast and hard as the calendar flips to the month of June. Almost before we really start getting to work adding peas, strawberries, and spring onions to the menu, it's time to close down. It's a frustrating setup and it feels as if we miss out on the most gratifying time to cook.

That's why in 2014 we plan to change our policy and stay open during July. Summer is all about abundance here, but unlike other places where you can take the sun for granted, in the northern countries I believe we appreciate it much more. Just look at how the Danes attack the outdoor spaces of their city when Copenhagen is hit by its first warm days in spring. In the same way, in the kitchen, we live for the moment of abundance that is short but greatly appreciated. Our creativity is toned down slightly, letting the produce speak for itself without requiring too many adventurous preparations. As fall approaches, we get busy pickling, salting, and preserving for the colder months ahead, and the countryside shows its best side. We just really enjoy cooking in this period and will probably continue to do so in many future Julys.

Fall

Most organic farms in Denmark celebrate fall around the first of September by inviting the public out to the countryside to appreciate the harvest and the land. This is when all their hard work through the year pays off, and they get to display it all to us cooks and chefs, as well as general consumers. We all get to admire the array of summer squash and pumpkins of all sizes and colors. Young root vegetables in every shape and type thinkable. Tender cabbages and leeks. Hazelnuts and walnuts that are ready to be picked and will stay crisp and crunchy for another month or so.

As a trace of Denmark's agricultural heritage, all schools and institutions are granted vacation for a week in the middle of October. Originally it was time for everyone to participate in the great potato harvest, and now most Copenhageners grab the opportunity to travel abroad and maybe catch another glimpse of sunshine before winter sets in.

Cookingwise, fall is a very satisfying time. It feels as if summer's green tenderness and winter's deep, dark, and comforting flavors overlap all through the season with the addition of wild mushrooms, berries, and game. After several months of chasing young shoots, crisp vegetables, and greens, it seems natural to slow down, soften things, and go toward a mellow flavor profile. We might leave the small roots with a crunch after cooking and add the occasional roasted carrot or cauliflower to the menu. Sauces become a bit more stock-based, more reduced and hearty, and the flavor spectrum goes more toward toasty and nutty while still staying light. Game will make its appearance, and with it comes pears and apples worth paying attention to. The splendid varieties of fruit along with their slow growth in our northern climate assures great flavors and a lot of excitement both in the pastry as well as savory sides of the kitchen.

Fall also offers the very last chance to preserve and pickle the harvest of crab apples, plums, and sour cherries before winter, making for busy hands cleaning, prepping, fermenting, and preserving before the frost hits the country, signaling winter's arrival.

Winter

Copenhagen does not exactly have polar conditions in winter. Our Scandinavian neighbors have a much more "Nordic" climate than we do, and at times I would prefer for our winter to be filled with blizzards, knee-high snow, and temperatures way below freezing. Instead, we are wrapped in a depressing blanket of gray rain and windy days for months and months. The occasional snow will normally last for just a few days and the fluctuating temperatures turn it into a halfway-melted traffic challenge rather than a charming landscape of pine trees covered in fluffy white crystals.

But in the kitchen, winter is a time of reflection and slowing down the often way-too-hectic rhythm, and with space to think at a deeper level. Time moves slower in a good and bad way; at times you feel as if you won't make it to spring, but with the years I have started to appreciate that slower pace. In spring, asparagus start shooting, and then as soon as you start appreciating the green, juicy stalks, the season is almost over. Spring and summer are all about being ready for action, whereas in winter, the produce challenges us in a very different way. Root vegetables stare at you day after day, challenging you to look at them differently, find another secret they hide. It takes time, and that is all you have, months and months with very little variation.

When we opened the restaurant in late August 2010 we were quickly confronted with winter and its limitations, a situation that I believe had a great part in defining the cuisine we do. We had planned the first menu for ages, the first rocambolesque month didn't let us think many creative thoughts, and before we knew it we were stuck with carrots, Jerusalem artichokes, and celery root for a very long time. During that winter, we came up with great dishes such as poached celery root sliced thinly and rolled around sea lettuce and served with a black olive sauce. We had a new approach to the chokes, baking them for very long periods on well-ventilated trays, making our "chewy Jerusalem artichokes" served with veal hearts and a black pepper sauce. We took the charring of carrots to the next step by cooking round carrots until very caramelized, almost blackened, in a pan and serving them with braised beef and a sauce with *söl*, the Icelandic tobacco-like seaweed.

If you want to try out the inventiveness of a restaurant, go there in winter when the chef has very little to work with. With a policy of going 100 percent organic restricting us even further during the winter months, our focus on vegetables really poses some challenges for us that we happily wander into during the month of November. Those challenges, I believe, have made the difference for us in the long term. Winter is still a call for creativity, and that's what comforts us through the long and dreary—if relatively mild—Danish winter.

Water
Wine
Fruit Vinegars
Extra-Virgin Olive Oil
Lamb
Fat
Chicken
Hindsholm Pork
Butter
Buttermilk
Jerusalem Artichokes
Carrots
Horseradish
Celery Root
Herbs
Cresses
Citrus
Unripe Strawberries
Elderflower
Crab Apple
Nuts
Seeds
Olives
Mussels
Coastal Fish
Mackerel
Sea Lettuce
Anchovy
Söl
Kelp
Fermentation
Pickling Fruits and Vegetables
Pickling Fish
Cooking in Butter Emulsion
Cooking Salads
Precision Cooking
Barely Cooking
Stocks
Nut Milks
Hiding on the Plate

Herb Bouquet
Celery Root Taco
Grilled Jerusalem Artichokes
Grilled Corn
Shallots and Nigella
Kornly Cracker
Oxalis Roots
Unripe Strawberries, Cress, and Buttermilk
Sheep's Milk Yogurt, Radishes, and Nasturtium
Cucumber, Caraway, and Lemon Balm
Smoked Beet "Fish" and Elderflower
Beet, Crab Apple, and Söl
Cooked Onions, Buttermilk, and Nasturtium
Lumpfish Roe, Daikon, and Almonds
Oysters, Cabbage, and Capers
Mussels, Seaweed, and Allumettes
Squid, Mussels, and Seaweed
Raw Beef, Anchovies, and Ramsons
Lamb, Shrimp, and Dill
White Asparagus and Anchovies
Pickled Skate, Mussels, and Celery Root
Pickled Mackerel, Cauliflower, and Lemon
Cod, Kohlrabi, and Skins
White Onions, Crayfish, and Fennel
Turnips, Chervil, and Horseradish
New Potatoes, Warm Berries, and Arugula
Potato, Seaweed, and Pecorino
Lettuce, Smoked Almond, and Olive Oil
Asparagus, Sunflower Seeds, and Mint
Jerusalem Artichoke, Quinoa, and Coffee
Sunflower Seeds, Kornly, and Pine
Baked Potato Puree
Barley, Cauliflower, and Black Trumpet

Contrasting Temperatures
Crunch!
Chewy
Leathery
Dehydrating/Rehydrating
Vegetable Skins
Salting and Brining Vegetables
Salting and Brining Meats and Fish
Juiciness, the Natural Sauce
Butter and Bitter
Charred and Grilled
Toasted and Nutty
A Touch of Umami
Meat with Seafood
Minerality
Building onto a Dish
Evolving a Technique
Snacks
Challenging the Guest
Vegetarian
Vegetables over Meat
Intertwining Flavors
Savory Desserts
Nose-to-Tail Cooking
Leaf-to-Stem Cooking
Acidity
Creativity Is in All of Us
Where Is the Cheese Trolley?

Italy
Denmark
France
elBulli
Thailand
Spring
Summer
Fall
Winter

Carrot, Elderflower, and Sesame
Charred Cucumber and Fermented Juice
Romaine, Egg Yolk, and Nettles
Enoki, Kelp, and Seaweed
Fennel, Smoked Almond, and Parsley
Dried Zucchini and Bitter Leaves
Fried Salsify and Bergamot
Salted Carrot and Oxalis "Béarnaise"
Pork from Hindsholm and Rye
Lamb, Turnip, and Samphire
Cauliflower, Veal Sweetbread, and Basil
Chicken Wings, White Asparagus, and Anchovies
Wild Duck, Elderberries, and White Onions
Salad, Beef, and Bronte Pistachio
Veal, Grilled Sauce, and Anchovy
Whipped Goat Cheese and Parsley
Nordlys, Carrots, and Orange Zest
Chanterelles, Apple, and Granité
Mandarin, Buttermilk, and Egg Yolk
Milk, Kelp, and Caramel
Rhubarb Compote, Almond, and Vinegar
Jerusalem Artichoke, Malt, and Bread
Sheep's Milk Yogurt, Beets, and Black Currant
Hokkaido Pumpkin and Mandarin
Corn, Bread Crumbs, and Marjoram
Elderflower and Rhubarb
Jerusalem Artichokes, Coffee, and Passion
Coffee Table

Chapter 3

Dishes

To present the dishes that mean the most to me—the ones that make best examples of all of the ideas and theories I have talked about so far—I decided to organize them here in the same way that we serve them at the restaurant.

We offer both an omnivorous and vegetarian four-course menu at Relæ. When guests arrive, they can order a snack (see pages 176–77) right away if they like, which is not part of the set menu. Then they receive the first course, which is either vegetarian or omnivorous and most often light and refreshing. The second course is vegetarian and shared by both menus. My original idea was that this second course would be the filling one, and together with the bread, it would take care of business and guarantee filled-up bellies by the end of the night. Still, most diners consider the last dish before dessert to be their main course, and with that comes expectations that it will be somewhat filling.

On both menus, we solve that conundrum by serving a third course that may surprise guests with its lightness but can still satisfy them with its complexity. These "main courses" aren't heavy on protein; in fact, the proteins in most of the omnivorous dishes are entirely hidden from view by a vegetable.

The cheese course follows, but like the snack, it's optional (see pages 198–99). Finally comes dessert, which will probably not have traditional components like custard or caramel or be as sweet as most desserts. Still, the guest should experience it as the natural outcome of the courses that came before it. Then they can finish the meal with coffee and a small sweet item that is as simple and clearcut, yet as thoughtfully carried out, as all of the previous dishes.

Dishes
Snacks

Herb Bouquet

At the original MAD Symposium in 2011, René Redzepi introduced Michel Bras to a roaring crowd; the standing ovation lasted almost five minutes. René focused his introduction on Bras's biggest contribution to modern cuisine, a dish that was possibly the greatest contribution made by a single person to modern cuisine ever: his *gargouillou* salad. Comprised of sixty different herbs and vegetables intertwined beautifully, this perfect expression of his cuisine has been copied countless times and inspired chefs around the world.

The Bras-inspired "wilderness" plating was probably at the peak of its popularity when Relæ opened in mid-2010, and because of its ubiquity, even pondering that direction was a complete no-no in our kitchen. The thought of Michel Bras taking a daily walk in his garden just seemed so far from our everyday experience on Nørrebro, I feared that trying to do something similar at Relæ would just end up as a fancy salad. But as the years went by, we loosened up on dogma a bit and tried to get his multiple-component approach on a dish, but never with any luck. We tried multiple gels, purees, you name it, but none worked out for us, since we both wanted to make a little tribute to Bras and reflect our restaurant's own personality at the same time.

Finally, one day I had the idea of serving a sort of bouquet garni. Traditionally, you tie up this "bouquet" of herbs, stems, and seasonings to infuse into a cooking stock. The idea of swapping the stalks of parsley, rosemary, and bay leaves with fresh and crisp edible herbs and flowers sounded great to us in the green abundance of June 2012. As time went on, it slowly started to shape into a juicy green bite of a snack.

We wanted our Herb Bouquet to be easily edible but still voluptuous and generous, so building the many layers of flavor required a good amount of structure and logic. We started out with a juicy lettuce leaf that we spread with a pistachio puree. The creaminess of the nuts gives substance to the mouthfeel and a richness to balance the bitterness and acidity of the herbs. On top of the leaf we added a few stalks of slightly blanched celery to give crunch and a foundation to build on and then came all the other herbs we could find. We used a few thin ribbons of celery softened in brine to tie up the bouquet just tight enough for it to be held together but to allow the herbs and flowers to show their diversity. Several sprays of our fruity pear vinegar and a sprinkle of salt made for the crucial last tang and gave the bouquet a fresh and moist look, making it one of the most popular snacks we have ever served.

When looking at the final result, I must say it ended up being quite far removed from the *gargouillou* inspiration. It was distant enough for me to feel that we had made something of our own, and in that way, we have truly made a small tribute, even though humble, to the great Michel Bras.

Dishes

Celery Root Taco

This snack was one of many results of a fast food–inspired trend we had going for a good while. We were frying onion rings for snacks and baking pizza for the cheese course, and eventually we ventured into doing tacos as well. I had just been on a trip to California that had introduced me to the greatness of Mexican cuisine for the first time. The soft tacos I tasted there were a revelation.

The whole idea of eating with your hands (see pages 176–77) is a recurring theme in our food, so finding a new "vessel" or a different way of transporting food to your mouth is always a welcome challenge.

In this case, I was also inspired by the taco's function because, in reality, this dish has nothing to do with a taco. As with all simple things, quality lies in the basics, and a good taco is judged by its masa and tortilla. Our "tortilla" is celery root, which flavorwise can't compare to a corn-based dough, but texturewise it has some similarities in its elasticity and stretch.

We came to understand that it is really no less complicated to do a tortilla based on a celery root than to nixtamalize corn and hand-knead a masa dough. To get the texture that would bring me back to California, we decided to first bake the celery root, wrapped in foil, for about an hour until it was cooked through but not too soft. After cooling it down, we sliced it on a meat slicer about 1.5 mm thick and recooked the slices on a very hot cast-iron pan. The "tortillas" would occasionally char in spots, but they stayed soft, juicy, and elastic. This was all a balancing act because a too-thin slice would burn and a too-thick slice would never be bendable enough to serve its purpose.

For the filling, which was also made of celery root, the vegetable needed to be a whole lot softer, so we baked it for 30 to 45 minutes longer than the ones we used for tortillas. After baking, we cooled, peeled, and julienned the celery root, which was extremely juicy, and mixed it with buttermilk, crème fraîche, salt, and lemon juice. Almost inspired by a French celery root rémoulade, this filling would give both a comforting and umami-like feel, and its acidity would also add plenty of freshness. We filled a still-warm "tortilla" with the celery root mixture and topped it with a few different types of cress to counter the natural sweetness of the root vegetable and to add a variation in texture.

In the end, we sprayed the herbs with a few rounds of lemon juice to add a final acidic touch and grated heavy amounts of salted and cured egg yolk on top. The almost golden egg "flakes" would allude to the traditional grated cheese that can top tacos. We folded the "tortilla" as you would a taco, and its handy size makes for two or three small bites, a moment of Mexican inspiration with a very locally grown flavor profile.

Dishes

Grilled Jerusalem Artichokes

When we first got our hands on the Japanese *kamado*-style grill named the Big Green Egg, it sparked a period when we were grilling absolutely everything. For a second, we even considered getting a grill installed in our kitchen, which is way too small for that pipe dream to ever come true. Charred and burnt was very much the theme that winter, and the produce available in that particular moment was well suited for it. Older root vegetables with a mature flavor and a lot of natural sweetness react well to the high and aggressive heat that comes from smoldering coals. We were surprised at how well Jerusalem artichokes did in the grill; in fact, they were the wintertime vegetable that gave us the most interesting result. We charred them on the grill at extremely high heat for a short period, and the burnt outside created a crunchy crust that concealed a softened, creamy inside.

It is surprising how discreet the bitterness is, even when you completely char this vegetable. We wanted to amp up the flavors, so we added a tangy and bitter lemon skin puree to turn up the bitterness of the choke's charred skin, which provided a counterpoint to the soft, fatty, sweet, and comforting flesh inside. Brown butter would align with the white interior, enhancing its "creaminess" while adding its own type of toasted bitterness.

The grill needs to reach a considerably high temperature—around 300°C (575°F)—before we cook the chokes for 15 to 20 minutes, turning every few minutes. While cooking, the tuber expels a good amount of steam and the chokes' insides start to soften. To facilitate this process, it is a good idea to poke a few holes in them with a skewer or a needle after the initial cooking and tenderizing, which lets the steam evaporate more easily.

We make the lemon puree simply by cooking lemon skins until soft and pureeing them, then adding some of their juice back for freshness. As soon as they are cooked, the chokes must be halved and seasoned with salt. We add a good dash of warmed brown butter and then generous amounts of the lemon puree, right before serving the finished dish very warm.

The bitter punch this snack gives serves as a great start to the meal. It awakens the palate and shows so much character. And as the first thing served at the table, it sparks the guest's curiosity. It's exactly how we want all of our meals to start at Relæ.

Grilled Corn

The greatest reactions to this dish come from our American guests, who tend to say, "Wow, corn on the cob!" But it surprises all of our customers to receive something as common and well-known as grilled corn on the cob, but as a tiny version made with baby corn.

When we first conceived of the dish, we'd unwrap whole baby corn from its husk, remove the corn silk, and slather the kernels with a dressing made of crème fraîche and marjoram, my favorite companion to corn. We then returned the husk to its place and served it. The guest would pull the husks off and eat the raw corn inside. Because baby corn is less sweet and quite anisey and fresh compared to the full-grown version, eating it whole, and raw, is very satisfying.

But something was missing. It was as if the dish was both too simple and too complicated at once. It felt stupid to keep the corn in the husks if they didn't serve a purpose other than just looking good. So we came up with another way to use the husks. I had once created a recipe for a Danish newspaper in which I wrapped up an entire mackerel with marjoram and sweet corn husks. I put it on the grill, and as the husks burned, the fish inside smoked and steamed. The delicious flavor and perfume of the fish popped up in my mind as we were working on this snack.

We unwrapped the cobs as before, removed the corn silk, and added marjoram leaves, this time leaving out the crème fraîche. We replaced the husks, leaving a small opening to expose a strip of kernels, tied up the bundles, and grilled them for a few minutes on a very hot grill. The grilled corn is still crunchy, flavorful, and slightly smoky. To finish, we add a small amount of melted butter and salt to some of the exposed corn kernels. The guest pulls the cob out of the husk and eats it by hand.

That was it. With just a few touches, we made the dish even simpler but also quite a lot sharper. The flavor was both comforting and appetizing, exactly what a snack should be.

Dishes

Shallots and Nigella

A meal at Rumi during the Melbourne 2012 Food & Wine Festival was incredibly inspiring to me. Many of the flavors at the Australian-Lebanese restaurant were unknown and exotic to me at the time, but what struck me most was the combination of aromatic, toasted nigella seeds with the lingering acidity of yogurt, something I wanted to pursue once I was back on home ground.

Much later, this flavor combination became the core of a wintertime snack we make with batter-fried whole shallots, which were themselves inspired by the Chinese taro dumplings often served in dim sum restaurants. Those dumplings combine a soft interior with a lacy shell, and I have always been amazed by how the batter seems to just stay together within a fluffy network of crispiness. We wanted to re-create that crispiness and decided on a beer-based tempura batter charged in a siphon to do it.

Of course, we still needed to decide what we'd batter and fry. Since we were serving this dish in winter, we chose shallots. After much trial and error, we found the right combination of baking the shallots in their skins before peeling, just long enough to soften but not turn to mush during the final frying. We bake them at 200°C (400°F), then carefully peel the skin away from the bulb while keeping it fixed at the root end. Then we return them to the oven at 150°C (300°F), just long enough to dry out the surface, which prevents the tempura batter from sliding off when it hits the fryer. We use the pulled-back skins as a handle to submerge the shallots in the batter and dump them in the fryer two at a time. During frying, it's crucial to dip them into the hot oil a few times before releasing them, which helps the batter shape around the onion, protecting it and keeping it from overcooking. After pulling them from the fryer, we allow the shallots and especially the skins to drip off any excess oil. Then we make a small incision in the center of each shallot and insert a good amount of strained sheep's milk yogurt to refresh the palate. Finally, we dust the whole thing with toasted powdered nigella seeds, giving bitterness, aroma, and a great Mediterranean feel to the snack. Best of all, the guest can use the fried skins as a handle and eat the shallot without cutlery.

Kornly Cracker

Filled with mushrooms and topped with cheese, this airy cracker is another offspring of fast food. After doing a small pizza for a cheese course, we wanted to turn that concept into a wintertime snack. Soon enough, we transformed our sourdough-based pizza dough into a cracker inspired very closely by the "air baguette" at elBulli. During my time there, those crazy Catalans turned a puffy pizza dough into an inflated, thin-crusted mini-baguette they served with a thin slice of Ibérico ham. The crackling texture of it really stayed with me, and I wanted to utilize that technique to create a vessel for this snack.

To make that doable, we needed to take it a step further and open up the crackers after baking them. As with the elBulli original, we flattened the cracker dough in a pasta machine until very thin and then simply cut it into squares. When baked immediately over high heat, they puff up into golden pillows that, once cooled, we cut in half to open up.

To fill them, we add thin slices of button mushrooms lightly pickled with 1.5 percent of their weight in salt. This procedure breaks them down, making them as juicy as if cooked yet still maintaining their raw mushroom flavor and umami. After adding the raw mushroom "compote" and fresh mushroom slices that we season with salt and brown butter, we cover everything in generous amounts of Kornly, a Danish cow's milk cheese, and top with a few turns of the peppermill. The Danish cheese has a mature flavor but is soft enough to add a pleasant texture once grated onto the mushrooms. Because the cheese isn't melted, the fattiness of the brown butter is crucial to prevent it from tasting dry. Thus, we are generous with the butter.

The flavor profile of this snack stays very much in the pizza realm, so it's a comforting and appetizing way to start off the meal, yet the layers of texture and flavor are complex and interesting. There is the light and crispy cracker exterior, the juicy middle, the soft slices of raw mushrooms, the warm nutty brown butter, and the superlight cheese for garnish. The black pepper gives a few top notes, enlivening the softer, umami-based flavors.

Dishes

Oxalis Roots

This simple yet exotic-flavored snack was another outcome of our relationship with Lars Jacobsen of Offside farm (see pages 94–95). His research and experiments with obscure and rare vegetables and herbs had given us the opportunity to work with these roots, called *lykkekløverrod* in Danish. Oxalis root has tart and acidic characteristics and is extremely crunchy and succulent to eat in its raw state. Cooking it felt completely unnecessary, as the structure is so interesting on its own. Biting into it for the first time reminded me of the fragile and crispy structure of an Asian pear—just as succulent but less sweet and slightly tart. To enhance the feeling of biting into an exotic fruit, it made sense to serve it as a snack to be eaten out of hand, just like a pear or apple.

We scrubbed the roots to get rid of the dirt and cut off the fibrous tips. With the tip of a knife, we removed the central part of the remaining bulb, which is also very fibrous, leaving us with the most succulent part of the root. The cavity in the middle created space for a filling, and we started to experiment with what could season and supplement the juiciness of the root.

We wanted something savory, vegetal, and appetizing, and our experimental batch of salted mirabelle plums came to mind. The pulp of these plums, which we had stored in brine for about 6 months, was very soft. We just needed to spread it on a bit of the oxalis root to experience how well the crunchy and tart root was complemented by the fruity and savory condiment.

However, the plums had turned a brown-greenish color that wasn't very appetizing, so we decided to find another garnish that would complement and support the natural tartness of the dish. We chose a relative to the oxalis root, French sorrel, which brings its own share of oxalic acid, a chemical component naturally found in many vegetables that adds bitter flavor and a slightly greener note. The tiny green leaves covered up the pureed plum and were highly decorative. Because the oxalis was such a rarity, we would display it untrimmed at the table when bringing the snack to the guests so they would know more about what they were eating.

Lars brought only a bag of the oxalis roots that first time, but his production has since expanded. We can now count on getting the roots in reasonable amounts throughout the summer months to hand to our guests like a piece of ripe, exotic fruit.

Dishes
Herbivorous
Starters

Unripe Strawberries, Cress, and Buttermilk
Sheep's Milk Yogurt, Radishes, and Nasturtium
Cucumber, Caraway, and Lemon Balm
Smoked Beet "Fish" and Elderflower
Beet, Crab Apple, and Söl
Cooked Onions, Buttermilk, and Nasturtium

Dishes

Unripe Strawberries, Cress, and Buttermilk

This is one bitter mouthful, and I love it. It was the beginning of summer in 2012, and we had finally got our hands on the first green, unripe strawberries. We had warmed them up to use as a component of other dishes before, but I felt that their intriguing mix of sweetness and acidity deserved a spot in the limelight.

To build around the juiciness and acidity of the warmed green strawberries, I wanted to add bitterness at different levels, with nasturtium leaves and stems and a watercress puree, which would be tempered by a buttermilk snow. The result is a superbly fresh dish that starts the menu on a very green, alive, and refreshing note.

The watercress puree that's spooned onto the bottom of the plate consists mostly of watercress, with a bit of spinach added to give body. Rather than slicing the berries, we cut them in half to keep their texture soft and juicy and to showcase them as the dish's main component. The nasturtium leaves and stems that we drape on top have a slight sweetness that helps them partner successfully with the berries, despite being cressy and bitter. The watercress puree, which is very green and almost aggressive on its own, becomes very pleasant when mixed with the ice-cold buttermilk snow that finishes the plate. The buttermilk's gentle acidity is similar to that of the strawberries and serves as a counterbalance that reins in the dish's bitterness.

There is an interplay between temperatures in this dish that I believe is crucial for sweetness and bitterness to work well together. Because the berries are warmed to about 50°C (125°F) and the snow is about -20°C (-4°F), the outcome can be disastrous if the timing isn't right. As soon as we add the frozen snow to the ice-cold plate, it is crucial to serve the dish immediately. The unexpected flavor contrast of the frozen snow and the warm berries (which are normally served cold) adds an element of surprise during the first few bites.

Dishes

Sheep's Milk Yogurt, Radishes, and Nasturtium

This dish is a story of contrasts. A story of peppery, bitter, and crunchy radishes in alliance with meaty green nasturtium leaves, pushing up against a velvety, creamy, and light sheep's milk yogurt mousse. This kind of balance is the key to turning seemingly insignificant and low-profile produce into a very interesting dish.

To give a lighter structure and texture to the dish, we just barely cook the radishes, since cooking tones down their peppery freshness. We blanch the radishes for about 30 seconds, then halve them and mix them with lemon juice, olive oil, and salt. This is the base for the dish, which we cover with a generous amount of sheep's milk yogurt mousse. We then top the whole white cloud in small, spicy green nasturtium leaves turned upside down, which complement the peppery radishes.

Cucumber, Caraway, and Lemon Balm

This dish is as close as you can get to soup on our menu. It came about one day when we were looking for a truly summery first course. We wanted something ice-cold, refreshing, and aromatic to cleanse the palate and get the menu started on the right foot. Cucumber is the ingredient that best meets those criteria, and it ended up forming the base of what became a wonton-inspired yet cold vegetable composition.

Cucumber has an incredibly versatile flavor, and its juice and crunch always provide textural complexity. For this dish, we wanted to capitalize on its juiciness without literally juicing the vegetable, so we finely grated peeled cucumber into a moist, green, almost slushy texture. We left the cucumber mixture to drain, and then we reserved the excess juices, seasoned with lemon juice, as a fragrant broth to later add to the dish. Then, we seasoned the grated cucumber with salt, a small amount of pear vinegar, and freshly chopped lemon balm to liven up the aromatics of the dish and underline its freshness.

We wrapped up the grated cucumber in salted and sliced kohlrabi "wrappers" so that the guest would experience a small explosion of juice and flavor in every bite. The small, almost dumplinglike fold that we use seemed interesting *and* functional, even if it does take agile fingers to get the job done.

Though we rarely make use of spices, here we add a few toasted caraway seeds for complexity, which forms a solid alliance with the flavors of cucumber and lemon balm. The caraway's slight toasted note really lifts the dish. We finish this cold-cucumber take on wonton soup by spooning the reserved cucumber juices over the top and adding a few drops of extra-virgin olive oil, which helps bind everything together and provides a slightly grassy and bitter note that accents its fresh and light flavor profile.

Dishes

Smoked Beet "Fish" and Elderflower

My first memory of how we conceived this dish was when my creative sous chef John Tam said, "Look! It looks just like tuna!" The last time we had an experiment that looked like tuna was when we braised a pork shank for way too long and it looked like cat food at best. But this time John wasn't thinking of Chicken of the Sea but of a beautiful slice of tuna sashimi. It had that same leathery and fulfilling texture and was slightly translucent, and if it I hadn't known that he had been fiddling around with baked beets for a few days, he could have tricked me.

John had spent days doing every thinkable thing to beets for a vegetarian first course. This was back when we had a Josper, a charcoal-fired oven that never found a permanent spot in our small kitchen, as it was too big, too warm, and not adaptable to our needs. But when we still had it, we were charcoal grilling just about anything we could think of, including those big round beets. The technique that proved to give the best results was to char the beets for about an hour or so over the coals and then bake them at a low temperature for 8 to 12 hours. I imagined that this would simulate the effect of tossing the beets into a roaring fire and then covering them in the ashes after an initial charring.

The low temperature and prolonged cooking of the beets, while sealed in their burnt shells, intensifies the flavor while retaining most of the moisture. The result is dense, savory, and packed with umami.

So we had the technique, but it still wasn't a finalized dish. That said, we knew we wanted to serve this simple piece of baked beet with the same respect and awe that a sushi chef would put into a slice of perfect toro tuna. To further underline the "fishy" feeling of the dish—in more of a Danish than a Japanese way—we slightly smoke the beets after peeling off the charred edges. We then dehydrate those charred peels and grind them into a powder that we sprinkle around the "fish," which gives a bitter, roasted flavor that complements the smoky notes.

To break through the dense texture and umami flavor, we add a few bits of pickled elderflower, which has enough acidity to balance the dish and cleanse the palate. The flowery aroma really picks up beautifully on the smoke, creating a very interesting flavor combination. In the end, it's just some beet slices, but the smoke, flowery aroma, bitterness, and dense texture gives it so many layers of complexity.

Beet, Crab Apple, and Söl

The earthy tones of red beets and the tobacco-like umami of the Icelandic dulse *söl* were a match that was meant to be. Here, we weave the two flavors together in a sauce made from beet juice and seaweed, which holds the cooked beet slices upright, interspersed with torn pieces of crab apple leather of different colors and flavors and more *söl*.

In a way, this dish is an amalgam of two vegetable dishes from our first menu at Relæ. The *söl* started as part of a sweet carrot dish with crushed black currants. We also had a vegetarian first course that featured juicy slices of poached celery root wrapped tightly around sea lettuce and sliced into small rolls. Served with a black olive sauce, its bitter and salty notes complemented the briny, juicy, and mineral mouthfeel of the celery root and sea lettuce. When it was time to change the menu, we wanted to keep the vegetable-seaweed template—and since winter was approaching, beets seemed an obvious choice. We knew that beets' earthiness would be way too dominant for sea lettuce, so we swapped in the more assertive *söl* and had a new dish.

It was as simple as the first two—and had the same basic ideas—but very different in flavor.

The following year, we started working with Lars Jacobsen from Offside farm (see pages 94–95), who was filling our fridges to overflowing with crab apples of numerous varieties, sizes, and colors. We tried to stay on top of them by pureeing and preserving them, and we began experimenting with drying them into fruit leathers. The combination of beets and *söl* resurfaced as a base onto which we could add the crab apple's acidity and bitterness.

We didn't want to repeat the same format we used for the original dishes, so instead of rolling everything up, we tried to display all of these different colors and textures by spreading them out evenly and intertwining them. The slightly varying flavors and lingering acidity of the crab apples added much more complexity, and the tobacco-like, salty seaweed gave a depth and warmth to a dish that was very suited to kicking off a menu in the cold Danish winter.

Dishes

Cooked Onions, Buttermilk, and Nasturtium

When reading through old notes, I am reminded how often our team at Relæ fights for some of our ideas to come to life and find their spot on the menu. Trying to find the right balances, distilling ideas, and pinpointing the right proportions for a dish could take weeks and weeks of experimentation. And then there is a completely different category of dishes that instantly make sense, as if they are born under a lucky star. That is the case with this dish, or rather its first iteration.

We had stumbled upon the wonderful combination of lemony Bronte pistachio puree with peppery cresses and were trying to figure out how to turn it into a first course on the vegetarian menu. It just wouldn't click for us, until, during a tasting of other dishes with the sommeliers, I was struck by the idea of folding soft-baked onion shells—the inner layers of an onion that separate during baking—and lining them up side by side on top of the pistachio puree. In between the puree and the onions I hid a few leaves of nasturtium and pot cress, giving a refreshing spice to the dish. When a soccer player strikes a goal from far out he knows immediately whether the shot felt right or not, and I had that same feeling of triumph long before I finished plating the dish.

This dish was conceived in the winter, and the following summer we decided to bring it back to the menu. But even though we considered it one of our greatest creations, it didn't make the same impression as it had in the colder months, when the comforting deep onion flavor worked so well. Now, we had freshly harvested onions at hand, so an update was necessary. Slightly blanched fresh onions are one of my favorite summertime treats, as their natural sweetness combines with their crunch and slight bitterness in a truly addictive way.

To add a gentle acidity, we replaced the sweet and heavy pistachio puree with a buttermilk and crème fraîche dressing. On top of that, we placed the onion shells rolled around ripped leaves of nasturtium, giving us that combination of cress and lactic acidity we're so fond of. To make the best use of the herb, we added the tiny stems as well, giving a fun texture with beautiful plating. We seasoned the onions with extra-virgin olive oil and a good amount of lemon juice, making everything tangy, fresh, and summery.

Dishes
Omnivorous
Starters

Lumpfish Roe, Daikon, and Almonds
Oysters, Cabbage, and Capers
Mussels, Seaweed, and Allumettes
Squid, Mussels, and Seaweed
Raw Beef, Anchovies, and Ramsons
Lamb, Shrimp, and Dill
White Asparagus and Anchovies
Pickled Skate, Mussels, and Celery Root
Pickled Mackerel, Cauliflower, and Lemon
Cod, Kohlrabi, and Skins
White Onions, Crayfish, and Fennel

Dishes

Lumpfish Roe, Daikon, and Almonds

When the waters start warming up in spring, the lumpfish, or lumpsucker, heads closer to the Danish shores to mate. That migration greatly benefits local fishermen, who land tons of the roe-bursting females every year. The roe's pink color, fresh and briny flavor, and lightly explosive crunch make it extremely popular in April and May. The flesh of the female fish is worn-out, watery, and bland, but the males, which are smaller, are much more firm-fleshed and actually very tasty, as long as they are very fresh, since the fish's high amount of fat turns rancid very quickly. We have worked hard to make a dish based on the males' creamy flesh, but their smaller size makes them a rarity in fishnets, which aim for catching the bigger females and their roe.

In this dish, we strive to underline the crunch and salinity of the roe. Flavorwise it makes a good connection with nutty, fatty, and bland flavors, which is why it's traditionally served on buckwheat blinis with crème fraîche or similar variations. With this in mind, we enjoy pairing it with a fatty, velvety nut milk, in this case an almond milk made with aromatic Sicilian almonds that's set in a smooth and creamy curd. We make the curd by gelling a base mixed of cow's milk and almond milk with iota, a seaweed-based gellificant. To give a slight temperature contrast to the final dish, we cook and set the gels to order so that they are slightly warm when served.

The almondy and nutty feel of the soft-textured curd can come across as almost sweet to some people, even though we add no sugar whatsoever. To enhance the salinity of the roe and keep the dish in balance, we found that the briny and complex flavor of lacto-fermented daikon—daikon that ferments in salt brine with a splash of whey—was the perfect savory boost we needed. By slicing the daikon fairly thinly, the radish's juicy crunch complements the pink lumpfish roe elegantly.

The roe needs to be kept very cold and stored on ice before serving, but the plates that we set the gels on must be at a warm room temperature so that the warm gel can contrast with the cold roe. As we cook the custard components and the gelling is activated, we add a few spoonfuls of it to a fairly shallow bowl to set. We then quickly arrange the julienned daikon around the gel. For a binding element that underlines the softness of the curd, we add drops of sauce made from almond milk seasoned with the fermenting brine from the daikons. On top of that, we add a fair amount of the roe and a few slices of almonds to give crunch and bitterness. To finalize it, we add a sprinkle of crunchy flaked salt and a few sprays of tangy lemon juice.

Oysters, Cabbage, and Capers

As with so many others, the idea for this dish was sparked by nibbling on a vegetable. White cabbage hardly seems like an interesting ingredient, but in the middle of the cold winter of 2010 to 2011, we were tasting quite a few different types of white cabbage, and we got the idea to make a fresher, modernized version of sauerkraut, or choucroute. After spending 2 or 3 days vacuum-sealed with a vinegar, sugar, and salt brine, the transparent but still crisp cabbage takes on a dimension of funkiness and umami, resulting in a fresh iodine flavor that just screams for oysters.

In reality, this dish is all about the flavor of oysters, even though it's mainly based on cabbage as it only includes one oyster per serving, sliced thinly. The brined vegetable's "intimation" of a marine oyster flavor made us want to enhance just that, instead of masking it or downplaying it, as I often see in oyster dishes. A caper puree blended with water and vinegar provides an almost metallic backbone, and the lingering spice of the horseradish mellowed out by acidic yogurt makes those slivers of beautiful, velvety Danish oysters taste like a million oysters in just a few bites.

There is definitely some bitterness in this dish, and that needs careful handling, which is why that slight bit of sweetness from the cabbage is crucial for the harmony of all the flavors. The cabbage's juicy and mouthwatering texture is also important, which it will achieve after marinating for a few days.

While we were playing around with the plating, we came up with the idea to add a thin slice of raw cabbage stem, which helps us use up the entire vegetable and also creates variation in texture. From there, we were inspired to recompose the pieces of brined cabbage so that they resembled a perfect slice to lay over the pieces of oyster.

This dish is served cool but just a bit warmer than fridge temperature to allow the oyster flavor to shine through. First we add a spoonful of yogurt and a few strips of scraped horseradish, and carefully position a few dots of caper puree, one for each mouthful. Next comes the oyster, sliced into spoon-fitting sizes, and then there's the time-consuming work of reconstructing a cross section of what is, at least in this case, an inspirational cabbage.

Mussels, Seaweed, and Allumettes

The flavor profile of this dish really stands out compared with the other cold courses we've had on the menu. Normally we pair shellfish with freshness, acidity, and crisp textures, but the sweetness of the blue mussels we were working with called for something more comforting and well rounded in flavor. The inspiration must have jumped out of a *moules frites* conversation in the kitchen, which made us want to pair up the soft texture of very lightly cooked mussels with the flavor of fried potatoes.

After briefly cooking the mussels and chilling them in a mussel stock, we rest them on the bottom of the plate and then slowly add matchstick potatoes, or *pommes alumettes*, that we brine and then very briefly blanch to retain a good bite. Though they aren't fried, their remaining crunch works very well with the soft and creamy mussels.

To bind everything together and add a briny and refreshingly green touch to the dish, we add a cold broth made of mussel juices blended with sea lettuce. As a textural contrast, we fry up a few potatoes until they're extra crispy and add them to the plate just before serving so they don't soak up the bouillon and get soggy. A few drops of pork fat at the very end enhance the umami feel of the dish and its pleasantly greasy quality gives the diner a french fry flavor but in a light and elegant way.

Somehow this dish also reminds me of minestrone, with small bits of broken spaghetti floating in a savory bouillon with pearls of fat on its surface. Serving what normally would be considered warmer flavors in a cold context really gives a playful dimension to a dish that's made from very basic ingredients.

Dishes

Squid, Mussels, and Seaweed

Squid was a tough nut to crack. It is not really a part of the traditional fishery or gastronomy in Denmark, and what is caught is almost always exported to Mediterranean countries, a common story for many fish that land in Denmark. Maybe that is why it is so undervalued here—only a single Danish word, *blæksprutte*, covers the whole array of squid, octopus, and cuttlefish.

Prior to opening Relæ, the only Danish squid I had worked with was the pearly white specimens we diced and served raw at Noma. But squid came to play a significant role as the focus of the very first dish I planned to put on Relæ's menu. I had the idea of cleaning the meat, stacking it up, and slicing it very thinly. For years, both elBulli and the San Sebastian restaurant Berasategui were making ravioli with this type of thinly sliced squid and filling them with squid ink, coconut, and whatnot. But I wanted to cut the squid even thinner and originally was going to just lay the slices over a soft-cooked cauliflower to give a creamy and velvety texture to accent the slight snap of the seafood.

Working with locally caught squid that have bodies about 30 centimeters long, we clean the bodies and halve them, then we stack them in five or six layers and freeze them in blocks no bigger than about 12 centimeters.

But instead of slicing it lengthwise, we flip the block of squid and slice it while still frozen to create an almost transparent handful of "tagliatelle." After bringing these thin slices to room temperature, we cook them for just a few moments in a generous amount of warm brown butter and then drain them off. Having enough fat is crucial for the squid "noodles" to be evenly cooked.

The tender and velvety texture of squid cooked this way is absolutely incredible. While still experimenting, we dropped the cauliflower concept and tried dressing the squid with sea urchins that we happened to have in-house, but sourcing those proved to be out of our reach. A sweet marine flavor was obviously the theme we wanted to accentuate, so we swapped sea urchin with mussels and squid ink and made an emulsion to serve as the base layer.

We frame the deep and umami-packed emulsion with a few leaves of sea lettuce and add the warm squid at the last second. We season the brown butter that has mixed with the juices expelled from the cooked squid with lemon juice and pour it over the top, creating a sauce that gives tang and fattiness all at once. It's a presentation that really celebrates Danish squid, in a fairly un-Danish way.

Dishes

Raw Beef, Anchovies, and Ramsons

In spring, ramsons—sometimes called wild garlic—shoot up all over the city of Copenhagen, attracting young Nordic chefs to forage the local parks like bees in chef's whites. But eating raw ramsons on their own is a painful experience. More garlicky than garlic, the green leaves (which resemble the poisonous lily) are truly packed with flavor.

Most often, we blanch ramsons and then puree them to add flavor to sauces. But it was not until we tried wrapping this wild chive around raw beef that we found the antidote to its aggressiveness. It seems like the bloody, irony raw meat can't get enough of the green pungency.

The meat we use for this purpose is high-quality organic beef that we buy in whole or half animals. We prefer the leaner cuts like the tenderloin, and most of the back leg when slicing it raw, since we want to avoid sinew. (And of course, Manfreds gives us an outlet to use the other cuts that are more suited for braising or longer cooking.)

To give the dish more depth and salinity, we add anchovy emulsion to the bottom of the plate. On top, we place a good amount of the thinly sliced raw beef that's been seasoned with olive oil, lemon juice, and salt. Next up we add a few leaves of spinach and sorrel, the latter of which contributes the acidity that is so crucial for making the raw meat come to life.

We tear the ramson leaves into smaller pieces still kept pointy and arrange them carefully on top of the rest of the meat. It is a work of great precision, both for the sake of aesthetics but also to assure that the leaves don't tangle up into one big piece when the guest takes a bite.

To finish off, we give the entire surface five sprays of lemon juice and a sprinkle of salt, and we also add a few drops of a lemon and olive oil vinaigrette between the leaves to give the meat its last seasoning. It is tempting to season the meat before building on the leaves, but it's too risky, as the acidity of the vinaigrette would cook the meat to a gray and rubbery mush by the time the plate made it to the guest's table.

Balance is key here, as too much or too little ramson could spoil every single bite. With this dish, our servers take a lot of care explaining that to our guests, though everybody ends up trying the ramsons on their own anyway, which probably encourages them to listen a bit more carefully when the next dish arrives.

Dishes

Lamb, Shrimp, and Dill

I have always steered away from cold lamb meat. Waking up on a Sunday morning to its wool-like aftertaste (after a long night out that ended with an obligatory kebab on Nørrebrogade) might have had that effect on me. Yet at one point I started wondering what lamb would turn out like if served raw. Both die-hard fans as well as lamb haters know that the fat is where all the action is, both good and bad. At Relæ we found that the key to serving thin slices of raw lamb would be in the balanced play between the meat's temperature and its flavorful fat.

We realized that we wanted the flavor of roasted lamb fat but also to keep the gamy characteristics of the meat in its raw form. So we decided to roast the fat from all the scraps left from butchering the animals and use it to brush on the finished dish. We cut these surplus bits into small pieces and roasted them slowly, until the fat rendered as much as possible. We then added an equal amount of neutral vegetable oil and let the concoction slowly simmer for about 30 minutes. The oil would keep the fat from glazing the cold meat when brought down in temperature.

The other components of this dish were partly inspired by a trip to Thailand, when my newfound obsession with dried shrimp led us to the idea of pairing it with raw lamb. It's a combination that is also loosely the base of a traditional Danish dish, *lam i dild og rejer*, a stew of soft-boiled lamb with tiny peeled fjord shrimp and plenty of dill. That's where the idea of adding generous amounts of dill came from, and even though dried shrimp has a very different flavor profile than cooked and peeled shrimp, conceptually it gave us a starting point.

To add juice, texture, and lightness, we started off plating sautéed sliced onions seasoned with plenty of lemon juice. We cooked the onions at very low heat just until their slightly aggressive bitterness turned into sweetness, leaving a crunch. Then came good amounts of roughly picked dill, with the thickest stems cut into small rounds. Just before dressing the sliced meat we added great amounts of dried fjord shrimp powder. The juiciness of the onions would be crucial to balancing this powder. The slices of raw lamb would be up next with their brush of lamb fat.

We kept the lamb fat warm during service, and when sending out the dish, we mixed the lamb fat with lemon juice, brushed it onto the meat, and heated it for a few instants with a flame torch. That ensured the lamb would keep safely above room temperature and thus enhance the depth and complexity of the dish.

Somehow this dish brings you on a quick trip around the world, from the funky Asian umami of the shrimp to the pleasantly dry and refreshing anise aroma of the dill so well represented in traditional Danish cooking. At the table, we don't bother our guests by explaining that the inspiration came partly from the Danish classic. That makes it even more rewarding when, from time to time, Danes smile as they put the puzzle together.

Dishes

White Asparagus and Anchovies

The balance between vegetables and protein in this dish really shows where we put our priorities. This was the first course on our omnivorous menu, and most people ordering it would expect a piece of fish or meat to take center stage. But to me, asparagus—which is hard for us to source organically in Copenhagen (see page 37)—is as precious an ingredient as any meat, so it felt right to focus on the vegetable.

Our preliminary idea was to serve the dish cold and keep the asparagus raw. But I was concerned that the dish would be monotonous, and I knew that asparagus had more to offer beyond its raw fibrous self. We blanched the peeled, white, juicy stalks so they would readily release their juices when bitten into and then cut them into slices of about 3 millimeters and then reconstructed them as a whole asparagus stalk when placing them on the plate. To retain some of the raw flavor and texture, we added the same amount of very thinly sliced, peeled raw asparagus in the same direction as the cooked one. Slowly we combined the two by building the raw slices on top of blanched asparagus and intertwining them precisely. In the end, we would add a tip to one end to make it look like a whole stalk.

To finish this dish, we pickled anchovy fillets in pear vinegar and cut them into small pieces to disperse around the asparagus. We also juiced the raw bottom stems of the asparagus. While the asparagus juice is quite liquid, the smooth and velvety anchovy emulsion acts as a binder. The diner can pass his spoon through the cut asparagus slices and then through the raw asparagus juice spiked with the dots of emulsion, maybe picking up a small piece of pickled anchovy along the way.

It goes without saying that the asparagus must be of very high quality and freshly harvested. A slight bitterness is great here, but you need the sweetness of fresh, top-quality asparagus to balance it out.

Dishes

Pickled Skate, Mussels, and Celery Root

Skate has a texture like no other fish when cooked. When you skin it and cut it off its soft bones, the remaining sinew left under the skin shrinks and curls the pieces into a convex wavy pattern as they cook, almost resembling the inside of a white seashell. When I first considered putting skate on as a cold starter on the menu, my first thought was to slightly cook it and fill up the cavity that forms under the "curl" with a garnish of some sort.

I thought back about how we halfway cook and pickle mackerel, and we tried a similar approach with this much leaner and more fibrous fish. However, because of that fibrous texture, it is very difficult to precisely cook skate. The lean flesh sits in a network of sinew that demands a longer cooking time than the pearly, almost lobsterlike meat. When the sinew is cooked until tender, the remaining parts often overcook and dry out.

To prepare the flesh for a gentler and slightly longer cooking time, we started off by brining the fillets in a 7 percent salt brine, which keeps them juicy and tenderizes them slightly. It's very important to sort the skate into pieces of similar size and texture to begin with, as a small skate has much finer fibers while a bigger and rougher specimen requires longer cooking. After brining and cooking, we chill the skate so that the juicy and shiny fibers of flesh are very easily detached from their sinewy frame, which we discard. This flesh has an incredibly elegant texture and fine flavor. Pulling all those fibers apart can be very time-consuming, but the result—

an almost crustacean-like quality—is definitely worth the trouble.

To complete the dish, we keep things simple. We wanted the velvety texture in the foreground, and the light flavors of the slightly tangy pickled fish needed only a slight supporting act. We kept my idea of filling the "curl" and decided to do so with celery root baked until soft and grated and then folded with an emulsion made from blanched mussels. The similarity of the soft textures between the fish and the vegetable enhances the fish even more, while the mussel emulsion gives a deeper and slightly sweeter sealike flavor, making something akin to a briny and light "rémoulade." Acidity is key in this context, as the mixture would turn out bland if not seasoned with the proper amount of lemon juice. As a final dressing, we prepare something between a thick sauce and a thin puree made with generous amounts of bright green blanched parsley and spinach blended with mussel stock.

As with many of our best dishes, we caught ourselves in a moment of wanting to do more, to add another component—a sprinkle of dried parsley, some seaweed, another texture. We soon realized that our impulse only came out of a moment of self-doubt, and that it would only spoil the beauty behind the dish's simplicity. It is truly a rewarding feeling when you know when enough is enough, that you have the experience and self-esteem to let a dish be naked, focused, and cut to the bone.

Dishes

Pickled Mackerel, Cauliflower, and Lemon

At first, I didn't think this dish from our original menu would make the cut for this book. We've developed so much since our beginnings that it didn't make sense to include dishes that we never serve today. But as my sous chef Lisa Lov, who is also my helping hand in making this book, said, "When I see these pictures of the dishes, I see the faces of the people making them."

She's right. Looking back at this dish brings me right back to our first weeks on the line, with all the expectations, the reviews, and the people I shared it with, some who don't work with us anymore. We created it while we were halfway prepping for our pantry, talking to contractors, and stressing out about what everybody would think of what we were doing. It was long before a fancy food lab would become our creative motor. But it is probably the one original dish that pointed us in the direction where we are today. It has everything I want a dish at Relæ to show: an intelligent approach to humble produce,

a way of showcasing my mixed heritage, clever technique, and high quality hiding underneath simple plating.

The escabèche-inspired technique we use to pickle the mackerel gives us a light tang to cut through the natural fattiness of the fish. This acidity, along with the way we gently cook it, firms up the flesh a bit, making it utterly delicious. Showing off my Italian heritage on that first menu was quite important for me, and accompanying the fish with a tangy and creamy lemon skin puree seemed like a great way to do that.

We plate the dish by making a few lines of lemon skin puree, topping it with the mackerel, and then we add a smooth and velvety cold puree of cauliflower that we splatter on top. To wrap things up, we add a few slices of crunchy cauliflower stem that we have tossed with extra-virgin olive oil and lemon juice, adding a refreshing touch to the dish. A great dish. The first dish.

Dishes

Cod, Kohlrabi, and Skins

We've put cod on the menu on and off ever since we bumped into Max Christensen (see pages 104–5), the fisherman who delivers fish of incredible quality. Cod is so incredibly lean that it can mistakenly be thought of as bland and dry. Cooking it *is* difficult, and building a cold dish around it required some elements that would underline its qualities rather than its flaws. Before we approached this dish, we had poached, cooked, and marinated it, and this time I wanted to focus on the actual skin. Most of the fat you will find on this northern predator is in the skin or just underneath it, so in a quest for texture and a creamy mouthfeel we started working on ways to incorporate the cod skin into the dish.

Cod is covered in tiny scales, so there is plenty of work just to get the skins thoroughly cleaned. After cleaning the skins, we blanched them for about a minute in salted boiling water and spread them out to cool. Once cooled, a light gel formed around them that was quite stiff when cold but very creamy if slightly warmed.

I was intrigued, and I started thinking about just putting the warmed skins on a vegetable, and that would be it! I remembered Ferran Adrià saying that the true flavor of the zucchini is in its seeds, which is why elBulli made a zucchini seed risotto (and why I, like other stagiaires, spent long hours squeezing the seeds from cooked zucchini). In the same way, I posited that the true flavor of the cod was in its skin, so we would serve just the skin.

But as my staff pointed out, that was pretty ridiculous. Manfreds could take some of the excess cod but we would have to butcher unheard of amounts of fish just to yield their skins, which didn't really make sense, did it? We decided to just slightly salt the beautiful loins of Max's pristine cod to firm them up, which would go on the plate uncooked, in translucent, firm, appetizing nuggets hiding underneath the skins.

Now that we had the basic concept, we thought of adding thinly sliced kohlrabi that had just been salted, which makes it release some of its juices while still keeping a crunch, qualities we thought would be well suited to the cod skin and flesh. As we added the salted cod to the plate, we would brush it with our "mushroom soy sauce," the dark juice of salted mushrooms, which enhances the umami of the fish. We also added a bit of cod stock and finally a generous amount of horseradish. The spice from the horseradish would really enhance the firm texture of the fish. We would then cover the fish with those waves of thinly sliced kohlrabi and the fish skins.

As a final touch, we give the skins a short burst of heat with a flame torch, which makes the gel creamy and the clean fish flavor come out even more clearly, bringing all the attention to those skins, just like I wanted. A splash of pear vinegar gives the dish a last dose of acidity.

White Onions, Crayfish, and Fennel

When we celebrated another incredible year at our summer staff party in 2012, our friends from Radio restaurant, Jesper Kirketerp and Rasmus Kliim, prepared an amazing feast for us inspired by the crayfish boils that traditionally take place in Sweden in August. The freshness and quality of these freshwater crustaceans were still clear in my mind several days afterward, even though the flood of natural wine kept me from remembering most of that night. We got in contact with the trapper Jesper and Rasmus work with, and we were soon privileged to have these incredible crayfish in our kitchen too.

The low yield and high cost of local freshwater crayfish in Denmark really challenged our concept and menu pricing, so it felt like a real treat and luxury to put them on the menu, even for a short period of time. To afford it, we needed to compose a dish that would be true to our ideals, where vegetables would be the main character and this seasonal delicacy would act as a supporting player.

I wanted the flavors to go in a fairly classic direction, and we found inspiration in the aromatics that are often added to the cooking liquid for the crayfish: onion and fennel. The anise notes in fennel always suit the sweetness of crustaceans, and the sweetness of in-season new white onions made their addition obvious.

To yield a maximum flavor from the crayfish, we blanch them very briefly and peel them. Then we meticulously crush the heads to extract the flavorful insides and use the liquid as a seasoning for the lightly cooked flesh, which we dice into small pieces. To add texture and sweetness to this mixture, we add diced brined raw fennel and finely chopped and sautéed onions.

As we plate the dish, we start with a small amount of the refreshing fennel puree. To balance the proportions between shellfish and vegetables, we build slices of soft-cooked white onions around the small mounds of crayfish, sort of re-creating the onions' shape. The flavors may be familiar, but the play on texture really completes the dish and keeps it interesting.

Dishes
Herbivorous
Seconds

Turnips, Chervil, and Horseradish
New Potatoes, Warm Berries, and Arugula
Potato, Seaweed, and Pecorino
Lettuce, Smoked Almond, and Olive Oil
Asparagus, Sunflower Seeds, and Mint
Jerusalem Artichoke, Quinoa, and Coffee
Sunflower Seeds, Kornly, and Pine
Baked Potato Puree, Two Ways
Barley, Cauliflower, and Black Trumpet

Turnips, Chervil, and Horseradish

Admittedly, *comforting* is a word I tend to look down on. In our eyes, the idea of serving something that's *only* comforting is like opting for the easy way out, such as a steak with sauce, an egg on toast. But honestly, cooking a "comforting" meal at a high level requires a specific skill set, especially if you're serving an adventurous crowd. With most dishes, I try to keep a small percentage of the flavors or textures comforting and familiar, to help contextualize the rest of the dish—or at least make it seem more approachable.

But with this dish, we took the opposite approach: most of it is quite familiar, and we added just an edgy detail for something different.

When we plated this dish for the first time, I was transported to a traditional Italian trattoria for a brief second, as if I were diving into a bowl of buttery maltagliati. But though the dish had nothing to do with pasta, it led us to the discovery of a brand-new texture. After turning slices of turnips into dried disks in the dehydrator, we then resoaked them in water and cooked them. The rehydrated slices turned into these bits of spongy vegetable "pasta" that were ready to suck up any kind of sauce.

I knew that this fascinating texture deserved to be the focus of its own dish.

Dressing the turnips with something creamy and buttery seemed an obvious approach for this pasta-style dish. We decided to go for a very thick beurre blanc–style sauce that would allow us to add a good amount of lemon juice without it liquefying completely. The viscosity of the sauce is very important to the dish, so we often add another knob of butter at the end to make sure it coats the turnips completely.

Without heating the sauce too much, we season the turnips with salt and a generous amount of chopped chervil and arrange them on the plate. The chervil gives an anise hint to slightly lift the heavy butter base and lighten the dish. To support the original radishy flavor of the raw turnip, we add both toasted mustard seeds and a good amount of grated horseradish, giving it that spicy, fresh, and bitter edge.

This super-simple dish really lets the diner indulge in the great texture of the vegetable and somehow manages to be both unexpected and comforting at the same time.

New Potatoes, Warm Berries, and Arugula

Danes have a special relationship with new potatoes. Copenhageners know that spring is finally here when the very first ones start appearing on menus around the city in the month of May. In fact, it has almost turned into a national sport to be the first to serve them, and restaurants on all levels pay sky-high prices to get their hands on the tiny spuds. We don't participate much in that pseudo-gastronomical race, but we certainly enjoy the virgin freshness, crunch, and aroma that the newly dug potatoes bring to the plate.

Traditionally, new potatoes are cooked just until still snappy and slightly crunchy, then tossed with butter and chopped lovage, which really enhances the natural aromas of these Danish favorites. The green herbal note in lovage was our initial inspiration when we approached the small spuds, but we opted for the more grassy, peppery tone of arugula and sea lettuce.

We blend the two greens, creating a base to emulsify with oil, mustard, and pear vinegar. After passing it through a fine-mesh sieve, the sauce is a beautiful green base for the potatoes to lie in, and adds an incredible tang with both minerality and peppery notes all at once.

We select potatoes of slightly varying sizes but still small enough to eat in one bite. Then we blanch them for just about a minute, keeping them quite crunchy.

To serve, we quickly reheat the potatoes in boiling butter emulsion, strain them, and dust them with powdered dried sea lettuce. As a fruity, juicy contrast, we add white and unripe strawberries, carefully sliced so they will easily combine with the smaller potatoes on the fork. The berries' flavor is undeniably strawberry, but the lack of sweetness creates a great connection with the minerality and tang of the new potatoes in their fresh herbal sauce. We think the potatoes—and the strawberries—are worth waiting the long winter for.

Dishes

Potato, Seaweed, and Pecorino

Most often when focusing on potatoes, people mash, bake, or maybe roast them until caramelized, but I wanted to find another way that was fresher and crisper, and our experiments were going in a million directions. What seemed like a confusing bunch of ideas on paper surprisingly turned into a network of cleverly connected flavors and textures. The dish we came up with transforms potatoes into bundles of "noodles" and serves them in a warm pecorino sauce with pickled fresh seaweed and clarified seaweed butter.

Even though it was winter, we were looking for the crisp and snappy texture of tiny, perfectly cooked new potatoes combined with the more mature, rounded flavor of winter's big old spuds. We knew that too much starch would cause a gritty and mealy mouthfeel and prevent us from achieving the crisp texture we were looking for. So we used the Japanese-style turning vegetable slicer to cut the potatoes into a fine, noodlelike shape, then brined them overnight, which washes away as much of the starch as possible. Brining also begins to break the potatoes down slightly, which helps us shape them into bundles, without them oxidizing, as we are ready to cook them. We added small julienned bits of Gracilaria seaweed to the bundles and steamed them in a bamboo steaming basket. They need only a few minutes of cooking to achieve a cooked potato flavor that retains a slight crunch.

To maintain their moisture during this short but hard and direct cooking, we coat them with clarified butter, which further protects the potatoes from browning during the few hours of cold storage until serving.

We picked an unusual pair of companions to go with the steamed potatoes, opting for salinity, umami, and a marine brine from slightly pickled sea lettuce, plus a comforting and soothing pecorino cheese sauce that's a natural match for potatoes and acts as an improbable link between the sea lettuce and potatoes, with its acidity and salt.

We make the sauce by simply combining chunks of Pecorino Romano with filtered water in a blender. Thinning the cheese this way tones down its fattiness and creamy texture and softens the acidity and the saltiness we are so fond of. We just slightly heat this "soup" for service by blending it several times during the night in the Thermomix at 60°C (140°F), which keeps it warm, preventing it from separating.

As a final touch and a binding flavor element between the seaweed and the cheese, we add butter spiked with powdered dried green seaweed. You could almost say the butter is inspired by Indian ghee, as it returns the bit of fattiness we removed from the cheese by adding water to the sauce and ties all the elements, however surprisingly connected, together.

Dishes

Lettuce, Smoked Almond, and Olive Oil

Ever since we started cooking lettuce, that grassy and green bitterness has been one of my favorite points of departure for a dish. Then, sometime in the beginning of 2012, we started to get interested in fermentation, and it was only a question of time before we would try to combine the two methods, as we do here. This take on salad features fermented lettuce hearts flavored with gently warmed smoked almond milk and covers them in meticulously "julienned" fresh lettuce leaves.

The initial idea for this dish was for it to be a snack. After the lettuces ferment for a few days, they pick up a juicy and crunchy texture similar to when we would cook it sous vide. We wanted that crunch at the start of the meal, thinking that the guest would pick up lettuce leaves garnished with frozen almond granité. That idea turned out to be very crunchy and very refreshing but just a bit too weird. The frozen almond milk brought a confusing sweetness, making it hard to understand if it was sweet or savory. We want a meal to start off fresh and alive and to show a clear idea from the very first mouthful, and this dish just wasn't doing that.

Even though it felt as if we were hitting a dead end on the snack idea, the richness of the almonds and the slight tang, umami, and crunch of the lettuce linked up very well. We knew we had to pursue this a little further.

We moved the lettuce to the second course, which meant it no longer had to be eaten by hand, and it didn't have to be cold. The frozen almond granité became a smoked almond milk. We cut the fermented salad into smaller bits and warmed them in a small amount of the fermenting brine, which created an aroma that almost reminds me of fermented grass. We put a spoonful of the lettuce hearts on the plate, then topped with warmed almond milk, which created a real flavor bomb with a long finish on the palate. The combination of the umami from fermentation and the richness of the almond milk flips this dish from being a "salad" to something incredibly deep, complex, and warm, basically everything a salad is not.

To finish the dish off, we covered the main elements entirely in the outer leaves of fresh lettuce sliced very thinly. The fun texture of the fluffy chiffonade adds variation and a binding element to the other components, in addition, of course, to offering a very aesthetic way of plating the dish. We drizzle a little extra-virgin olive oil on just before serving; grassy, spicy, and fruity, it supports the feeling of eating "grass" from a very tasty pasture indeed.

Dishes

Asparagus, Sunflower Seeds, and Mint

Asparagus completely reigns over spring and early summer in Denmark, and its quality here can be very impressive. It's a beautiful vegetable, and the instinct is always to display it in its entirety on the plate. But at Relæ, we rarely serve anything that isn't cut into pieces and ready to be spooned up.Most of our dishes are strongest when the components are consumed together, so to facilitate this, we plate things so they are easy to eat and there is less guesswork for the guest.

For this reason, we decided to simply slice the asparagus quite thinly so that it easily could be mixed with the other components. The idea for this dish was to make a stew of some sort with the asparagus and a few other elements but with much fresher flavors and crisper textures than you normally find in a stew. We would cook the asparagus only in a warm butter emulsion, essentially keeping them almost raw but cooked enough to give a juicy mouthfeel. To freshen up the dish, we added a mint puree that, along with a lemony beurre blanc, would act as the binding element and underline the idea of a "stew" when the guest mixed everything together by the spoonful.

The incredible texture of pressure-cooked sunflower seeds supplements the crunch of the asparagus, and a dash of olive oil, fresh mint leaves, and a spoonful of crispy buckwheat add the final complexity.

Dishes

Jerusalem Artichoke, Quinoa, and Coffee

As I've said, I love challenging our guests with plating that leaves them curious and somehow doesn't tell them the whole story. Serving a savory dish that looks like a dessert, probably followed by a dessert with lots of savory notes, sends a pretty clear message about how little we care about the usual notions of what makes a proper meal. This dish is a perfect example. Its main component is a Jerusalem artichoke puree dressed with garnishes that all have golden color tones, and it does appear very much like a sugary dessert, maybe even chocolate chip cookie dough. That said, the dish is not about provoking preconceptions, but about finding a great balance between soft and crunchy and sweet and bitter.

Bitterness and texture are the two key elements that contrast with the rich, sweet, and round flavor of Jerusalem artichokes, which I consider to be one of the most versatile ingredients in the kitchen. Though we often emphasize the chokes' snappy texture, in this particular dish, we remove the vegetable's inherent crunch, reducing it to a comforting and smooth puree. It's packed with a satisfying, slightly caramelized flavor that comes from first baking the chokes and then boiling them in vacuum bags until thoroughly soft. To underline the soft texture even further, we thin the puree slightly and charge it into a siphon, making it light and fluffy. Then we set about bringing back some texture to the dish with a few variations of crunch.

The first textural contrast comes from crosnes, the small white larva-looking tubers—there's no better way to describe them—that have a crisp texture and nutty flavor. We cut the crosnes up into small, rounded pieces, making for a more refined chew than we could obtain with square-cut pieces of Jerusalem artichoke. For a more crackling crunch, we add golden crispy quinoa, which we first cook until soft, then dehydrate, and then fry until puffed and crunchy.

While the textural profile of the dish was spot-on at this point in our testing, repetitive tastings revealed that we needed some bitterness to cleanse and awaken the palate while still supporting the fundamental nutty flavors. So we scattered finely ground coffee from the light roast of the Coffee Collective over the top of the dish, which manages to keep the flavors together without leaving a dry and unpleasant mouthfeel and aftertaste. Finally, to add acidity, we sprinkled on a bit of our caramelized yogurt, which is simply yogurt reduced until the curd naturally caramelizes and then dehydrated until crispy.

The bitter tone that grasps the palate from the first bite balances everything very well and leaves the flavors to stand in clear succession: first comforting and lightly sweet chokes, then toasty quinoa, and finally the lingering coffee finish and the cleansing acidity from the yogurt. In the end, being able to pull the guests out of their comfort zone for a few short minutes—they may think that they are being served a dessert until they bite into the savory complexity awaiting them—just makes everything a whole lot sweeter.

Sunflower Seeds, Kornly, and Pine

Whenever we had *Asparagus, Sunflower Seeds, and Mint* (page 292) on the menu, I would always jump in to season those tiny soft seeds with olive oil and salt during service. As I stirred them around, making sure the seasonings were evenly spread, I always ended up tasting them a few times too many. I just find the seeds addictive, with a structure that somehow magically stays together in small individual bursts of tender softness. I decided they deserved to play a more significant role on their own, to be front and center and not just be a backdrop to an asparagus dish.

I wanted to keep the seeds' singular and individual structure, and taking a cue from a risotto or maybe a perfectly cooked bean stew, I wanted that same feeling of small pearls suspended in a tasty sauce.

As we developed the dish, summer was around the corner, so we mixed in an herbal puree, which turned the "risotto" vividly green.

But the result was surprisingly muddled; the elegant and delicate sunflower seed flavor just didn't shine through.

Finally, we used a dense puree of the sunflower seeds themselves to thicken a light beurre blanc as the creamy sauce to suspend the seeds in. It was rich but not too fatty, and we seasoned it with a very generous amount of lemon juice, freshening things up to get that summery feeling we were going for.

As the seeds were suspended in a lightly flavored, buttery, and tangy sauce, we continued further down the classic Italian path with a light grating of Kornly, the lightly flavored Danish cow's milk cheese. As the final touch, we scattered pine shoots on top. They provide a foresty, resinlike acidity that suits the creamy components elegantly and gives the dish—with its surprisingly classic approach and flavor profile—a significant edge.

Dishes

Baked Potato Puree, Two Ways

When Relæ first opened, I gave our kitchen team a big challenge. I wanted to serve an incredible potato puree, with the qualification that the potatoes should be baked rather than boiled, to give us a golden, slightly caramelized flavor. That toasted flavor would help us build a base onto which we would pair acidic components that matched and contrasted the flavors of the potato.

We would do everything we could think of to actually make the baked potato taste baked, which is more complicated than you might think if you also want the texture to be smooth and creamy, which means adding milk and butter. To best accomplish that, we bake potatoes until the skins are very crisp and the interior is very soft, then remove the skins and bake them further, until completely dried out, golden, and crisp.We gather this toasty flavor in the skins by infusing it into the milk we later use to make the puree. To do this, we had to create a routine of cooking a batch of potatoes a day ahead to obtain the skins, since they have to infuse in the milk for 24 hours. After infusing the milk, it morphs to a cappuccino-like light brown and absorbs the caramelized flavor of the skin. We strain and warm this milk, add butter, and fold it into the warm potatoes. Next, we pass the mixture through two different strainers while keeping it rigorously warm, creating a velvety and appetizing texture.

Inspired by the contrast of spooning heavy cream over a classic Danish rhubarb or strawberry compote, I wanted to add buttermilk as a lactic sauce with a lingering acidity. We can't heat the buttermilk without the risk of curdling it, so we just pour it onto a warm plate next to the puree for the guest to gather in their spoon along with each mouthful. To intensify the buttermilk flavor and add a crumbly crunch, we sprinkle on caramelized buttermilk powder. Then finally, to avoid everything taking on a too-sweet tone, we add dehydrated black olives that come out clear on the palate with their salty flavor and have a crumbly texture that creates another great contrast to the comforting texture of the puree.

The following winter, we went in a slightly different direction with the combination of caramelized and acidic flavors. Instead of buttermilk, we added dried citrus to give a chewy but highly acidic punch to the potato flavor, including dried mandarin, grapefruit, orange, blood orange, and kumquats. The acidity was so aggressive that we had to warm the citrus in brown butter to balance it out. The citrus also provided the bitterness the olives had given before, and we added toasted and dried bread crumbs instead of the caramelized buttermilk powder for that last fine crunch.

I like how we managed to build another combination onto a base that we had experience with and took it a step further, swapping out flavors but keeping the basic composition of the dish. I wouldn't be surprised if a third variation appears on our menu in the future.

Barley, Cauliflower, and Black Trumpet

Porridge is another one of those antique dishes revitalized by the New Nordic movement. Elevating it from poor man's fodder to restaurant fare has become an exercise in gastronomical creativity. Noma turning oatmeal porridge into a crisp snack back in the day was pure genius, and us chefs have all come a long way since then by testing that method out on different cereals and in varying contexts. It has been taken so far, in fact, that a couple of young cooks opened Grød on Jægersborggade, which serves only porridge in all its thinkable variations. It's definitely a one-of-a-kind place.

I love the comforting and warming feel of a bowl of warm and buttery porridge, and its pleasing texture can be very interesting as a base for a dish. It can occasionally come out a bit heavy, though, so the challenge is to lighten it up with proper amounts of acidity and to contrast it with varying textures.

In this dish, the barley porridge is really only the base, as it is covered entirely with chopped cauliflower so that the two are easily mixed and give you a less starchy and sticky sensation, forcing you to chew more as you eat through it.

We use barley flakes for the porridge, to which we add a good amount of Per Kølster's incredible apple cider to give it a complex, fruity, and aromatic acidity and then fold in a splash of smoked almond milk. The milk thickens and enriches the porridge, taking the place of the traditional knob of butter. The cider's acidity and the creamy and smoky nut flavor are an incredible match. We cover the porridge in finely chopped cauliflower cooked for a few seconds in boiling butter emulsion. The mild flavored bits of cauliflower suspended in the buttery liquid gives texture to the complex flavors of the porridge and help prevent the stickiness that often happens when cooking porridge.

We finish the dish off with a few toasted and salted smoked almonds, which surprises the palate with their occasional crunch and bite. Finally, to underline both acidity and the toasted notes, we add two types of black trumpet mushrooms: one dried and pulverized into a powder and the other pickled in a slightly acidic brine. They add an almost leathery meatiness and umami that is well suited to a dish way more complex in flavor than its origins as a poorhouse breakfast.

Dishes
Herbivorous
Mains

Carrot, Elderflower, and Sesame
Charred Cucumber and Fermented Juice
Romaine, Egg Yolk, and Nettles
Enoki, Kelp, and Seaweed
Fennel, Smoked Almond, and Parsley
Dried Zucchini and Bitter Leaves
Fried Salsify and Bergamot
Salted Carrot and Oxalis "Béarnaise"

Carrot, Elderflower, and Sesame

After we successfully dried and rehydrated turnips, creating a texture that was a revelation to us, we began the hunt for the next great vegetable to use with this technique. We had already peeled carrots with a Japanese-style turning slicer so that we could dry and crisp the skins for another dish. We thought we could use that same tool to slice the sweet root into long and irregular slices, and then dry it as we did the turnips, combining those two ideas into one dish.

Carrots can be quite tough on the machine, as the hard roots challenge its blade severely, but the result is the longest imaginable slice of carrot. Since drying shrinks down the vegetable quite a lot—to as little as one-tenth of its original weight—we thought a large and wide piece of raw carrot would be necessary to achieve a broad pastalike piece that would be about 3 centimeters in the finished dish. We dried the carrot slices in the dehydrator until very dry, for about 10 to 12 hours at 65°C (150°F) and found they could be stored at this stage for quite a long time.

Even though drying intensifies the sweetness of the carrots, it also gives them a slightly bitter flavor, which is key to making sure this dish is not overwhelmingly sweet. To play on that balance of sweetness and bitterness, we added bitter sesame seeds and sesame cream, a naturally sweet carrot sauce, and pickled elderflower stems, which give floral and acidic qualities. The aroma of elderflower and the toasted, bitter notes from the sesame are an incredible match to the fruitiness and sweetness of the carrots.

At service, we briefly rehydrated the carrots to give them a soft and slightly leathery texture. We then toss them with reduced carrot juice and season with salt and a few sprays of the elderflower pickling liquid. We spoon warm carrot sauce on the plate, then the bitter sesame cream along with a teaspoon of pressure-cooked sesame seeds. We then arrange the carrots on top with some small elderflower stems all around to add acidity to every bite.

The intense flavor and the chew from the carrots make this a surprisingly filling dish, yet all the flavors stand quite undisturbed and clear, assuring lightness and a clean aftertaste. The sweetness is quite pronounced, but bitterness and acidity hold it in balance.

Charred Cucumber and Fermented Juice

This dish was presented as the third savory course on our vegetarian menu, and I must admit that serving seemingly raw cucumbers during what many would consider their main course called for careful explanations at the table. We challenged that notion and basically served raw cucumber slices, though great complexity hid underneath.

The starting point of the dish was the deep and complex brine we used to ferment cucumbers. With a 5 percent salt solution, garlic, horseradish, and cucumbers (and a small amount of whey we used to get the process started), magic would happen in 5 or 6 days. The flavors turned toward a briny and addictive umami juice. Most of us crave deeper umami flavors when we reach the high point of a meal, just before dessert. The intensity of the brine combined with its juicy freshness opened up the idea that a main course could be somewhat uncooked, as well as vegetarian and light, though still satisfyingly packed with umami flavors.

Offering only the pickled cucumber, though, would leave us with too blubbery a texture, and we decided that adding a raw or barely cooked element to the plate would result in more complexity. We started by chopping up some of the pickle, reserving the brine, and mixing the pickle with cooked tapioca pearls to give a filling structure.

To serve the dish, we warmed the brine, added the chopped pickle and tapioca pearl filling, and poured everything into a bowl that we topped with thinly sliced raw cucumbers. To step further away from a cold and simple dish and toward something more filling and complex, we then flamed the raw cucumbers with a kitchen torch for a few minutes. The outer layer charred and increased its bitterness by a notch, while the rest just cooked slightly and softened. That touch of heat in the last second enhanced all the flavors and the dish was ready—satisfying, complex, and still sort of raw.

Romaine, Egg Yolk, and Nettles

I had always wanted to take romaine lettuce—a vegetable that is usually a lowly vessel for Caesar dressing and crispy croutons—and place it in the driver's seat.

I have long been intrigued by cooking lettuce because I've noticed that simply poached but very fresh romaine seems to be even juicier once cooked. Poaching with a good amount of butter weakens the lettuce's fibers, which readily release a warm and pleasantly bitter juice when bitten into, but the texture is quite varied from one end to the other, making it interesting to eat. The heart gives a firmer crunch than the rest of the lettuce, and the leaves are more juicy, containing fewer fibers. Normally, you would try to control the cooking of a vegetable so that it has the same texture throughout, but in this case, the sequence in which the lettuce is eaten serves as the narrative of the dish, complemented by the additional flavors sprinkled on top.

The butter we poach the romaine in is crucial for keeping the salad moist because it almost glazes it during cooking; its fat also helps to control the lettuce's bitterness. When serving, we cover the lettuce entirely in grated salted egg yolk, a nod to the classic Caesar preparation that gives the dish extra umami without stealing the lettuce's show. The soft pillow of fluffy egg yolk is joined by a few salty and crispy dried black olives, varying the texture and enhancing the flavors.

Because the bitterness of the lettuce is somewhat diminished by the cooking, we looked for a sauce that would grab on to that bitterness. Stinging nettle came to mind because of its similar characteristics to lettuce. The stinging nettle becomes vivid and green once blanched and blended with water, reduced white wine, and a good amount of lemon juice. That necessary lemony jolt helps maintain the balance between fat and bitterness. It's the grassy green bitterness combined with a creamy and umami fattiness that are the central components of this dish, and, as it happens, in a Caesar salad.

Dishes

Enoki, Kelp, and Seaweed

With my Italian background, I know how important it is to tread lightly when you're dealing with strong culinary traditions. This dish has clearly been inspired by the Japanese dashi, a complex preparation that defines a great Japanese chef in the same way a perfect consommé does for the French. So when I set out to make my own version of dashi, I knew I had to serve it with great reverence when Japanese guests came to the restaurant. That reverence turned into tension one night when the highly respected Junya Yamasaki of the Japanese restaurant Koya in London visited Relæ. We happened to have our dashi-inspired enoki on that evening's menu: a simple dish of steamed local enoki served in a hot and briny broth.

We had already used local enoki in another dish with charred onions, which underlined their texture with depth and bitterness. This time around, we wanted a clearer, less muddled flavor profile. John Tam had been experimenting with Icelandic kelp in the food lab and found that cooking kelp in vacuum bags at 60°C (140°F) for about an hour would give a clear extraction of the seaweed's umami. To add seasoning, we continued along a Japanese path by adding our mushroom

"soy sauce," which contributes a full-bodied mouthfeel, umami, and a delicate but deep background flavor.

When serving the enoki, to underline the salinity and add even more complexity, we add crunchy and bitter seaweed and herbs to the plate. But we struggled with how to serve the broth. At first, we poured it onto the plate just before serving, but the amount of liquid made it impossible to reach the table and still have an orderly plating. I didn't want to pour the bouillon tableside, as it always feels like an unnecessary way of taking up the guest's time. It wasn't until I bumped into small Japanese pouring cups in a tea shop that we had a solution that would suit both the dish and our philosophy. We started placing the cup at the table for the guest to pour, which fits in well with our DIY approach to cutlery.

Chef Junya is a young and progressive chef, and when he came in, he told us that he appreciated our personal take on a Japanese classic. I was relieved. Thanks to its Japanese inspiration, I believe this is one of the most complex dishes we have ever had on the menu.

Dishes

Fennel, Smoked Almond, and Parsley

This vegetarian main course is one of the oldest dishes in the book, but its simplicity and the strong alliance between its three main flavors makes it one of the most interesting plates we have ever served at Relæ. Salted and lightly cooked young fennel forms the centerpiece of a plate dressed with both long-cooked fennel puree and bright, fresh parsley puree, with smoky almond milk adding a hint of depth, fat, and the needed umami.

When we first conceived this dish, we made it with slices of large fennel bulbs, which we vacuum-sealed in a 3 percent brine and then cooked in a butter emulsion until tender but still snappy. As the fennel season wound down, Ask from Kiselgården, our biodynamic vegetables supplier, had harvested most of his fennel. Then he noticed that the first ones he harvested had sprouted another set of small tiny bulbs. He told us he would start a second harvest shortly, and with that, the dish mutated into one consisting only of those tender shoots.

The flavor of the shoots was less intense, but the texture was incredible. The young bulbs had only two layers or so and were much less fibrous than the "grown-ups." We would brine them in the same 3 percent brine and just let them hit the boiling butter emulsion for a minute or two to warm through.

To keep the intense anise flavor profile, we cooked a puree from bigger fennel bulbs, which we sealed in vacuum bags and boiled until very soft. After passing the puree through a very fine strainer, we blended and seasoned it with reduced white wine. We also added complexity and a green flavor note to the final dish with a splash of bright green parsley puree. The two purees contrast well with the crunch of the fennel shoots, while the flavors stay alive and green.

This was a vegetarian main course and the last savory dish on the menu, so a certain level of richness was critical to make it satisfying. We found this dimension by liquefying smoked almonds into a rich and filling milk we could add as a sauce. We heated it only a slight bit to avoid it curdling, and the smokiness came through very well and grabbed on to the green and anise notes. The smoky milk was best described by a member of the staff as "pure vegetable bacon," which were words of truth indeed.

Dishes

Dried Zucchini and Bitter Leaves

This dish represents the most complex texture we have ever achieved in our kitchen, and it is also one of our more unique presentations. We take whole peeled zucchini and dehydrate them, then reintroduce juiciness with a butter emulsion and remake their "peels" with a coating of dark green herbs. The result is a combination of leathery and juicy at the same time, and it creates a sensation that feels nothing like eating a simple summer squash.

We started off dehydrating zucchini after peeling them. The dehydrating process slightly broke them down and softened them on the inside, just as the outside layer tightened up and became more and more leathery. It's almost like the skin that forms on the outside encapsulates the inner juices while the squash flavors slowly intensify and turn sweeter.

Usually we compose our dishes so that it is obvious how to eat them and so that they don't require much cutting by the guest. We prefer cutting up the vegetables or slicing up the meat so that we can be sure that every bite will be well composed and balanced. Nonetheless, as we continued working on this dish, I realized that it needed a different approach. After dehydrating the zucchini for about 6 hours, we poked plenty of holes in each one, then cooked them whole in boiling butter emulsion. This rendered the inside extremely juicy while the outside tenderized enough to offer a pleasant chew. As the squash is cut into, a warm, sweet juice mixed with the buttery cooking liquid runs out and acts as a natural sauce. We realized that this was a key moment for the eating experience, and that to cut the squash up before serving it would ruin things for the diner.

After cooking the zucchini, we pat them dry to remove the excess butter and dust them with a mixture of dried seaweed, dried sorrel, and dried purslane leaves. These provide bitterness and acidity and coat the zucchini with a new sort of skin, making it look as if it hadn't been peeled or had been reunited with its peel after cooking. The tight bitterness and acidity, almost tealike and tannic, really constrains the sweetness of the inside and plays well with the soft and chewy texture.

To complement those bright green notes, we add spinach, amaranth, and sorrel leaves, sautéed in a very hot pan, and French sorrel and oxalis added raw, giving a fresh acidic touch. The oxalic acid (see page 242) highly present in the spinach, sorrels, and oxalis gives an almost metallic note that suits the opulent sweetness of the zucchini. Even extremely bitter amaranth leaves, which normally need to be used very carefully, work well in this preparation. The zucchini is so sweet and fruity that it feels as if you could throw all kinds of bitterness at it without regret.

Considering the fact that we usually cut up the components of a dish, even meat, into smaller pieces, this seemingly humble but quite complex vegetable dish is probably the closest you get to slicing a steak on our menu.

Fried Salsify and Bergamot

I love the buttery and creamy mouthfeel of unctuous and pearly white salsify puree, and I wanted to see if we could find the appropriate contrasts for that flavor and texture in the salsify itself. We had worked with salsify a few times, and in the process of rethinking it for a warm wintery dish, I wanted to try including the skin. This would keep the dish simple and precise in flavor but still contribute what I saw as necessary complexity.

As an apprentice at Røgeriet, north of Copenhagen, I remembered scrubbing the salsify completely free of dirt, then slicing it very thinly and frying it into golden and crispy chips. I couldn't think of another time I had seen the skin left on that particular root vegetable. We began experimenting with getting that skin cleaned and cooked in a way that we could discover whether it had any special qualities to be revealed.

After meticulously scrubbing the salsify, we tried different cooking methods, including roasting them whole. It turned out that we just needed high heat for a few minutes, and by deep-frying, we could uniformly cook the long and rounded roots. After frying the salsify whole for a few minutes, we remove them from the oil just as part of the skin starts to detach. As they cool, we scrape off most of the outer layer of skin, which is the bitterest part and can be gritty and unpleasant to eat. Then we pull the salsify apart and fry them again in hot oil. The ends where the white inside flesh is exposed crisp up nicely as the inside warms up and turns creamy. The twice-fried skin has a very delicate texture that's somewhere between leathery and crispy, adding a lot of complexity to the final texture of the dish.

We also make my beloved puree out of peeled salsify that we boil until totally soft, and then combine with butter and reduced white wine. To plate the dish, we put a good scoop of this puree on the plate. The puree helps to balance out the skins' bitterness and texture, but we also needed a high amount of acidity to balance that level of bitterness, and we decided citrus would give us the whole package at once. Bergamot has almost no sweetness but brings a lot of aroma and top notes, plus loads of its own bitterness to connect to the salsify's bitterness, as well as acidity. Initially, it felt a bit like turning the volume up on the bass player to fix an excessively dedicated drummer, with the risk of everybody just pushing each other offstage. But it actually worked very well. We turned the bergamot skins into a puree that we fold into a beurre blanc–style sauce in the last second, as we season both the sauce and the fried salsify with the tangy bergamot juice.

This dish features just a single root vegetable, yet it comes out with so many qualities— fattiness, a crisp bitterness, toasted notes from the fried skins, and citric acidity and a mellowing mouthfeel from the puree. All contribute to the overall dish's great complexity while using very few resources.

Dishes

Salted Carrot and Oxalis "Béarnaise"

This is one of those dishes that is just as enjoyable to cook as it is to eat. When we cook the carrots in a pan with butter and garlic, they slowly caramelize and the aroma of cooking garlic fills the room with a wonderful perfume. Since Relæ has a completely open kitchen, it's the first thing that hits the guests as they walk in the door. No one thinks of a simple sautéed carrot having the ability to trigger this olfactory sensation; instead, everyone, including me, thinks of a roast or a steak as soon as the perfume hits their nostrils. And that is the paradox we playfully work with in this dish.

We prepare the carrots almost as if they were a steak: After slicing them thinly lengthwise and salting them, we make small stacks of the slices and roll them as tightly as possible. We secure the bundle with butcher's twine and trim the top and bottom flat.

As the carrot "steak" hits the pan, multiple layers touch the surface, slowly caramelizing and softening. We add butter to the pan and a few crushed garlic cloves in the beginning of a cooking process that stretches as long as 40 to 45 minutes. We never flip the carrot bundle but just keep basting the warm and foamy butter over it, allowing it to cook from the underside. This gives a slight crunch to the bottom and a soft interior.

As we were testing out different types of carrots, we opted for the purple variety, which gave us reduced sweetness and a slight bitterness that worked well for our illusion of "steak." After resting the carrot stacks for a few minutes on the cutting board, we would just slice them into two and put them back together with the cutting surface facing upward. As we pressed the two halves together you could see how the buttery juices permeated the surface and revealed how juicy this "steak" had turned out.

To complete the cheeky illusion, we served a "béarnaise" on the side. Instead of traditionally whisking egg yolks over the stove and emulsifying clarified butter into it, we made the "béarnaise" in a siphon without any butter and seasoned it with apple cider vinegar. Instead of the classic tarragon, we opted for chopped oxalis stalks and a few leaves sprinkled on top.

When this dish was on the menu, we actually received a complaint by email from a French lady who was upset that we would try to pass off carrots as steak! I guess she got caught up in the illusion but truly missed the point.

Dishes
Omnivorous
Mains

Pork from Hindsholm and Rye
Lamb, Turnip, and Samphire
Cauliflower, Veal Sweetbread, and Basil
Chicken Wings, White Asparagus, and Anchovies
Wild Duck, Elderberries, and White Onions
Salad, Beef, and Bronte Pistachio
Veal, Grilled Sauce, and Anchovy

Pork from Hindsholm and Rye

After we hit it off so well when visiting Poul at his pig farm in Hindsholm (see pages 70–71), the following winter, in a spontaneous moment of inspiration, he brought us a bag of the rye that he occasionally feeds the pigs during the coldest months of the year. Grown on the farm, the grain's nutty and flavorful qualities were very much in line with the flavor profile we wanted to accentuate in the meat. It made great sense to have the dish go full circle in flavor and concept by marrying the meat with what was used as the animal's fodder.

Rye can be cooked for more than an hour and still be slightly too dense, so we went for a more gentle approach and sprouted the grains. Sprouting breaks down some of the complex carbohydrates and fibers and make the grains softer and slightly sweeter—perfect for this dish. We also boiled some of the rye, as their crunch adds a great texture in a controlled amount.

We poach the bigger pork roasts such as the neck, the shoulder, and the leg for this dish.

The rest is used for charcuterie and various braised dishes at Manfreds. We cook the neck and shoulder for about 2½ hours in a vacuum bag at 55°C (131°F) and then finish them in the pan to get a beautiful caramelized coating. At Relæ, we often treat the legs similarly, but we complement that meat with pieces of roasted jowl or other very fatty bits.

On the plate, we dress a nice slab of one of these cuts with a generous amount of sauce made from chicken and pork bones, with reduced white wine for acidity. We heat the boiled and sprouted rye in a small amount of the sauce, then strain and season it before covering the meat with it. To enhance the porkiness of this incredible pig, we finish with a generous amount of roasted pork fat and small bits of cracklings, as well as malted buckwheat that we sprout, just like the rye, and then dehydrate. After all, we like to remind ourselves and our guests of the raw materials our products are made of and maybe even once ate themselves.

Lamb, Turnip, and Samphire

Thinking back to when this dish was first on the menu awakens great emotions in me. It was during the first year that René Redzepi's MAD Symposium hit the city like a storm, and journalists, bloggers, foodies, and some of the greatest chefs in the world were coming into the restaurant when this dish was on the menu. I'm still proud of its simplicity, the greatness of its ingredients, and a cooking approach that showcased both.

The idea to pair lamb and samphire came when Henriette Guld, who rears beautiful Havervadgård lambs, called to ask whether we would be interested in *kveller,* the samphire or sea bean that grows on the marshes where she leaves her sheep and lambs to roam and graze. "I heard fancy restaurants use this," she said. "Well, less fancy ones too," I responded, and off she went to forage the juicy and savory sea plant by the beaches of southern Jutland.

Just like with the *Pork from Hindsholm and Rye* (page 322), since Henriette's lambs graze on these marsh plants, it made perfect sense to incorporate the samphire into the dish to underline the subtle salinity they give to the meat. To avoid blurring the meat's mineral profile, we wanted to add a vegetable that wouldn't carry too much sweetness or too distinctive a flavor. By cooking turnips whole, cooling them, and slicing them thinly, we had a soft but appetizing texture that would be a great support to the lamb's flavor.

At Relæ, we make use of the entire lamb for this dish, so the cuts vary from roasted shoulder to braised breast, and we always mix up the different types so that each diner gets to try a few different expressions of the meat. (However, the recipe in this book calls only for lamb loin for simplicity's sake.)

We place the slices of meat on the bottom of the plate, then the cut-up pieces of the samphire, and then we dress everything with a lamb sauce with roasted young garlic. The roasted garlic is a classic combination with lamb and perfumes the sauce with a deep caramelized flavor that's well embraced by the minerality of the dish.

To finish, we briefly reheat the cooked turnip slices in a butter emulsion, just long enough to keep them warm and comforting. We completely cover the rest of the dish with the white turnip slices, placing the vegetable front and center—after all, the white turnip is equal to the greatness of the lamb that rests underneath.

Cauliflower, Veal Sweetbread, and Basil

I like to think of sweetbreads as "beginner's offal," since it is not as bloody or liver-y tasting as many other "off cuts." I enjoy sweetbreads quite a bit myself, and this dish came about because I wanted to showcase the ingredient exactly as I like it: soft, creamy, and tender on the inside and crunchy, savory, and caramelized on the outside.

We do that by brining the sweetbreads in a vacuum bag overnight and then cooking them sous vide the following day for an hour at 63°C (145°F). After cleaning the sweetbreads, we brown them in a pan in oil, then add butter and continue cooking and basting them until crisp.

Cauliflower has a delicate and mild flavor that I thought would suit the elegant nature of sweetbreads. Eventually we decided to place a creamy and comforting cauliflower puree on the bottom of the plate to create the base of the dish. To that, we added a few bits of crunchy cauliflower stems just briefly touched by a hot butter emulsion. Next came the sweetbread, and for the texture to come through clearly I wanted it to be in pieces just big enough to fit into a spoon. We then covered the whole thing in a blanket of soft-cooked and finely chopped cauliflower, so that the sweetbread would catch the guest by surprise as its crunchy exterior broke through the monotony of the vegetable that hid it.

With this covering of finely chopped cauliflower, the dish resembles a simple bowl of rice on first glance. That idea had us looking east to find the flavors that would complete the combination of fatty meat and creamy, buttery cauliflower. We added a selection of several types of basil, which permeate the dish with top notes and freshness once they are doused in the warm sauce. The light and citrusy sauce also reminds me of Asia—and combined with the ricey presentation and fragrant basil, the dish evokes fresh Thai cuisine while still keeping its earthy Danish roots clear and distinct.

Dishes

Chicken Wings, White Asparagus, and Anchovies

A favorite flavor-play of ours is to pair chicken and anchovy, presented here in the best version we have made so far. After poaching chicken several different ways and using it in various dishes, this time around we wanted to focus on the wings, the fattiest cut of all. And though chicken wings are plenty tasty on their own, we enhance the flavor more by adding diced chicken livers sautéed with shallot and chives. The combination of the wings and livers represent to me the best possible way to present the most flavorful and fatty part of the animal, and when combining it with the anchovy, this is as complex and complete a chicken flavor as you can get.

We poach the wings, to keep them firm but tender and still very juicy. That juiciness is due in part to us brining them for 24 hours in a 3 percent solution, and of course from the carefully planned timing and cooking. Taking care that the meat doesn't cool down too much before serving, we pull the meat off the bone in a few quick movements.

We tried this dish with different garnishes, such as zucchini and baby corn, but we found that the sweetness of white asparagus brings out the fine and elegant flavors of the chicken the best. We cut the asparagus into very fine lengthwise slices and weighed and portioned it out into small bunches for service.

After placing the anchovies on the plate, we add the picked meat and livers and cover the whole thing with the slices of asparagus. We then pour on the sauce, a light chicken stock with reduced white wine with a consistency almost like a light bouillon, which allows the flavors to combine well and further enhances the elegant characteristics of the chicken while slightly cooking the asparagus. Finally, we top everything with a few drops of our favorite extra-virgin olive oil, which brings out the vegetable's fruity notes.

328

Dishes

Wild Duck, Elderberries, and White Onions

This dish was created by fusing two other dishes. Actually, it was two vegetarian dishes—steamed spring onions with elderberries, and roasted spring onions with charred onion puree—that we crossed with a roasted meat to form a main course. Eventually it turned into a dish I am very proud of, as it mixes old and new techniques: roasting wild duck in a classic way while using more modern and innovative techniques to cook vegetables.

We wanted to have game on the menu, and since hunting season had just started, wild duck seemed like the best choice. We cooked the ducks, which are considerably smaller and leaner than the farmed species, in every conceivable way. It was great to realize that for once no vacuum bag or immersion circulator could compete with straight-up, old-school pan roasting. Duck is all about the flavor and texture of the roasted and slightly crispy fat juxtaposed with the cooked-rare, tender meat, and direct high heat is the only way to make it happen.

We first detached the legs (which went to Manfreds), cut off the backbone to roast for sauce, and removed the wishbone from the breasts to facilitate carving. We seared the rest of the double-breasted body on all sides for a few minutes and left it to rest at room temperature. Coordinated carefully before service, we roasted the duck in the oven for about 6 or 7 minutes and then let it rest again. After resting, it should reach about 52°C (126°F) in the thickest spot and be appetizingly bloody and rare.

Pairing up game with a bit of fruit and sweetness is always a safe way to go, and cooking onions seemed like a clear way to get that sweetness. The shape and texture had to be comforting and juicy, so we cut up white onions into noodle shapes on the Japanese-style turning vegetable slicer and brined them overnight. This loosened their texture and released moisture, so that we could cook them for just a couple of minutes in a boiling butter emulsion, which allowed them to hold together with a slight crunch but become tenderized enough to be soft and sweet. We also added elderberries to the duck-based sauce at the last second, releasing their characteristic flavor, tannic bitterness, and acidity all at once.

As a final binding element we added the grilled onion puree, connecting all the other components with its balance between sweet and bitter, and dusted charred onion powder over the buttery, rolled-up noodles. The noodles went right next to the duck slices with the elderberry duck glaze.

Dishes

Salad, Beef, and Bronte Pistachio

This is another dish that started out as a vegetarian main course. We built it up around juicy stems of cooked and smoked celtuce and added a fulfilling depth with a creamy pistachio puree.

But the celtuce had a very short-lived season that year. We felt that there was more to pursue with the original dish's combination of smoky, green, and slightly bitter juice mixed with a rich pistachio puree that had a tangy and lemony acidity. Combining the puree with a beef braise seemed as if it would enhance that richness even further, and we thought our juicy poached romaine could stand in for the celtuce. The end result would become an original hybrid that falls somewhere between a stew and a salad.

Again, after testing several braising methods for the beef, we found that a fairly traditional approach gave us what we needed. We braise the short ribs in a simple braising liquid made of red wine, water, and salt for 4 to 6 hours. We leave the whole pieces of meat to cool down in the braising liquid, which allows them to retain their juice and texture. After chilling in the fridge overnight, we cut up the big braised cuts into slices about 2 centimeters wide. To serve, we roast the cold slices until they became soft and warmed through and intensely caramelized on one side.

As a juicy element, we add our poached romaine lettuce, but instead of leaving it in halves as we do with the *Romaine, Egg Yolk, and Nettles* (see page 308), we chop it slightly thinner than the beef slices. This gives us varying textures and a lot of juice for a stew-like sensation.

For yet another textural component, we decided to add a crispy beef floss. This idea was just another great benefit of having several members of the staff with Asian heritage and cultural connections. A traditional Chinese technique using pork and beef requires you to braise veal or beef shanks until they fall off the bone, then pulling them apart to discard bones, cartilage, and tissue. You then return the meat to the pot with water to cook and reduce while constantly stirring. After hours of tenderizing, reducing, and eventually drying, the result is fluffy, caramelized, and crisp.

The sauce is made by halving raw romaine heads and charring them until blackened on one side. We then liquefy them in the juicer, making a smoky and savory juice that we thicken with a puree of peeled raw pistachios. We heat the sauce and add a good amount of lemon juice before serving; the tangy lemon balances the bitterness of the charred romaine.

To finalize the dish with a fresh element, we spread small romaine leaves with the pistachio puree and then sprinkle them with the floss. After plating the short ribs with the romaine hearts and sauce, we then flip the leaves, floss side down, so that the impression is that of a salad. This extra dimension intensifies everything else going on and overall is a great addition to a dish with so many stewlike—and saladlike—qualities.

Dishes

Veal, Grilled Sauce, and Anchovy

Though not everyone will readily order tongue, guests who do brave the unknown are always surprised and pleased by its comforting texture and flavor. When we were devising this dish, we already had put poached tongue on the menu, and this time we wanted to elevate the pink and tender meat by adding grilled, charred, and bitter notes.

To achieve the bitterness and char we were looking for, we decided to grill the tongue over high heat. After brining for 24 hours in a 7 percent salt solution and then cooking for 24 hours at 62°C (144°F), all in vacuum bags, we tried to cut it up into individual portions and char it over very high heat on a grill. The problem is, the tongue's high level of moisture made it impossible to char the surface without completely overcooking it. We even tried to grill the whole thing with the tough skin on, hoping the skin would crisp up and tenderize while protecting the juicy inside. Unfortunately, we found out that the tough skin stays tough no matter how long you cook it.

In the end, we realized that the charred flavor, bitterness, and smoke had to come from something other than the tongue. We grilled onions until fairly blackened but then crumbled them instead of grinding them into a fine powder. Our grilling method leaves some bits less cooked (and thus sweeter) than charred, which balanced the bitterness very well. Then we added the onions to a light veal sauce that dispersed the charred flavor all over the meat when poured onto it.

As a counterpoint to the charred flavor, we wanted something soft, tender, and mild, and sweet salsify, often called "the poor man's asparagus" in Denmark, seemed to be the perfect middleman between the meat and the sauce. We decided to use salsify two ways: We added a puree of the peeled salsify boiled in vacuum bags, and we also sliced very thin rounds of salsify and cooked them in a butter emulsion for about 30 seconds. They were just softened enough so we could then strain them and season them with lemon juice and salt.

To plate the final dish, we use the salsify puree and an anchovy emulsion as a base, with the salsify discs, meat, and charred onion sauce added on top. The complex combination of fruity root vegetable, the bitter sauce, and the sweet umami from the meat turned this into a dish that even a tongue-averse diner could love.

Dishes Cheese and Desserts

Dishes

Whipped Goat Cheese and Parsley

The first time we made a proper cheese dish that went beyond just putting a simple slice on a plate, we added olive oil and freshly chopped herbs to fresh goat cheese. With time, it transformed into this dish, which has a few sharper details and honors our original intention of presenting cheeses in a more inventive and fun way.

The goat cheese we use from Swedish producer Hagelstads Gårdmejeri is an incredible fresh farmstead cheese made from unpasteurized milk. It has a lingering lactic acidity and complexity that can hardly be found in pasteurized cheeses, making it a perfect fit for our cheese course.

As we started working with the cheese, I tried simply whipping it, expecting it to react somewhat like butter and become fluffy and appetizing. That was not the case— the cheese fell completely onto itself and liquefied. After the first few moments of quiet despair, I tasted it and my mood changed instantly. Swapping a dense and pasty texture for a smooth liquid suited the acidity and full-bodied flavor and funk of the cheese brilliantly. We dipped our bread in it, and it was a great success among the kitchen staff.

I'm not sure what exact physical reaction occurred when we whipped the cheese, but we have developed the technique a bit since that first discovery. We used to blend the cheese with water, but now we do it without, since the liquefying comes from the cheese breaking down rather than thinning it with water. I have obtained similar results when trying it with other fresh cheeses, such as a local, and brilliant, goat cheese I served at a dinner at Attica in Melbourne.

To support and garnish the cheese, I originally tried sprinkling the same old chopped herbs on top, but soon the idea of liquefying the garnish, too, became obvious. We decided on parsley puree because of its deep grassy notes and slight sweetness. It's not too overpowering or spicy and would support the cheese's flavor.

When it comes to plating, I have a bit of a cheeky go at it. First I splash a few spoonfuls of the cheese on the plate, then lob on a spoonful of parsley puree. The result is great— as messy as a Jackson Pollock but so simple and tasty.

Nordlys, Carrots, and Orange Zest

About 10 years ago, a Danish-Swedish dairy giant that is one of the biggest cooperatives in the world ventured to make cheese of the highest quality as a sort of R & D project. Called Arla Unika, the project was supposed to make up for our region's lack of the small-scale artisanal producers that had kept cheesemaking culture alive for generations in the rest of Europe. Inspiration was found in both forgotten Danish traditions as well as the funky French cheeses and hard Italian cheeses that, up until then, had monopolized the cheese platters of the better Copenhagen restaurants.

One of my favorites among the eight or ten varieties coming out of this project is called Nordlys, which means "Northern Lights" in English. Nordlys is very much a funky Époisses-style washed-rind cheese, with a slightly fruity and ammonia flavor and a soft and almost runny texture.

We like serving a cheese course that moves beyond just putting a slice on a plate, but in this case, we had to constrain ourselves and just let it be. We realized that trying to manipulate Nordlys by blending, mixing,

or freezing it, as we do with other cheeses, would just spoil its flavor and its already quite complex structure.

I am fascinated by the controlled funk and ammonia that lingers on the palate after tasting a washed-rind cheese, so we worked on garnishes that would accentuate that yet still control it. A touch of sweetness is often used to accompany cheese for the same reason, and to get that, we reached for a vegetable with a pronounced natural sweetness that we already used in desserts: carrots. Using a technique we developed for an earlier dish, we cut unpeeled carrots into strips with a Japanese-style turning vegetable slicer, tossed them in brown butter, and then roasted them in the oven until crisp. The toasted, buttery carrot chips also bring a slight crunch that embellishes the cheese's soft interior.

To finalize and freshen things up, we add grated orange zest to the cheese. The aroma and top notes really bring out the creamy cheese's texture and flavor. While the sweet carrot chips support the long finish of a cheese of this kind, the zest cleanses and awakens the palate.

Dishes

Chanterelles, Apple, and Granité

One of the first ideas that Carol Choi came up with when she was our newly appointed pastry chef was to use chanterelles in a dessert. I have to admit that my first reaction was a forced smile and raised eyebrows. But when an idea eventually becomes something that you are really proud of, you often question why no one else had thought of it before. That's the feeling this dessert gives me. Carol's original idea came out of nowhere and ended up being a revelation of flavors. It became a classic in our kitchen.

To begin with, Carol experimented with ice creams and sorbets based on a puree of sautéed chanterelles. In all honesty, the texture of those first attempts at ice cream was awful, since the mushrooms turned slimy after they were blended and the mushroom flavor never really materialized. It was only when we tried to turn the brown puree into a lightly set mousse that the flavors really started to pop.With the fluffy and airy texture of a mousse, the aroma of the mushroom was incredibly clear and the addition of cream, egg whites, and a pinch of salt made this simple mousse taste more of chanterelles than the mushrooms did on their own.

I have heard that some people consider this small, slightly orange, and beautiful mushroom to have flavor notes similar to apricots, and in this dessert, I really agree. The chanterelle's fruitiness takes on another dimension when paired with a fresh and addictive apple granité, creating an incredible synergy.

To complete the dessert's flavor profile, we wanted to add a salty and crunchy note to underline the savory quality of the mushrooms as well as something fruity to bring out their hidden sweet tone. We made a granité by simply freezing freshly juiced Collina apples and scraping it into a granité-like texture, which added natural sweetness, aroma, and textural complexity. On top, we sprinkled a baked crumble with black trumpet mushroom and blackberry powders, adding a deep, foresty bitterness. A few pieces of dried chanterelles to finish added another texture and also gave proof that yes, we were not kidding, we *did* put mushrooms in your dessert.

Dishes

Mandarin, Buttermilk, and Egg Yolk

One day, I was thinking back on the iconic elBulli dessert that displays a perfectly round sphere of mango resting on a white chocolate shell, filled with coconut foam. It looks *just* like an egg. And I thought, why not really put an egg in there? I mean, you can hardly find a classic French dessert without large numbers of eggs hiding in the crème anglaise, brioche, and mille-feuille, so . . . ? I wanted to make a dessert with a poached egg in the middle of everything.

The poached egg has been on and off our menu since the beginning, but somehow moving it into a dessert felt like crossing a line. My fears proved to be completely ungrounded, though, as challenging the guest is not always as dangerous as many of us restaurateurs make it out to be.

How to successfully combine that runny yolk with other components and leave the diner thinking that she actually had a dessert on her plate proved to be quite challenging. Egg yolk has a dominant texture and it can easily take over the palate. If you combine it with something highly acidic and bitter like charred cabbage, you can control it a bit, but when you push it in a sweeter direction, it becomes somewhat more complicated.

So I had to look for a good amount of bitterness, high acidity, and a crisp texture to complete the egg yolks' transformation into dessert. I also wanted to play on the temperatures, leaving the egg yolk warm so it could be as runny as possible while combining it with frozen elements that would be refreshing after eating the intensely eggy centerpiece. Mandarin seemed like a great companion, bringing together acidity, sweetness, and zesty bitterness all at once.

We prepared a mandarin curd with a light texture and zesty flavor. The curd acts as a textural bridge between the intense egg yolk and the frozen granités or snows we would sprinkle around it. We froze freshly squeezed mandarin juice and grated it into a snow and then did the same with frozen buttermilk. The tang of the buttermilk is quite aggressive, and alongside the mandarin's citric acid, they lighten up the mouthfeel and overall flavor of the dessert.

When I served this dessert to a highly respected colleague, he asked, half ecstatic and half incredulous, "What *do* people say to this?" I assured him that people were actually very excited about it. Nobody ever threw the eggs back at us, though some do just eat around the yolk. But I strongly believe that the few people who do that would have also done so if we had served the egg yolk on a tartare or on sautéed cabbage and toast.

In the end, dishes like this have shown us that it takes much more than most of us chefs think to cross the line for our guests. They come to us to have a great dining experience, and part of that is to be challenged, even if that means finding egg yolks in all kinds of weird places.

Milk, Kelp, and Caramel

This is probably one of the dishes of which I am the proudest, and it's certainly one that implements several of our core principles to greatest effect. On the surface, it's as screamingly simple as a soft-serve ice cream with sprinkles—a familiar-looking frozen dessert with a comforting caramel topping. But dig a bit deeper, and you'll discover an intense flavor and complexity that is very hard to find in desserts.

When we first thought to infuse a milk-based ice cream with Icelandic dried kelp, we weren't sure what to expect. Kelp has some natural gellifying attributes that contribute to the texture of the ice cream, but those attributes can also create challenges when not controlled. When infused and softened, a heavy gel forms around the actual kelp bits, which have a soft but very slimy texture that you don't want to mix into the base. We underwent a lot of experimentation to find the balance to pull this off, taste- and texturewise, and finally settled on adding the kelp to the cooled ice cream base in vacuum bags and infusing it for only 13 minutes. To make maximum use of the quite costly kelp, we

remove it from the base and cook it a further 40 minutes, then rinse it to remove any gel, and dry and candy it for a crunchy garnish to top the ice cream.

We were thrilled with the results of the ice cream: a milky soft texture with a deeply satisfying, filling, and complex umami-packed kick. A classic caramel topping provides a hint of bitterness, and the small amount of candied kelp garnish gives a crunch that diversifies the texture. A couple of sprays of pear vinegar gives this dish a fruity acidity that makes it well suited to pairing with a dry and light cider.

Most of the time, an ingredient as umami-forward as kelp would be considered strictly savory and kept away from sweeter contexts. While we've always opted for low sugar and integrated a lot of vegetables into our desserts, we decided to take things a step further by adding a high-salinity seaweed. And again, because we have such a small menu, we were free to gently push our guests toward taking a chance with their dessert. I hope they'll agree that the result was an eye-opening experience.

Rhubarb Compote, Almond, and Vinegar

Rhubarb is the easiest vegetable to pull off in a dessert, in part because its main characteristic is its acidity. Instead of toning down the acidity with lots of sugar and sweetness, we tried to add another very acidic component, a vinegar sorbet, to harmonize with it. It's a similar method to matching a highly acidic and mineral wine with a highly acidic dish. Then, to balance all the acidity, we added almond milk as a creamy and fatty component that also introduced a powerful temperature contrast.

The oxalic acid and the high acidity of rhubarb call for some sugar to be added and for gentle cooking to bring out its best aroma, so we made a rhubarb compote by just slightly cooking the chopped rhubarb with a splash of lemon juice and sugar so that it keeps a light bite and crunch. For a successful pairing with this fresh compote, the vinegar in the sorbet must be fruity and not too aggressive. We originally used a light Moscatel vinegar, but later experiments with pear vinegar worked just as well, and really, any fruit vinegar would probably work fine.

We place finely grated almonds and the fresh sorbet on the bottom of a frozen plate and cover it with a milk gel, which is just to insulate the sorbet from the warm compote and barely adds any flavor. On top of the gel, we scoop a spoonful of the warmed rhubarb compote and add a fair amount of creamy almond milk. We then add a few almond pieces to give a little more crunch to the dessert's otherwise porridgy mouthfeel.

The presentation of this dish is partly inspired by some of the platings I saw at elBulli, where some dishes looked like a child's drawing yet hid all kinds of innovative techniques and flavors under the scattered surface. I've always remembered that, and I enjoy splashing rhubarb compote on a plate and dousing it with almond milk that often spreads out all over the plate. The qualities of the dish are to be found just underneath that milk gel, in all the contrasts and flavors.

Dishes

Jerusalem Artichoke, Malt, and Bread

My hope is that when guests look at this dish, with its quenelle of creamy Jerusalem artichoke ice cream and candied Jerusalem artichoke skins, it reminds them of a vegetable broken down and put back together as a slightly different version. I can't help but think of Wario in the classic Nintendo games—he's basically Super Mario, but way more muscular and dangerous. Similarly, I feel like this dish is more an evil twin than a copy or inspiration.

The base of the dessert is a totally innocuous ice cream made of peeled, cooked, and pureed Jerusalem artichokes folded into a base of crème anglaise. Besides flavoring the ice cream, the chokes make the texture wonderfully creamy. We wanted to add contrast to that soft texture, so we decided to add the crunch of candied Jerusalem artichoke skins.

The skins added a welcome toasted element, but we still wanted to turn the bitterness up a notch to really sustain that contrast in textures. In fact, the inspiration for this dessert came when we were grilling and charring Jerusalem artichokes for savory purposes and decided we wanted that same bitterness in a dessert. We had already paired ground coffee with Jerusalem artichoke in another dessert, but here we found that completely blackened malt was more reminiscent of the charred surface of the choke, making a direct and pungent connection.

To incorporate the malt flavor, we first make a malt oil by combining malt powder, vegetable oil, and powdered sugar in the Thermomix. To ensure that the malt's bitterness hits the palate in bursts, we soak small bits of day-old sourdough bread in it. The bread sucks up the oil and turns chewy and adds a savory acidity, bumping up the dish's complexity even more. As in many of our desserts, these more savory flavors prevent the sweetness from becoming overpowering. When eating this dessert, the sequence of bitterness of the malt oil–soaked bread cubes, the creamy and fatty ice cream, and the crispy and flavorful candied Jerusalem artichoke skins rolls out in a very elegant and tasty way that is only the slightest bit dangerous.

Sheep's Milk Yogurt, Beets, and Black Currant

You're not mistaken, the warm red sauce splashed onto a fluffy white base does indeed resemble the classic Danish Christmas dessert *risalamande*. For non-Danish readers, the traditional dessert is rice pudding mixed with lightly whipped cream and vanilla that's served with a warm and sweet cherry sauce.

Risalamande a tradition that all Danes, big and small, look forward to every Christmas Eve for a reason: it is damn tasty. Originally the dessert was a way of using the leftovers of *risengrød*, a warm rice porridge served with a knob of butter and sprinkles of sugar and cinnamon throughout December. The next day, the cold leftover porridge is lightened up with whipped cream and sprinkled with almond slivers. I am honestly not a fan of having a sweet rice porridge for dinner, but I will always grab seconds when it's time to pour hot cherry sauce on a creamy dessert.

The flavor profile of this classic is so solid that we barely tweaked the original. Sure, we messed around with details, but the backbone of vanilla, cream, and a fruity sauce remains intact.

We swapped candy-striped or Chioggia beets for preserved cherries, moving the dish away from almondy and sweet toward earthy and deep. The beets are cooked, dehydrated, and finally rehydrated in reduced juice from the sweeter red beets. Candy-striped beets turn less earthy and heavy when their flavor is intensified in this way, and they get a satisfying chew.

To plate the dish, we start with a small amount of vanilla ice cream that we cover with a light and tangy sheep's milk yogurt mousse. We sprinkle on freeze-dried black currants to give an extra crunch to every bite, and then cover the whole thing with a light gel of beet juice that we brush with black currant vinegar. Made with gellan, the gel protects the fragile mousse from the final dousing of the warm and chewy beets and reduced red sauce.

As I look back at this dish, I realize it's the only time we ever put vanilla on the menu, which always seemed too classic and obvious to me. But in this dish, the vanilla represents just that, a superclassic foundation that we manipulate into an enjoyable, fun, and interesting dessert.

Hokkaido Pumpkin and Mandarin

This dessert got its start when I was working on a recipe using pumpkin seeds for a local newspaper. The recipes I've published there tend to be more home cook–oriented than the ones found in this book, and they are normally simplified versions of the techniques and ideas that we use in the Relæ kitchen. For this recipe, the tables were turned. My excitement about the airy and light pumpkin seed parfait I wrote about for the paper became the fundamental idea for something we later served at the restaurant.

As the dish evolved, we changed the parfait into a creamy ice cream and made it more densely flavored and textured by using toasted pumpkin seeds. We served it with some juicy frozen and thawed Hokkaido pumpkin, which was in season at that moment, and some sweet pumpkin pieces cooked in syrup.

The idea to freeze and then thaw something came about just because we wanted to see what would come of it. Pumpkin was the perfect candidate for our little experiment, as it's a bit too mealy to eat raw. It turned out that freezing and then thawing it made it extremely juicy, whereas blanching or cooking the pumpkin softens it too much.

The deeply flavored pumpkin seed ice cream comes out a very appetizing light green, speckled with darker green spots. The base is just a mix of milk, sugar, trimoline, the toasted pureed pumpkin seeds, and lightly poached egg whites. Our hope was that if we added a lot of pumpkin seeds, which are both rich in fiber and high in fat, we could leave out the egg yolks. Since the whites would already be lightly cooked, our "ice cream" would almost be an uncooked sorbet base. The egg whites definitely balance the intensity of the pumpkin seeds and lighten up the ice cream's texture, and the flavor is clear and unspoiled.

Because of the pumpkin's natural flavor, the last component of the dish needed to have high acidity followed by fruit, or sweetness. Mandarin, with its light bitterness, was an obvious fit, so we vacuum-sealed the defrosted pumpkin slices with mandarin juice to infuse them, making a kind of "pumpkin salad." We also added frozen mandarin granité to the plate and topped everything with a few crunchy candied pumpkin chips.

The bitterness from the toasted pumpkin seeds is picked up by the mandarin, which in return freshens up the fatty profile of the ice cream. Together, they make a much more complex dessert than the original and still maintain the full-blown pumpkin flavor we wanted.

Corn, Bread Crumbs, and Marjoram

Corn and marjoram is one of my absolute favorite flavor combinations. At Røgeriet, the Danish restaurant where I apprenticed, I clearly remember how we would cut the kernels from the cob and sauté them in brown butter, then toss in marjoram leaves at the last second. That bright green, pungent, and almost camphorlike perfume would instantly spread all over the kitchen. I loved the way it complemented the slightly sweet and caramelized flavor of the sautéed corn. In those days, the corn was just a garnish for chicken or sautéed fish, but even back then, I had toyed with the idea of using the combination in a sweet version.

Like many other vegetables that are high in carbohydrates, corn hides its natural sweetness, offering true potential in the pastry kitchen. It turned out to be very straightforward to transform that sweet corn flavor into a fundamental part of dessert. We decided on a corn ice cream as the centerpiece of this dish, and found that the natural starches in the corn made the texture and mouthfeel very pleasant, so that we didn't need to add any stabilizers. We removed the kernels from the cob and sautéed them in butter, and we also roasted the scraped cobs on their own. Once roasted, the roasted cobs are infused in milk overnight. The next day, the infused corn milk and roasted kernels are blended into a fine puree that's ready to be frozen and spun into a velvety ice cream.

But I wasn't satisfied with just "hiding" the corn in an ice cream quenelle. I wanted it to be obvious that it was the centerpiece of this dessert, so we needed to find a way to plate up the kernels in their natural state. We tried just caramelizing them and even adding them raw to the plate. The best solution was dehydrating boiled corn kernels, which intensified their flavor, and then quickly blanching them so that they would soften slightly while still keeping a nice chew. To further enhance the corn flavor, we blended some of the dry kernels into a deep yellow powder to sprinkle on top.

The addition of freshly picked marjoram leaves gave me that flavor combination I had been longing for in a dessert. To create a bridge between the corn and the marjoram, we added just a bit of acidity. A meringue with vinegar plays on the savory notes and also brings in a sugary sweetness. As a final note, we add our own bread crumbs, simply toasted and blended into a powder, another savory addition that is salty, acidic, and crunchy all at once.

We end with a sprinkle of salt, something I do anytime a dessert has a savory element. All told, it's definitely a dessert, but it still brings me back to my days of sautéing corn in brown butter and tossing it all in herbaceous, fragrant marjoram.

Dishes

Elderflower and Rhubarb

Rhubarb and elderflower are a classic Nordic combination, and here I bring the flavors together in multiple layers, with elderflower appearing both in a cream and granité, and the rhubarb in the form of a compote and leather. The base of this floral dessert is the elderflower cream, made of milk and cream infused with fresh elderflowers. We add a small amount of black cane sugar to give the cream a deeper, caramelized note, and thicken it with iota, a gelling agent that creates a smooth curdlike texture. To lighten it up even further, we pour it into a siphon to introduce more air and make it fluffy.

We start with a spoonful of rhubarb compote, then siphon on the elderflower cream. Then come 4 or 5 pieces of the chewy and tangy rhubarb leather no bigger than a tiny spoonful; we often curl them up and insert them strategically into the cream so one is a part of every bite.

To add an element of crunch, we add a yogurt crumble, a spin-off of the signature milk crumble from Momofuku Milk Bar in New York City, which provides a lactic acidity that works very well with both the cream and the rhubarb. We cover the entire thing in a granité made from the vinegar we use to pickle elderflowers and then sprinkle the dessert with fresh elderflowers. The granité gives a much more acidic but also deeper and slightly more oxidized tone that grabs on to the delicate savoriness of the dessert and lifts all the flavors brilliantly.

This play on floral elderflower; deep and mature acidity from the rhubarb; and the milky, buttery, and baked tones from the yogurt crumble and cream was very well received by guests the entire time it was on the menu.

Dishes

Jerusalem Artichokes, Coffee, and Passion

In the days before we saved enough money to buy a blast freezer, liquid nitrogen was a great thing to have on hand. When preparing granité, snows, and sorbets for a considerable number of guests, our regular freezer would often leave us hanging. In many situations, freshening up a granité in nitrogen saved us, as it did with this dish.

I based this dish on an old apple mousse recipe with meringue and whipped cream. I had used liquid nitrogen for the apple mousse and knew I'd use it again here. When you put spoonfuls of a mixture into liquid nitrogen to instantly freeze it, the outside solidifies while the inside can remain runny. The trick here was to account for the starch and solids in Jerusalem artichokes, which would impact the texture of the frozen mousse. My solution was to start with a very light and fluffy mousse that was almost runny, because I knew that it would get a crisp shell in the liquid nitrogen, and the two textures could contrast very well. We scooped spoonfuls of the mousse into a container of liquid nitrogen. After flipping the "dumplings" a few times, a crisp exterior shaped up around the inside. As we pulled them from the liquid we slightly crushed them prior to plating so the difference in textures would be obvious for the guest.

In New Nordic kitchens, Jerusalem artichokes are often combined with sea buckthorn, but my rebellious approach convinced me to choose passion fruit over the local orange berries. Everybody always described sea buckthorn as "almost like passion fruit," so why not just put the real thing on the plate?

We made a passion fruit curd to line the ice-cold plate and then added the quenelles of frozen Jerusalem artichoke mousse. We finished it with some ground black coffee, which added a toasted bitterness and brought out the nuttiness of the Jerusalem artichokes, while giving everything a slightly gritty crunch.

Whenever our staff walks the ice-cold plates through the dining room, thanks to the liquid nitrogen the frozen mousse gives off wafts of fog, which never ceases to be a showstopper. I love when there's a visual surprise when a dish is served, but as with all surprises, it must be backed up by thought and substance to avoid turning into a gimmick—it's the kind of substance that we easily find in the flavors and textures of this dessert.

Dishes

Coffee Table

Recently I visited a friend's brand-new restaurant, and one of the things he was most excited about showing me were some Japanese siphon coffee makers that no one else had used in Copenhagen before. These shiny bad boys were going to be the base of their coffee program. I was amazed, but I am not sure whether it was by the discovery of a new and mysterious brewing tool or because he actually even cared about it. Chefs used to think of coffee as black gasoline for their tired bodies, and now it's all about fixie-biking down to your local microroastery to pick up the blend they roast for you, and only you.

Perhaps my favorite perk of being located on Jægersborggade is our proximity to Coffee Collective, an artisanal coffee roaster that I credit with my own coffee awakening. My Italian heritage and years of working long hours had given me plenty of occasions to drink espresso of dubious quality, but I had never met anyone as knowing, passionate, and dedicated about coffee as these neighbors of ours. Most of my preopening meetings were in the far corner of CC's tiny café, where the roaring Probat coffee roaster never seemed to bother us as long as we were sipping on Aeropress, French press, or the crema of their incredibly balanced espresso blend.

When it came time to plan our own coffee service, we ditched our initial idea of having an espresso machine, since a complicated menu with a bunch of foamy milk-brews had the potential to throw us around in every direction whenever someone ordered coffee. Instead we went with serving Coffee Collective's Kenyan Kieni roast, which is light and fruity with a pronounced acidity, using a very simple French press brewing method. The guys at the Coffee Collective helped us figure out how to assure a consistently high quality without too many variables.

After a few years, we decided to up the ante and see if we couldn't improve the brew even more. It was at the same time that we were gunning for an organic certification, so we already had the Coffee Collective scouting for great raw material that met our ethical standards and their quality criteria. We switched to making pour-over coffee with a Kalita Wave dripper, a slightly more complicated brewing method that essentially gives us a similar style but a by far improved result. The Kalita offered us a high-standard filter brew that would bring out the best qualities of the Bokasso, the organic Ethiopian coffee we switched to. Aromatic and tannic, and maybe slightly more masculine than the Kieni, the Bokasso would drip through as clear as beef consommé in a matter of minutes.

Over the years, we've also taken a streamlined approach about what to serve with the coffee. We've never wanted to make a fuss about it and make a million different *mignardises*; we wanted to send people off with something slightly sweet, like a simple nougat with toasted hazelnuts and milk chocolate. Period. I feel that by the end of the meal a guest has not only filled his belly more than usual but also filled his mind with plenty of impressions. When I eat out, by the time I have gotten to the coffee I feel that it is time to regroup, to maybe think about what I have eaten and what I enjoyed the most. Maybe I could just get a second to look my girlfriend in the eyes without a waiter asking for our attention? I want our guests to be left to their privacy as much as possible.

Below I have picked out the three best bites we have done so far to serve with coffee. We would never serve three different things at once, but here they are.

Mosaic of Leathers
We dry the several types of crab apples we have at hand into leather and then rip them into slivers. We put these back together and add a bit of pressure to press them together, then slice into rectangles. The acidity is quite elevated on this and the flavor is reminiscent of a chewy *pâté de fruit*, so the coffee matched with it needs to have the same level of acidity, such as the Kieni.

Söl Tart
Our fetish with this sweet and tobacco-like seaweed stretches to the final bite of the meal with this shortbread topped with söl toffee and söl powder. The comforting and buttery notes of the shortbread shell mean that it tastes far less challenging than it sounds, and it makes for a great finale to the meal.

Bread Caramel
Based on the lactic acidity of our sourdough, we wanted to implement a chewy caramel to accompany the tannic Bokasso coffee. The caramel is flavored with water infused with our sourdough bread and with our sourdough starter, and when it's done, it's rolled in bread vinegar powder. I love how this sends the message that bread is so important to us that we serve it next to everything on the menu, even the coffee.

Appendix: Recipes

A Note on the Recipes, Tools, and Equipment

Whether you're a professional chef or an amateur one, the mission of this book is to inspire you and help you understand our cuisine at Relæ. The recipes that follow will show you exactly how everything is prepared at our restaurant, down to the smallest detail. Realistically, you will never be able to replicate exactly what we do in our kitchen—just as I would not be able to replicate what you do in yours. But my hope is that by carefully reading the recipes, you should be equipped to create your own take on our dishes.

You might not have a Pacojet to spin your ice cream, but try using a small household ice cream churner instead. Ideally you would cut a purple carrot on a professional meat slicer to get the most even slices, but an affordable mandoline can also do the job. You are probably cooking for your family or friends and not for seventy-five customers with high expectations, so just do your best and have fun with it. At the restaurant many tasks—such as blending spinach into a parsley puree—are easier and more efficient to do in large batches. But when you scale these recipes down to yield the exact four spoonfuls you need for your next dinner party, it becomes practically impossible to blend the spinach. We therefore often suggest that you make a larger amount of puree than you

might need—ultimately, a larger batch is less effort, and you can always enjoy the leftovers as a vibrant green sandwich spread the following day.

If you're curious about an unfamiliar ingredient, we encourage you to contact your favorite vegetable grocer or specialty store, or simply do what we do: use Google. I'll bet you will find a source for oxalis root and, if not, a million suggestions for an alternative.

Cooking at home should be fun and never pretentious. The food photographed in this book was prepared by professionals who probably have made each dish somewhere between five hundred and five thousand times. They get pretty good at shaping ice creams into perfect eggs or slicing lettuce into angel hair. You could practice forever to master some of these skills, but that would be missing the point. Take your time, read the recipe, and do things exactly as you want—you might want your lemon curd more tart or your veal tongue cooked longer. Go ahead. Only you know your "customer" and only you are the chef.

p.40

Sourdough Bread

Makes approximately 6 buns

Sourdough Starter

80 grams unbleached wheat flour or white bread flour,
plus more for feeding the starter

20 grams whole wheat flour or brown bread flour,
plus more for feeding the starter

80 grams water, plus more for feeding the starter

Combine the 80 grams unbleached wheat flour, 20 grams whole wheat flour, and 80 grams water in a bowl. Place a kitchen towel over the bowl and leave out at room temperature, out of direct sunlight, for 2 to 3 days, until bubbles have formed. If at the end of 3 days bubbles have still not formed, wait a few days longer.

Once bubbles have formed, you can start feeding the sourdough. Discard all but 40 grams of the starter. Add to this an additional 80 grams of unbleached wheat flour, 20 grams whole wheat flour, and 80 grams water, then stir to combine. Re-cover the bowl with a kitchen towel and leave out at room temperature. Repeat this feeding process every 12 hours (preferably once in the morning and once in the evening).

To test whether the starter is ready to use for bread dough, drop a spoonful of the starter into a small bowl filled with water. If the starter sinks, it is not ready and you should test again in 1 to 2 hours. If the starter floats, it is ready to be used for bread dough.

Bread Dough

480 grams water

130 grams Sourdough Starter

400 grams unbleached wheat flour or
white bread flour

130 grams whole wheat flour or brown bread flour,
plus more for dusting

16 grams fine-grain salt

In the bowl of a stand mixer fitted with the hook attachment, combine 400 grams of the water with the Sourdough Starter and the two flours. Mix on low speed until the dough comes together in a shaggy mass, approximately 3 minutes. Turn off the mixer and let the dough rest for 15 minutes.

Add the salt, then mix on low speed for an additional 3 minutes.

With the mixer on low speed, slowly pour in the remaining 80 grams of water over the course of 13 minutes (pouring the water in more quickly at the start of the 13 minutes than the end). Turn off the mixer and let the dough rest for 30 minutes.

After 30 minutes, fold the dough by grasping the front half of the dough mass, pulling it toward you, and then wrapping it over and behind the rest of the dough mass (tucking it underneath). Rotate the dough mass 90 degrees, then repeat this folding action. Rotate and fold a total of four times so that you've folded all four quadrants of the dough mass. Let the dough rest 30 minutes, then repeat the entire process. Let it rest for 30 minutes more, then repeat the folding process again. (You will have folded the dough three times, total.)

Transfer the dough to a covered plastic container and put in the fridge. Chill for 1 hour, then fold again. Re-cover the dough, put it back in the fridge, and chill for 20 to 24 hours.

The dough is ready to bake when it has risen by about 30 percent. If you have a pH meter, you can check for the ideal pH of 3.9 to 4.0.

Preheat the oven to 280°C (536°F).

Turn the dough out onto a floured work surface. Using a bench scraper, fold the dough, very gently, in half. Cut the folded dough into 6 (200-gram) squares and using the bench scraper and your hand as a guide, turn each square twice to shape it into a roughly round shape. It is important to be gentle during the cutting, weighing, and shaping of the dough so that you do not knock out any air. Place the dough rounds onto a parchment paper–lined baking sheet, separated by at least 3 cm. Dust the top of the buns with flour.

Place the baking sheet in the oven and inject some steam using the "steam oven" function, if you have it. Otherwise, use a spray bottle to quickly spray some water into the oven. Bake for 25 minutes with the oven vents closed, then open the oven vents and continue baking until the bread is darkly caramelized, approximately 5 to 10 minutes. If your oven doesn't have a ventilate function, simply open the door after 25 minutes, to allow some steam out, then close it again quickly so you don't lose too much heat.

Remove from the oven and cool on racks.

Herb Bouquet
Serves 6

Celery Sticks
1 large celery stalk, cut into 5-mm-thick and
    10-cm-long sticks

Blanch the celery sticks in boiling salted water for
10 seconds, then transfer to ice water to cool. Drain in
a colander.

Pistachio Puree
100 grams raw shelled pistachios
45 grams vegetable oil
15 grams extra-virgin olive oil
60 grams water
30 grams freshly squeezed lemon juice
Fine-grain salt

Combine the pistachios and oil in a Thermomix and
puree until smooth and the mixture reaches 90°C
(194°F), approximately 10 minutes. Allow the puree
to cool, then transfer to a large bowl. Add the olive
oil, water, and lemon juice and whisk until emulsified.
Season with salt.

Celery Ribbons
2 large celery stalks
200 grams 3% Salt Brine (page 438)

Hold the celery stalk by the thickest part and peel
long, thin strips of the celery using a vegetable peeler,
starting from the end that you are holding. Place the
celery with the Salt Brine in a single layer in a vacuum
bag and vacuum-seal it for 10 minutes. Drain the
celery ribbons in a colander.

Finishing
6 baby cos lettuce or romaine lettuce leaves,
    approximately 10 to 12 cm long
15 grams raw shelled pistachios, roughly chopped
6 large green spinach leaves
6 large red spinach leaves
6 large garden sorrel leaves
6 red oxalis sprigs with stems, leaves, and flowers
6 purslane sprigs with stems and small buds
6 nasturtium with stems
6 red basil leaves
6 green basil leaves
6 lemon basil leaves
6 Thai basil leaves
6 lovage leaves
6 marigold leaves
6 pieces bronze fennel top
6 watercress leaves with stems
6 pea shoots or pea leaves
1 bunch elderflowers or some marigold petals
Sea salt
Pear vinegar

p.230

Note: The lettuce leaves act as the backbone of
the bouquet, so it's important that they are the right
size and shape. The inverted teardrop shape we are
looking for is typical of baby cos lettuce and romaine
lettuce.

The types of herbs we use can vary from day to
day, depending on what is available, so you can use
any herbs that are available to you.

For each serving, on the inside of 1 lettuce leaf,
brush a thick layer of Pistachio Puree, then sprinkle
with pistachios. (Note that you will have more
Pistachio Puree than you need for the 6 bouquets.)
Start building a bouquet, starting with the largest
leaves, such as the spinach and sorrel leaves. Add
the Celery Stick and the larger greens with stems,
such as the oxalis, nasturtium, purslane, and pea
shoots, followed by the smaller herbs, such as the
basils, lovage, marigold, bronze fennel top, and
watercress. Use a Celery Ribbon to bind together
all of the herbs about 1.5 cm from the bottom of the
lettuce leaf. Rearrange the herbs so that each herb
can be seen and the bouquet looks complete and full.
Use scissors to trim the bottom of the bouquet and
sprinkle a few elderflowers on top. Finish the bouquet
with a sprinkle of sea salt and 8 sprays of pear
vinegar. Place the bouquet on a plate and serve.

Celery Root Taco
Serves 6

p.232

Salt-Cured Egg Yolks
1 kilogram fine-grain salt
6 egg yolks

Put half the salt in an even layer in a container.
Carefully place the egg yolks on the salt, leaving
space between each yolk. Completely cover the
yolks with the remaining salt and refrigerate for
24 hours, until firm. Using your hands, remove
the yolks from the salt and rinse them in a bowl of
cold water, scraping off any embedded salt with a
small knife. Place in a single layer and dry at 55°C
(131°F) in the dehydrator until dried but still pliable,
approximately 6 to 8 hours. The yolks should be
dried enough that when grated with a microplane,
you get a fine, flaky "snow" of egg yolk. If the yolk
becomes a thick gel when grated, they are not dry
enough and need to be returned to the dehydrator.

Celery Root "Tortilla"
1 large celery root (12 to 16 cm wide), scrubbed
    and trimmed
10 grams fine-grain salt

Preheat the oven to 180°C (356°F). Sprinkle the celery
root with the salt and wrap it tightly in aluminum foil.
Bake the celery root until cooked through, but not
too soft, 45 to 60 minutes. The celery root should be
80°C (175°F) in the center. Remove the foil and allow
the celery root to cool. Using a meat slicer, slice the
celery root crosswise into 1.5-mm slices, starting
from the top of the celery root. Use 6 of the largest
slices, from the widest part of the celery root. Preheat
a dry cast-iron pan over high heat, then cook the
rounds until slightly charred and dried, 30 to
45 seconds per side.

Buttermilk and Crème Fraîche Dressing
100 grams crème fraîche
15 grams freshly squeezed lemon juice
200 grams buttermilk
Fine grain salt

In the bowl of an electric stand mixer fitted with
the whisk attachment, whisk the crème fraiche
and the lemon juice to combine. Slowly pour in the
buttermilk, continuing to whisk, until the mixture is
slightly thickened, approximately 5 minutes. Season
with salt.

Celery Root Filling
1 large celery root
Fine-grain salt
Buttermilk and Crème Fraîche dressing
Freshly squeezed lemon juice

Preheat the oven to 180°C (356°F). Sprinkle the celery
root with the salt and wrap it tightly in aluminum foil.
Bake the celery root until cooked through and slightly
softer than the celery root "tortilla," 75 to 105 minutes.
Remove the foil and allow the celery root to cool.
Using a knife, peel the celery root, then julienne it.
Dress the celery root, julienne with just enough
Buttermilk and Crème Fraiche Dressing to evenly coat
it (note that you will have more dressing than you need
for the 6 tacos), then season with salt and lemon juice.

Finishing
1 bunch watercress, leaves picked and stems cut
    into 1-cm lengths
1 bunch nasturtium, leaves picked and torn in half
    and stems cut into 1-cm lengths
1 bunch garden cress, cut into 1-cm lengths
Freshly squeezed lemon juice

For each serving, place a large spoonful of the Celery
Root Filling onto a Celery Root "Tortilla" and top with
3 watercress leaves, 3 torn nasturtium leaves, and
4 pieces each of the nasturtium and watercress stems.
Using a microplane, finely grate half a Salt-Cured Egg
Yolk over the Celery Root Filling and the herbs to
cover, and sprinkle garden cress on top. Finish with
3 sprays of lemon juice and fold the taco in half.

Grilled Jerusalem Artichokes
Serves 6

Lemon Skin Puree
10 lemons, halved
2,050 grams water

Juice the lemons and place the juiced lemon halves in a pressure cooker with 1,000 grams of the water. Seal the lid and cook over high heat until it starts to steam, approximately 10 minutes. Decrease the heat to medium and cook 10 minutes more. Remove the cooker from the heat and release the pressure. Drain the lemons in a colander. Using a spoon, remove the lemon flesh and as much of the pith as possible, then discard. Return the lemon skins to the pressure cooker with 1,000 grams of the water, seal the lid, and cook over high heat until it starts to steam, approximately 10 minutes. Decrease the heat to medium and cook for 15 minutes more. Remove the cooker from the heat and release the pressure. Drain the lemon skins in a colander and rinse. Transfer the lemon skins to a Thermomix, add the remaining 50 grams water, and puree until smooth. Press the puree through a fine-mesh sieve and season with lemon juice.

Grilled Jerusalem Artichokes
3 large Jerusalem artichokes, scrubbed

Preheat a gas or charcoal grill to 300°C (575°F). Grill the Jerusalem artichokes until charred, 15 to 20 minutes, turning them every 5 minutes so that each side is charred evenly. After 10 minutes, use a skewer to poke some holes into the Jerusalem artichokes to release some steam. To test the Jerusalem artichokes for doneness, squeeze: there should be some fairly firm parts and some very soft spots. Remove from the grill and cut into halves.

p.234

Finishing
Sea salt
Brown Butter, melted (page 438)

For each serving, score the flesh of the cut side of a Grilled Jerusalem Artichoke half. Sprinkle with salt, brush with melted Brown Butter, and squeeze the Lemon Skin Puree all over the Jerusalem artichoke on the scored flesh side. Plate and serve.

Grilled Corn
Serves 6

6 ears baby corn, in the husk
1 small bunch marjoram, roughly chopped
50 grams unsalted butter, melted
Sea salt

p.236

Preheat a gas or charcoal grill to 300°C (575°F). With a knife make an incision in the husk around the base of each ear of corn, just above where the kernels start. Make another incision in the husk from here to the tip of the corn. Carefully remove the husk, keeping it intact, and remove the silk. Cut a 1-cm-wide strip of husk away from the vertical incision of the husk, making a kind of "open jacket" to encase the corn in. Fill the husk with marjoram and wrap the husk back around the corn. Use butcher's twine to tie the husk in place, leaving a strip of the corn kernels exposed down the length of the corn where you cut away the 1 cm of husk. Repeat with the remaining corn and marjoram. Grill the exposed side of the corn until charred, 1 to 2 minutes, then turn them over and grill until just cooked, but still crunchy, approximately 1 minute. Remove the corn from the grill and remove the butcher's twine. Open up the husk slightly, brush the corn with melted butter, sprinkle with salt, and enclose the corn back in the charred husk, leaving the charred surface of the corn visible through the opening of the husk.

Shallots and Nigella
Serves 6

p.238

Thick Sheep's Milk Yogurt
120 grams sheep's milk yogurt

Pour the yogurt into a strainer lined with cheesecloth set over a bowl. Keep in the fridge overnight, allowing the whey to drip out of the yogurt and into the bowl. The following day, transfer the thickened yogurt to a piping bag. Reserve the whey for another use.

Baked Shallots
6 large banana shallots

Preheat the oven to 200°C (400°F). Bake the shallots, skin on, until completely soft, 35 to 40 minutes. With a small knife, make 2 incisions to the skin, on opposite sides of the shallot, from the tip of each shallot to the root, and peel the skin back, leaving it attached at the root. Decrease the oven temperature to 150°C (300°F) and place the peeled-back shallots directly on the oven racks and bake until the outer surface of the shallots dries out slightly, approximately 10 minutes. Remove from the oven and allow to cool on the racks.

Tempura Batter
80 grams unbleached wheat flour
20 grams potato starch
2 grams fine-grain salt
8 grams baking powder
5 grams sugar
165 grams sparkling water

In a bowl, combine all the dry ingredients and mix well. Add the sparkling water and stir gently only a few times, trying not to flatten out the air bubbles. It is okay if there are still some small chunks of the dry ingredients not mixed in. It's more important that you don't overmix the batter; otherwise it will not be airy.

Toasted Nigella Seed Powder
100 grams nigella seeds

Preheat the oven to 160°C (140°F). Process the nigella seeds in a Thermomix until they become a fine powder. Spread the seeds onto a parchment paper–lined baking sheet and bake until lightly toasted, approximately 10 minutes. (Note you will have more powder than you need for this recipe.)

Finishing
3 kilograms vegetable oil
Sea salt

In a pot, heat the oil over medium-high heat until it reaches 210°C (410°F). Holding the shallot by the folded-back skins, dip the exposed part of the shallot into the batter to evenly coat it with a thin layer. Carefully dip the battered shallot into the oil two or three times, then drop the whole shallot into the frying oil and fry until golden brown, 1 to 2 minutes, turning it around in the oil every 5 seconds. Remove from the oil and allow to cool slightly on a rack, 1 to 2 minutes. With a small paring knife, make a 3-cm-long and 1-cm-deep incision along the side of the shallot, through the batter. Pipe the Thick Sheep's Milk Yogurt into the incision until the shallot is filled completely, then cover the shallot with a big sprinkle of Toasted Nigella Seed Powder and a pinch of salt. Place on the edge of the plate with the folded back skins hanging off the plate and serve.

Kornly Cracker
Serves 6

Sourdough Cracker
50 grams Sourdough Starter (page 370)

10 grams fresh yeast

150 grams water

375 grams unbleached wheat flour, plus more for dusting

75 grams durum semolina flour

15 grams extra-virgin olive oil

6 grams fine-grain salt

5 grams sugar

Note: This recipe makes about 80 crackers, which is more than you need for this recipe—however, leftover crackers can be stored for about a week in an airtight container.

Mix the sourdough, yeast, and water with your hands in the bowl of a stand mixer. Add 175 grams of the flour, the durum semolina, the olive oil, the salt, and the sugar. With the dough hook attachment, mix on low speed until just combined. Cover the bowl with plastic wrap and let rest at room temperature for 2 hours. At 30 minutes, fold the dough by taking the front half, pulling it up and over the dough, and tucking it into the back. Repeat the same action on the left, right, and back sides of the dough. Fold the dough in this manner every 30 minutes. When the dough doubles in size, let it rest covered overnight in the fridge.

The next morning, on low speed, with the dough hook attachment, mix the remaining 200 grams of flour into the cold dough until fully combined.

Preheat the oven to 300°C (575°F). On a floured work surface, divide the dough into 6 pieces. Cover the dough with plastic wrap so that it doesn't dry out. Use a pasta machine to roll out each piece of the dough. Start by taking 1 piece, dusting it with flour, and using a rolling pin to roll the dough out thin enough to fit in the thickest setting of the machine. Roll the dough through once, then dust it quite generously with flour, fold it in half, and roll it through the machine again at the same setting. Repeat this two or three times on the same setting. Once you have folded flour into the dough two or three times, the consistency of the dough should be firm like fresh pasta dough.

Then the dough will be strong enough to roll out all the way to the thinnest setting. Continue to roll the dough through the machine, gradually decreasing the thickness. When the dough has reached the thinnest setting, fold it in half so that there are two layers. Cut the dough into rectangle pieces of 2.5 cm by 11 cm. Transfer them to parchment paper–lined baking sheets, with 1 cm space around each cracker. Bake the crackers until they puff, approximately 2 minutes on one side, then flip them and bake for 1 minute on the other side, until golden and slightly charred. Allow to cool, then using a small knife, split each cracker into halves. Store in an airtight container for up to 2 weeks.

p.240

Salted Mushroom Slices
100 grams white button mushrooms, cleaned

1.5 grams fine-grain salt

Cut the mushrooms into 1-mm slices on a mandoline and transfer to a bowl. Sprinkle the salt evenly on the mushrooms and carefully mix them with your hands. Let stand for 15 minutes, until the salt draws out some of the liquid in the mushrooms. Transfer the mushrooms and their juices to a vacuum bag and vacuum-seal it for 10 minutes. When you are ready to use them, drain the mushrooms in a colander and use immediately.

Finishing
100 grams white button mushrooms, cleaned

Brown Butter, melted (page 438)

Sea salt

60 grams Kornly cheese

Freshly ground black pepper

Cut the white button mushrooms into 1-mm slices on a mandoline. For each serving, fill the hollow side of the cracker with Salted Mushroom Slices. Top with the raw mushrooms in a single layer that covers the Salted Mushroom Slices. Drizzle Brown Butter on the raw mushrooms and sprinkle sea salt on top. Finely grate a generous amount of cheese to cover the raw mushrooms and finish with a pinch of pepper.

Oxalis Roots
Serves 6

p.242

Salted Plum Puree
200 grams Salted Mirabelle Plums (page 440)

Drain the plums in a colander, reserving the brine. Halve the plums and remove the stones. Place the pitted plums in a fine-mesh sieve and, using a ladle, press gently to remove some of the liquid inside them. Reserve the liquid for another use. Transfer the plums to a blender and process until it has become a rough, thick paste. Add some of the salt brine, if necessary, to adjust the texture.

Finishing
3 large oxalis roots, scrubbed and trimmed
50 to 60 French sorrel leaves, with 2-cm stems

Cut the oxalis roots in half lengthwise. With a paring knife, carefully remove the cores and discard.

For each serving, spread a thin layer of the Salted Plum Puree on the cut side of 1 oxalis root half. Place 8 to 10 French sorrel leaves on top, with the leaf side down and the stems facing up, covering most of the root and the puree, but allowing a few gaps of the puree to show through.

Unripe Strawberries, Cress, and Buttermilk
Serves 6

p.246

Warm Unripe Strawberries
24 unripe strawberries, hulled

Preheat the oven to 50°C (125°F). Cut the strawberries lengthwise into halves, then place the pieces back together as if they were still whole strawberries. Warm the strawberries in a sealed heat-resistant container in the oven for approximately 1 hour.

Watercress Puree
180 grams watercress stems, roughly chopped
130 grams watercress leaves
150 grams baby spinach leaves
2 ice cubes
100 grams cold water
Fine-grain salt

In a Thermomix, puree the watercress stems, watercress leaves, spinach, ice cubes, and 50 grams of the cold water until smooth. You may need to add up to 50 grams more cold water to ensure that the puree blends thoroughly, but be careful not to add too much, as it should not be runny. Press the puree through a tamis lined with very fine-mesh cloth set over a bowl. The puree should hold a soft peak when spooned onto a plate. If the puree is too runny, pour it back onto the tamis and let it sit there, this time without pressing it through, to allow some of the water to drip out until it reaches the desired consistency. Season with salt and keep in the fridge. (Note that you will have more Watercress Puree than you need for this recipe.)

Buttermilk Snow
0.25 gram gellan
50 grams milk
750 grams cold buttermilk
Fine-grain salt
Freshly squeezed lemon juice

In a saucepan, stir the gellan into the milk and heat until it reaches 85°C (185°F). Strain the milk through a fine-mesh strainer set over a bowl. Allow the milk to cool slightly and then stir in the cold buttermilk. Season with salt and lemon juice. Freeze the liquid in a shallow, freezer-proof container overnight. Once the liquid is completely frozen, remove it from the container and transfer the frozen block to a large metal bowl. Using a rolling pin, or other heavy item, such as a pestle, smash the ice block into smaller pieces, 1 to 4 cm in size. Transfer a large handful of the frozen pieces to the Thermomix and process until it looks like a fine snow, approximately 30 seconds. Transfer the snow to a freezer-proof container and place in the freezer. Repeat for the rest of the frozen pieces.

Finishing
Sea salt
2 or 3 bunches of nasturtium with 6-cm-long stems

For each serving, place a large spoonful of Watercress Puree slightly off center and to the right on a frozen plate. Place 4 Warm Unripe Strawberries on and around the right side of the puree. Place a large spoonful of the Buttermilk Snow to the left of the strawberries and sprinkle with salt. Place 8 to 10 nasturtiums on top of the strawberries.

Sheep's Milk Yogurt, Radishes, and Nasturtium
Serves 6

p.248

Sheep's Milk Yogurt Mousse
125 grams heavy cream
200 grams sheep's milk yogurt

In a bowl, whisk together the cream and the sheep's milk yogurt. Pour into a siphon bottle and charge with one CO_2 cartridge. Shake the siphon bottle until the mousse is smooth and can hold stiff peaks.

Cooked Radishes
250 grams different colored small radishes, halved
    lengthwise
Extra-virgin olive oil
Freshly squeezed lemon juice
Fine-grain salt

Blanch the radishes in boiling salted water until just cooked, but still slightly crunchy, 30 seconds to 2 minutes, depending on the size. Transfer to ice water to cool. Drain in a colander. Season with olive oil, lemon juice, and salt.

Finishing
2 bunches of nasturtium, separated into leaves with
    3 cm of stem attached
Extra-virgin olive oil
Sea salt

For each serving, place the Cooked Radishes in a pile in the center of the plate. Siphon enough Sheep's Milk Yogurt Mousse on top of the radishes to cover them. Place the nasturtium leaves, with stems facing out, on top of the mousse, covering it completely. Finish with a drizzle of olive oil and a sprinkle of salt.

Cucumber, Caraway, and Lemon Balm
Serves 6

p.250

Salted Kolhrabi Wrappers
2 large kohlrabi, peeled and trimmed
1.8 grams fine-grain salt

Using a meat slicer or mandoline, slice the kohlrabi crosswise into 0.2-mm-thin rounds. Set aside 30 of the largest kohlrabi slices, each at least 8 to 10 cm in diameter, and sprinkle with salt. Let stand for 15 minutes, until the salt draws out some of the liquid. Transfer the kohlrabi and their juices to a vacuum bag, in one neat pile, and vacuum-seal it. After 20 minutes, drain the kohlrabi in a colander.

Cucumber Filling and Cucumber Juice
3 large cucumbers, peeled and trimmed
1 bunch lemon balm, leaves finely chopped
Pear vinegar
Fine-grain salt

Using a fine-mesh sieve set over a bowl, grate the cucumbers into the sieve so that the cucumber juice collects in the bowl. Let the grated cucumber sit in the sieve for 10 minutes to drain. Transfer the grated cucumber to a bowl and mix with the chopped lemon balm. Season with pear vinegar and salt. Season the cucumber juice with additional pear vinegar and salt.

Finishing
12 grams caraway seeds, toasted
Sea salt
Extra-virgin olive oil
Freshly squeezed lemon juice

For each serving, take 5 Salted Kohlrabi Wrappers and place a spoonful of the Cucumber Filling in the center of each wrapper. Fold the wrapper in half, enclosing the filling to form a dumpling. Using your fingers, make small folds along the edge of the wrapper and press it together so it stays closed. Place the dumplings in a shallow bowl and pour 5 spoonfuls of Cucumber Juice over the dumplings. Sprinkle each dumpling with a pinch of toasted caraway seeds and a little salt. Finish with a few drops of olive oil and 2 sprays of lemon juice.

Smoked Beet "Fish" and Elderflower

Serves 6

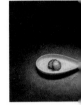

p.252

Smoked Beets and Beet Ash
6 large Chioggia beets, scrubbed
Smoke powder

Preheat a charcoal grill to 300°C (575°F). Grill the beets until charred, 15 to 20 minutes, turning them every 5 minutes so that each side is charred evenly. Preheat the oven to 300°C (575°F). Place the beets directly on the oven rack and bake until the beets reach 99°C (210°F) in the center, approximately 20 minutes. Decrease the oven temperature to 80°C (175°F) and bake the beets overnight, until they feel bouncy when you squeeze them. Remove from the oven and transfer to an uncovered tray and keep in the fridge for at least 12 hours. The following day, use a knife to cut away the burnt skins from the beets. To make the beet ash, place the beet skins in a single layer and dry overnight at 65°C (150°F) in the dehydrator. The following day, transfer the dried beet skins to a Thermomix and process until it has become a fine powder. Sift the powder through a fine-mesh sieve set over a bowl.

Put 2 handfuls of smoke powder in the bottom of a flameproof casserole dish. Set a rack inside the casserole dish. Place the casserole dish on the stove top and cook over high heat until the powder smokes, approximately 5 minutes. Allow the powder to smoke for 30 seconds, then place the beets on the rack, cover the casserole dish with a lid, and turn off the heat. Allow the beets to smoke for 10 minutes, then turn the beets upside down. Repeat the smoking and turning process two or three more times until the beets are smoky in smell and taste. Cut the beets into 5-mm slices, then place the slices back together as if they were still a whole beet.

Finishing
Elderflower vinegar reserved from Pickled
    Elderflowers (page 440)
6 bunches Pickled Elderflowers (page 440),
    small stems and flowers picked
Sea salt
Extra-virgin olive oil

For each serving, dust 1 Smoked Beet with Beet Ash, then lay each slice on a baking sheet and spray with elderflower vinegar. Place a few pinches of the mixed Pickled Elderflower stems and flowers onto each slice and spread them out in a thin layer. Leave one large slice without elderflower stems and flowers. Sprinkle salt on each slice. Layer the slices on the center of the plate, in a fan shape, and top with the large slice that's without elderflower stems and flowers. Brush the top slice with olive oil.

Beet, Crab Apple, and Söl
Serves 6

p.254

Cooked Beets
2 large red beets, peeled

Place the beets in a large vacuum bag and vacuum-seal them so that there is space around each beet. Place the bag in a saucepan with enough water to cover and bring to a boil over medium heat. Decrease the heat to low and simmer until the beets feel completely cooked, but not too soft, approximately 1 1/2 hours. Transfer the bag into ice water to cool. Once the beets have cooled, drain them in a colander. Using a meat slicer, slice the beets into 0.7-mm-thick slices. You should make at least 18 large slices in total from the widest part of the beets. Reserve the smaller slices and remaining pieces.

Beet and Söl Sauce
Cooked beet pieces left over from slicing
50 grams *söl* seaweed, rehydrated
Freshly squeezed lemon juice

Juice the cooked beet pieces in a juicer. Transfer the juice to a very fine-mesh cloth sieve set over a bowl and strain. Transfer the remaining pulp in the sieve to a superbag and over the same bowl squeeze the pulp with your hands until all the juice is extracted. Combine 250 grams of the beet juice and the *söl* in a saucepan and cook over medium-high heat until the *söl* is completely soft and the juice has reduced slightly, approximately 10 minutes. Transfer the mixture to a Thermomix and puree until smooth. Press the puree through a tamis lined with very fine-mesh cloth into a bowl, then allow to cool and season with lemon juice.

Finishing
9 pieces of each type of Paradise Apple Leather
    (page 436), each about 6 by 8 cm
30 grams *söl* seaweed, rehydrated
Sea salt
Extra-virgin olive oil
Black currant vinegar

For each serving, place 7 or 8 (2 cm) dots of the Beet and Söl Sauce in different places all over the plate using a squeeze bottle. Tear 3 slices of Cooked Beet in half, then fold each over and stand it upright on top of the dots of puree. Place 3 pieces of each type of Paradise Apple Leather, folded in the same way as the beets, around the plate to fill the spaces between the beets. Place 6 or 7 pieces of *söl* on top, laying the long strips horizontally over the beets and leathers. Sprinkle salt on the beets and finish with a drizzle of olive oil and 3 sprays of black currant vinegar.

Cooked Onions, Buttermilk, and Nasturtium

Serves 6

p.256

Blanched Spring Onions

1 kilogram small white spring onions, peeled and
    halved lengthwise
Extra-virgin olive oil
Freshly squeezed lemon juice
Fine-grain salt

Bring a large pot of salted water to a boil over high
heat. Add the onions to the boiling water and allow
the pot to come back to a boil. Decrease the heat
to low and simmer until the onions are just cooked,
but still slightly crunchy, 8 to 10 minutes. Transfer
the onions to ice water to cool. Drain the onions in a
colander and pick apart the onion shells, discarding
the tougher outer layers. Transfer the onions to a large
bowl and dress with olive oil, lemon juice, and salt.

Finishing

60 grams Buttermilk and Crème Fraîche Dressing
    (page 372)
2 bunches nasturtium, leaves picked and torn, stems
    cut into 1-cm lengths
Extra-virgin olive oil
Freshly squeezed lemon juice
Sea salt

For each serving, place a spoonful of the Buttermilk
and Crème Fraîche Dressing in the center of the plate.
Place a torn nasturtium leaf inside each onion shell
and place on top of the dressing. Starting from the left
side, plate 10 to 12 onion shells, one behind the other,
until the dressing is covered. Place 5 or 6 nasturtium
stem pieces between the onions, slightly angled
upward. Finish with a drizzle of olive oil, 3 sprays of
lemon juice, and a sprinkle of salt.

Lumpfish Roe, Daikon, and Almonds
Serves 6

Fermented Daikon
1 large daikon, peeled and trimmed
2 kilograms 3% Salt Brine (page 438)
60 grams Whey (page 438)

Cut the daikon crosswise into 3 pieces. Cut the daikon pieces lengthwise into 1-mm slices on a mandoline. Place the daikon in a glass jar or a food-grade plastic container with the Salt Brine and Whey. Use a plate to weigh down the daikon slices to ensure that they are completely submerged in the liquid. Seal the jar or container with a lid fitted with an airlock. Place the jar out of direct sunlight, where the ambient room temperature is 16°C to 18°C (60°F to 64°F), to ferment for 5 or 6 days. The fermentation is complete when the daikon has broken down, becomes soft, and tastes slightly soured. Once fermented, you can seal the jar or container and store in the fridge. Remove the daikon slices from the brine and julienne. Reserve the fermented daikon brine. Keep the julienne in neat lines for easier plating.

Fresh Almond Milk
250 grams blanched almonds, peeled
250 grams water
Fine-grain salt

In a bowl, soak the almonds in the water overnight in the fridge. The following day, transfer the almonds and the water to a Thermomix and puree until smooth. Transfer the puree to a superbag set over a bowl and squeeze the puree to extract as much almond milk as possible. Discard the solids in the superbag. Season the almond milk with salt and keep in the fridge. (Note that this makes more Almond Milk than you need for this recipe.)

Almond Gel
300 grams blanched almonds, peeled
450 grams water
255 grams milk
1 gram iota
35 grams unsalted butter, cut into cubes
Fine-grain salt

In a bowl, soak the almonds in the water overnight in the fridge. The following day, transfer the almonds and the water to a Thermomix and puree until smooth. Transfer the puree to a superbag set over a bowl and squeeze the puree to extract as much of the almond milk as possible. Discard the solids in the superbag. (This mixture will be a bit thinner than the Fresh Almond Milk you made in the step above.) In a saucepan, warm the milk over medium heat until it reaches 80°C (175°F), then whisk in the iota. Remove the saucepan from the heat and whisk in the butter, cube by cube, until emulsified. Allow to cool for 5 minutes, then stir in 130 grams of the almond milk and season with salt. Pour the gel into 6 shallow serving bowls and allow to set at room temperature, approximately 2 minutes.

Lumpfish Roe
250 grams lumpfish roe, cleaned and drained
3.75 grams fine-grain salt

In a bowl, mix the lumpfish roe with the salt.

Almond and Fermented Daikon Sauce
50 grams Fresh Almond Milk
25 grams brine from Fermented Daikon
Fine-grain salt

In a bowl, mix the Fresh Almond Milk and the brine. Season with salt and keep in the fridge.

Finishing
20 grams raw almonds with skin, cut lengthwise
    into 0.5-mm slices
Sea salt
Freshly squeezed lemon juice

As soon as the Almond Gel has set in the bowls, arrange 4 small bundles of the julienned Fermented Daikon on top of each. The bundles should not touch or overlap each other. Place spoonfuls of the Lumpfish Roe in small piles between the Fermented Daikon bundles. Place 12 drops of the Almond and Fermented Daikon Sauce around the roe and daikon. Sprinkle a few almond slices on top of the roe and finish with a sprinkle of salt and 3 sprays of lemon juice.

Oysters, Cabbage, and Capers

Serves 6

p.262

Pickled Cabbage and Cabbage Stem Slices
2,000 grams water
120 grams sugar
80 grams fine-grain salt
100 grams white wine vinegar
1 large white cabbage

In a saucepan, warm 500 grams of the water over high heat, add the sugar and salt, and stir until dissolved. Allow to cool, then stir in the remaining 1,500 grams water and the white wine vinegar. Place the cabbage upside down on a cutting board, so that the stem faces up. With a large knife, make a cut all the way through it directly to the right of the stem. Repeat this on all sides of the cabbage until you are left with the whole stem intact and 4 large pieces of cabbage leaves. Using a meat slicer or mandoline, slice the cabbage leaves lengthwise into 1-mm-thin strips, creating long, thin strands of cabbage. Slice the stem on the meat slicer or mandoline lengthwise into 1-mm-thin slices. Place the sliced cabbage and cabbage stems in separate vacuum bags with the brine and vacuum-seal them. Keep in the fridge for 2 or 3 days, until the cabbage has softened and tastes slightly soured, then drain in a colander. (Note you will have more pickled cabbage than you need for this recipe.)

Caper Puree
150 grams salted capers
600 grams water
45 grams Moscatel vinegar

In a bowl, soak the salted capers in 500 grams of the water for 30 minutes, then drain in a colander and rinse well. Transfer the capers to a Thermomix, add the remaining 100 grams water and Moscatel vinegar, and puree until smooth. Transfer to a squeeze bottle. (Note you will have more Caper Puree than you need for this recipe.)

Finishing
60 grams plain yogurt
1 horseradish, peeled
6 large shucked oysters, cut into 5 pieces
Freshly squeezed lemon juice
Sea salt

For each serving, place a large spoonful of yogurt in the center of the plate and flatten it out a little with the back of a spoon. Using a small knife, scrape 5 thin slivers of horseradish and place them on top and around the yogurt. Place 5 oyster pieces around the plate, in between the yogurt and horseradish pieces. Using a squeeze bottle, place 4 dots of Caper Puree on top of the yogurt. At the bottom left of the plate, place a Cabbage Stem Slice and fold a small section of the bottom part underneath itself. Arrange the Pickled Cabbage neatly over the top of the oysters and yogurt, creating what should look like a cross section of a whole cabbage. Finish with 3 sprays of lemon juice and a sprinkle of salt.

Mussels, Seaweed, and Allumettes
Serves 6

p.264

Clarified Mussel Stock
260 grams white wine
1 kilogram blue mussels, cleaned and debearded

In a large saucepan, bring the wine to a boil over high heat, then add the mussels and cover. When the wine returns to a boil, uncover, decrease the heat to medium, and simmer for 20 minutes. Strain the stock through a fine-mesh sieve set over a freezer-proof container, reserving the mussels and their shells for another use, and allow it cool. Cover the container and place it in the freezer overnight. Once the stock is frozen, remove it from the container, wrap it in cheesecloth, and place it in a fine-mesh strainer set over a large bowl in the fridge until melted, approximately 24 to 36 hours.

Blanched Mussels
20 large blue mussels, cleaned and debearded
250 grams Clarified Mussel Stock, chilled

Blanch the mussels, a few at a time, in boiling salted water, and remove them, one by one, as they open, 30 to 60 seconds. Remove the mussels from their shells and cool the mussels in the chilled Clarified Mussel Stock. Keep the mussels in the stock in the fridge.

Seaweed Bouillon
85 grams fresh green seaweed, washed
150 grams Clarified Mussel Stock
Freshly squeezed lemon juice
Fine-grain salt

Blanch the seaweed in boiling salted water until tender, 2 to 3 minutes, then transfer to ice water to cool. Remove the seaweed from the ice water and squeeze out as much water as possible with your hands. Transfer the blanched seaweed to a Thermomix, add the Clarified Mussel Stock, and blend until smooth. Transfer the mixture to a superbag set over a bowl and squeeze as much as possible to extract the bouillon. Discard the seaweed. Season with lemon juice and salt and keep in the fridge.

Pommes Allumettes
2 kilograms large baking potatoes, peeled
2 L 3% Salt Brine (page 438)
2 kilograms Pork Fat (page 414), melted
Fine-grain salt

Over a large bowl of water, cut the potatoes lengthwise with an allumettes blade on a mandoline. Remove the potatoes from the water, place in a vacuum bag with the Salt Brine, and vacuum-seal it. Keep in the fridge for 24 hours. The following day, drain the potatoes in a colander. Transfer one-quarter of the potatoes to paper towels and reserve for frying. Blanch the remaining potatoes in boiling salted water until just cooked, approximately 1 minute, then transfer to ice water to cool. Drain in a colander. In a saucepan, heat the rendered pork fat over medium-high heat until it reaches 190°C (375°F). Fry the reserved potatoes in the Pork Fat until golden brown, approximately 2 minutes. Drain on a layer of paper towels and season with salt.

Finishing
Sea salt
12 grams Pork Fat (page 414), melted

For each serving, place 4 Blanched Mussels around the center of the plate and sprinkle with salt. Cover the mussels with the blanched Pommes Allumettes, placing them horizontally. Spoon some of the chilled Seaweed Bouillon over the potatoes and top with a few drops of melted Pork Fat. Spray the fried Pommes Allumettes with some Pork Fat and place 5 or 6 pieces horizontally on top of the blanched Pommes Allumettes.

Squid, Mussels, and Seaweed
Serves 6

p.266

Green Sea Lettuce Powder
250 grams fresh green sea lettuce, washed

Place the sea lettuce in a single layer and dry overnight at 65°C (150°F) in the dehydrator. The following day, transfer to a Thermomix and process until it has become a fine powder. Sift the powder through a fine-mesh sieve set over a bowl. (Note that this yields more Green Sea Lettuce Powder than you need for this recipe.)

Squid Noodles
400 grams squid bodies, cleaned and skinned
100 grams Brown Butter, melted (page 438)
Freshly squeezed lemon juice
Fine-grain salt

Cut the squid bodies open and, with a knife, scrape away the membrane from inside the squid bodies. Cut the bodies into halves and stack on top of each other in a vacuum bag. Vacuum-seal the bag and freeze overnight. The following day, remove the frozen squid bodies from the vacuum bag. Using a meat slicer, slice the squid lengthwise into 1-mm-thin strips, making long transparent noodles. In a saucepan, heat the Brown Butter over medium heat until just warm. Add the squid noodles and cook, stirring constantly, until they start to curl slightly, separate from each other, and become slightly opaque, approximately 30 seconds. Strain the squid noodles using a fine-mesh sieve set over a bowl, and reserve the Brown Butter. Transfer the squid noodles into another bowl and season with lemon juice and salt. Add a few spoonfuls of the reserved Brown Butter and mix.

Squid and Caramelized Onion Puree
Vegetable oil
750 grams yellow onions, peeled and finely sliced
100 grams squid, finely chopped

In a sauté pan, heat a little vegetable oil over medium-high heat. Add the onions and sauté until softened, approximately 10 minutes. Decrease the heat to medium-low and sauté, stirring occasionally, until all of the onions are evenly caramelized, approximately 45 minutes. Meanwhile, in a separate pan, heat a little vegetable oil over medium-high heat. Add the squid and sauté until fully cooked and slightly browned, approximately 10 minutes. Transfer the caramelized onions and cooked squid to a Thermomix and puree until smooth. Press through a tamis lined with very fine-mesh cloth set over a bowl.

Mussel and Squid Ink Emulsion
600 grams blue mussels, cleaned and debearded
55 grams Squid and Caramelized Onion Puree
14 grams freshly squeezed lemon juice
140 grams vegetable oil, chilled
6 grams squid ink
Fine-grain salt

Blanch the mussels, a few at a time, in boiling salted water, and remove them, one by one, as they open, 30 to 60 seconds. Remove the mussels from their shells and allow the mussels to cool on a layer on paper towels in the fridge. Once cooled, transfer 100 grams of the blanched mussels to a Thermomix and puree until smooth. Add the Squid and Caramelized Onion Puree and lemon juice and puree until smooth. Decrease the speed to low, and add the chilled oil in a fine stream. Press the emulsion through a tamis lined with very fine-mesh cloth set over a bowl. Whisk in the squid ink and season with salt. Keep the emulsion in the fridge, but remove it from the fridge to temper 30 minutes before serving.

Finishing
30 grams fresh green sea lettuce, washed

For each serving, place a large spoonful of the Mussel and Squid Ink Emulsion in the center of a plate and surround it with 4 or 5 pieces of fresh green sea lettuce. Place 2 piles of the cooked Squid Noodles to the side of the emulsion, reserving the Brown Butter the noodles were cooked in. Pour 2 spoonfuls of the Brown Butter over the noodles and dust with a pinch of Green Sea Lettuce Powder.

p.268

Raw Beef, Anchovies, and Ramsons
Serves 6

Anchovy Emulsion
100 grams oil-packed anchovy fillets
1,040 grams water
8 grams pear vinegar
150 grams vegetable oil, chilled
Fine-grain salt
Freshly squeezed lemon juice

Remove the anchovies from the oil and soak them in 1,000 grams of the water for 30 minutes. Drain them in a colander and rinse under running water. Transfer the anchovies to a Thermomix, add the vinegar and the remaining 40 grams water, and puree until smooth. Decrease the speed to low and add the chilled oil in a fine stream. Press the emulsion through a tamis lined with very fine-mesh cloth set over a bowl. Season with salt and lemon juice and transfer to a squeeze bottle. (Note that this will yield more Anchovy Emulsion than you need for this recipe.)

Raw Beef Slices
250 grams beef tenderloin or back leg cut, trimmed of fat and sinew

Place the beef in a vacuum bag, vacuum-seal it, and freeze overnight. The following day, 1 hour before slicing, remove the beef from the bag and transfer to the fridge. Using a meat slicer, cut the beef, against the grain, into 0.5-mm slices. Arrange the slices in a single layer on parchment paper.

Finishing
50 grams freshly squeezed lemon juice, plus more
    for seasoning
50 grams extra-virgin olive oil
6 ramson stems, 4 to 5 cm long
Sea salt
12 baby spinach leaves, halved lengthwise
4 large garden sorrel leaves, cut into 2-cm pieces
15 to 20 ramson leaves, torn into long pointy strips

Combine the lemon juice and the olive oil in a squeeze bottle. For each serving, draw a long zigzag of Anchovy Emulsion, horizontally on the lower half of the plate. Place a ransom stem on the right of the Anchovy Emulsion, sticking off the plate slightly. Sprinkle salt on the Raw Beef slices and arrange 3 or 4 slices on top of the emulsion, in the shape of a broad ramson leaf. Drizzle the lemon juice–olive oil mixture over the beef, then place 4 pieces of spinach and 4 pieces of sorrel on top. Arrange the ramson leaf pieces so that they cover the beef, creating a natural leaf shape. Finish with 5 sprays of lemon juice and a sprinkle salt on top, then add a few more drops of the lemon juice and olive oil mixture between the ramson leaves.

Lamb, Shrimp, and Dill
Serves 6

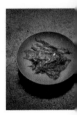

p.270

Dried Shrimp Powder
1 kilogram fresh small shrimp, unpeeled

Preheat the oven to 200°C (400°F). Place the shrimp onto two baking sheets and bake for 10 minutes. Place in a single layer and dry overnight at 65°C (150°F) in the dehydrator. The following day, transfer the dried shrimp to a Thermomix and process until it has become a fine powder. Sift the powder through a fine-mesh sieve set over a bowl. (Note that this recipe yields more Dried Shrimp Powder than you need for this recipe.)

Raw Lamb Slices
250 grams lamb loin, shoulder, or leg, trimmed of fat and sinew

Place the lamb in a vacuum bag, vacuum-seal it, and freeze overnight. The following day, 1 hour before slicing, remove the lamb from the bag and transfer to the fridge. Using a meat slicer, cut the lamb, against the grain, into 0.5-mm slices. Arrange the slices in a single layer on parchment paper.

Roasted Lamb Oil
150 grams lamb fat trimmings, with a little meat attached
150 grams vegetable oil
Fine-grain salt
Freshly squeezed lemon juice

Cut the trimmings into 2- to 3-cm pieces. In a saucepan, cook the trimmings over high heat until evenly caramelized, approximately 5 minutes. Decrease the heat to low and allow the fat to render slowly, stirring occasionally, for approximately 10 minutes. Add the vegetable oil and continue to cook over low heat for 30 minutes. Remove the saucepan from the heat and allow to infuse for 30 minutes. Strain the oil through a fine-mesh sieve set over a bowl and discard the cooked meat. Keep warm and season with a little salt and lemon juice. (Note that this yields more Roasted Lamb Oil than you need for this recipe.)

Sautéed Spring Onions
500 grams large spring onions, peeled and halved
Vegetable oil
Roasted Lamb Oil, slightly warmed
Fine-grain salt
Freshly squeezed lemon juice

Cut the onions crosswise into 1-cm slices. In a saucepan, heat a little vegetable oil over medium heat. Add the onions and cook until softened with a slight crunch remaining, but not at all caramelized, approximately 5 minutes. Decrease the heat to low and continue cooking until the onions are transparent and taste sweet, approximately 10 minutes. Allow the onions to cool. Season with Roasted Lamb Oil, salt, and lemon juice.

Finishing
1 bunch dill, leaves picked and stems finely chopped
Sea salt

For each serving, spread the Sautéed Spring Onions over the plate in a single layer, then sprinkle some dill leaves and stems and Dried Shrimp Powder on top. Cover with a single layer of Raw Lamb Slices, leaving a few gaps between the slices, so the onions, dill, and shrimp powder can be seen. Sprinkle salt on the lamb. Brush a thin layer of Roasted Lamb Oil onto the meat. Using a gas-powered kitchen torch, quickly warm the fat on the meat for 2 seconds, but be careful not to cook the meat.

White Asparagus and Anchovies
Serves 6

p.272

Pickled Anchovies
30 grams oil-packed anchovy fillets
600 grams water
100 grams pear vinegar

Remove the anchovies from the oil and soak them in 500 grams of the water for 30 minutes. Drain them in a colander and rinse under cold running water. Combine the remaining 100 grams water and the pear vinegar and soak the anchovies in the brine for 45 minutes. Drain the anchovies in a colander and cut each anchovy into 4 or 5 pieces.

Cooked and Raw White Asparagus
950 grams large white asparagus, peeled and
    trimmed, peels and trimmings reserved
Extra-virgin olive oil
Freshly squeezed lemon juice
Fine-grain salt

Blanch 600 grams of the asparagus in boiling salted water until just cooked but still slightly crunchy, 1 to 2 minutes. Transfer to ice water to cool, then drain in a colander. Cut the asparagus tips and reserve for finishing. Cut the stalks crosswise into 3-mm rounds. Cut the remaining 350 grams raw asparagus in the same way. Set aside 100 grams of the raw asparagus and mix the remaining raw asparagus slices with the cooked asparagus slices. Season the mixture with olive oil, lemon juice, and salt.

White Asparagus Juice
600 grams white asparagus trimmings reserved from
    Cooked and Raw White Asparagus
Pear vinegar

Juice the asparagus in a juicer and strain through a fine-mesh strainer set over a bowl and season with pear vinegar.

Finishing
100 grams raw asparagus reserved from Cooked and
    Raw White Asparagus
Reserved tips from Cooked and Raw White Asparagus
90 grams Anchovy Emulsion (page 386)
Extra-virgin olive oil
Freshly squeezed lemon juice
Fine-grain salt

For each serving, place the Cooked and Raw White Asparagus in a thin line approximately 10 cm long, on the top right of the plate, and place a few pieces of Pickled Anchovies among the slices. Cover the line of asparagus with the 100 grams reserved raw asparagus. Place 1 cooked asparagus tip on the left side of the line of asparagus, pointing out so that the whole asparagus mass looks like a spear of asaparagus. On the plate, below the asparagus, squeeze 5 or 6 dots of Anchovy Emulsion, then spoon the White Asparagus Juice around the dots. Finish with a few drops of olive oil over the White Asparagus Juice, and 3 sprays of lemon juice and a sprinkle of salt over the asparagus.

Pickled Skate, Mussels, and Celery Root
Serves 6

p.274

Grated Celery Root with Mussel Emulsion
600 grams blue mussels, cleaned and debearded
10 grams Dijon mustard
14 grams freshly squeezed lemon juice, plus more
　for seasoning
160 grams vegetable oil, chilled
10 grams fine-grain salt, plus more for seasoning
1 large celery root, scrubbed

Blanch the mussels, a few at a time, in boiling salted water, and remove them, one by one, as they open, 30 to 60 seconds. Remove them from their shells and allow to cool on a layer on paper towels in the fridge. Once cooled, transfer 100 grams of the blanched mussels to a Thermomix and puree until smooth. Add the mustard and lemon juice and mix well. Decrease the speed to low and add the chilled vegetable oil in a fine stream. Press the emulsion through a tamis lined with very fine-mesh cloth set over a bowl. Season with a pinch of salt.

Preheat the oven to 180°C (356°F). Sprinkle the celery root with the 10 grams salt and wrap it tightly in aluminum foil. Bake the celery root until soft, approximately 75 to 105 minutes. Remove the foil and allow to cool. Using a knife, peel the celery root, then grate it on a coarse grater.

Dress the grated celery root with the Mussel Emulsion and season with lemon juice and salt.

Pickled Skate
600 grams skate, skin and cartilage removed
500 grams 7% Salt Brine (page 438)
100 grams water
50 grams Moscatel vinegar

Place the skate with the Salt Brine in a vacuum bag and vacuum-seal it. Keep in the fridge for 24 hours. Remove the skate from the Salt Brine and rinse well under running water. Place the rinsed skate with the 100 grams water and Moscatel vinegar in a vacuum bag and vacuum-seal it. Cook the skate in an immersion circulator at 45°C (113°F) until it is soft and falls apart, 15 to 20 minutes, then transfer to ice water to cool.

Skate Stock
2.5 kilograms vegetable oil
1 kilogram skate cartilage

In a large pot, heat the vegetable oil over high heat until it reaches 175°C (350°F). Fry the skate cartilage until golden brown, 3 to 4 minutes. Drain on a layer of paper towels and allow to cool. Place the fried skate bones in a large stock pot and add enough cold water to cover. Bring to a boil over high heat and skim the fat and foam from the surface. Decrease the heat to low and simmer for 20 minutes. Strain the stock though a fine-mesh sieve. Return the strained stock to a clean pot and cook the stock over high heat until reduced by half, 45 to 50 minutes. Cool uncovered in the fridge. (Note that this will yield more Skate Stock than you need for this recipe.)

Parsley Sauce
100 grams Parsley Puree (page 410)
40 grams Skate Stock, chilled
40 grams Clarified Mussel Stock (page 384), chilled
Fine-grain salt

Combine the Parsley Puree, Skate Stock, and Clarified Mussel Stock and mix well. Season with salt.

Finishing
Sea salt
Extra virgin olive oil

For each serving, place 2 spoonfuls of the Grated Celery Root with Mussel Emulsion in two separate piles on the plate. Split the Pickled Skate where there are grooves in the flesh and cover the celery root by lining up the slivers of skate flesh over the celery root. Brush some Skate Stock onto the skate and sprinkle with salt. Place 3 large spoonfuls of the cold Parsley Sauce in the center of the plate between the two piles of celery root and skate. Finish with a few drops of olive oil.

p.276

Pickled Mackerel, Cauliflower, and Lemon
Serves 6

Sweetened Lemon Skin Puree
10 lemons, halved
2,395 grams water
1,415 grams sugar
Freshly squeezed lemon juice

Juice the lemons and reserve the juice for another use. Place the juiced lemon skin halves in a pressure cooker with 1,000 grams of the water, seal the lid, and cook over high heat until it starts to steam, approximately 10 minutes. Decrease the heat to medium and cook for an additional 10 minutes. Remove the cooker from the heat and release the pressure. Drain the lemon skin halves in a colander and allow to cool slightly. Using a spoon, remove the lemon flesh and scrape out as much of the pith as possible and discard.

Combine 1,400 grams of the sugar with 1,100 grams of water in the pressure cooker and bring to the boil over high heat, uncovered. Stir until all of the sugar has dissolved. Once all of the sugar has dissolved, return the cooked lemon skin halves to the pressure cooker, seal the lid, and cook over high heat until it starts to steam, approximately 5 minutes. Decrease the heat to medium and cook for an additional 15 minutes. Remove the cooker from the heat and release the pressure. Drain the lemon skin halves in a colander set over a bowl, reserving the liquid.

Transfer the lemon skin halves to a Thermomix, add 50 grams of the water, and puree until smooth. Press the puree through a fine-mesh sieve set over a bowl.

Combine 250 grams of this lemon skin puree with the remaining 245 grams of water, 110 grams of the reserved cooking liquid, and the remaining 15 grams of sugar in a Thermomix and puree until smooth. Season with lemon juice and transfer to a squeeze bottle. (Note that this will yield more Sweetened Lemon Skin Puree than you need for this recipe.)

Pickled Mackerel
6 mackerel fillets
Fine-grain salt
430 grams water
80 grams sherry vinegar
60 grams red wine vinegar

Place the mackerel, skin side down, in a shallow dish and lightly sprinkle with salt. Place the dish in the fridge, uncovered, for 1 hour. Combine the water and the vinegars in a saucepan and cook over medium heat until it reaches 38°C (100°F), approximately 15 minutes. Remove the mackerel from the fridge and flip them so that the skin side is up. Pour the warmed brine over the mackerel, so that it is completely covered. Return to the fridge for 1 hour. Carefully lift the mackerel out of the brine and transfer to a parchment paper–lined tray, skin side down. Return to the fridge, uncovered, until the skin dries out slightly, approximately 1 hour. Place each mackerel, skin side down, onto a cutting board and slice it, lengthwise, into 3 even slices.

Cauliflower Crudité
1 large head cauliflower
Extra-virgin olive oil
Freshly squeezed lemon juice
Fine-grain salt

Cut away the florets of the cauliflower from the stem. Reserve the florets for Cauliflower Puree. Cut the stem lengthwise into 1-mm-thick slices. Dress the cauliflower with olive oil, lemon juice, and salt.

Cauliflower Puree

100 grams cauliflower florets reserved from
    Cauliflower Crudité
10 grams heavy cream
Fine-grain salt
Reduced White Wine (page 439)

Place the cauliflower in a single layer in a vacuum bag and
vacuum-seal it. Place the bag in a large saucepan with
enough water to cover and bring to boil over medium-high
heat. Boil the cauliflower until it is completely soft, 35 to
45 minutes. Transfer the cooked cauliflower, its juices, and
the cream to a Thermomix and puree until smooth. Press
the puree through a tamis lined with very fine-mesh cloth
set over a bowl. Season with salt and Reduced White
Wine and cool in the fridge. (Note that this will make more
Cauliflower Puree than you need for this recipe.)

Finishing

Sea salt

Using a squeeze bottle, make 3 horizontal lines of
Sweetened Lemon Skin Puree on the bottom half of the
plate. Place 3 slices of Pickled Mackerel to cover the
puree. Sprinkle the Pickled Mackerel with salt. Splatter a
large spoonful of Cauliflower Puree onto the top right of
the plate. To either side of the Cauliflower Puree, place
2 or 3 slices of Cauliflower Crudité, resting each crudité
on the other so that they stand up on the plate.

p.278

Cod, Kohlrabi, and Skins
Serves 6

Salted Cod
1 large fillet of cod
Fine-grain salt

Remove the skin of the fillet and reserve for Blanched Cod Skin. Separate the belly, tail, and loin pieces, reserving the belly and tail for another use. Sprinkle the loins with a thin, even layer of salt on both sides and place in a single layer on a parchment paper–lined tray. Keep in the fridge, uncovered, for at least 6 hours or overnight. Slice the cod loin crosswise, on a slight diagonal, into 1.5-cm-thick slices. (Note that you will have more Salted Cod than you need for this recipe.)

Blanched Cod Skin
Reserved skin from Salted Cod

Scrape all the flesh and scales off the skin with a knife and rinse well under running water. Blanch the skin in boiling salted water until softened, approximately 1 minute, then transfer to ice water to cool. Drain in a colander. Spread the skins out in a single layer on parchment paper and cool them, uncovered, in the fridge for 1 hour. Cut the skins into 6 cm by 2-cm pieces. (Note that you will have more Blanched Cod Skin than you need for this recipe.)

Cod Stock
Bones from 1 large cod, cut into 3 pieces

Rinse the bones several times in cold running water. Place in a saucepan with enough water to cover and bring to a boil over high heat. Decrease the heat to low and simmer for 20 minutes. Skim the foam from the surface. Remove the saucepan from the heat and allow to infuse for 20 minutes. Strain the stock through a superbag into another saucepan. Bring the stock to a boil over high heat and reduce it to about three-quarters of its original volume, 10 to 15 minutes. Transfer to an uncovered container and allow to cool in the fridge. (Note that you will have more Cod Stock than you need for this recipe.)

Salted Kohlrabi
1 large kohlrabi, peeled and trimmed
1.8 grams fine-grain salt

Slice the kohlrabi on a Japanese-style turning vegetable slicer, making the longest strips possible. Cut the kohlrabi strips into 10-cm lengths. Weigh out 120 grams of the kohlrabi slices and reserve the rest for another use. You should have at least 24 to 30 strips. Sprinkle the kohlrabi with the salt. Let stand for 15 minutes, until the salt draws out some of the liquid from the kohlrabi. Transfer the kohlrabi and their juices to a vacuum bag, in one neat pile, and vacuum-seal it. After 20 minutes, drain the kohlrabi in a colander.

Finishing
Mushroom Soy Sauce (page 440)
Sea salt
1 horseradish, peeled
Pear vinegar

For each serving, place 3 or 4 slices of Salted Cod in a single layer on the center of the plate. Brush on some Mushroom Soy Sauce and pour 2 spoonfuls of Cod Stock over the cod. Sprinkle with salt. Using a small knife, scrape 5 or 6 thin slivers of horseradish and place them on top of the cod. Place 4 or 5 pieces of Salted Kohlrabi on top of the cod, folded in half lengthwise. Place 3 strips of Blanched Cod Skin between the pieces of kohlrabi. Using a gas-powered kitchen torch, warm the Blanched Cod Skin for 2 seconds each, without causing any burning or charring. Sprinkle salt on the skin and finish with 5 sprays of pear vinegar.

White Onions, Crayfish, and Fennel
Serves 6

p.280

Blanched White Onion Shells
1 kilogram large white spring onions, peeled and
    halved lengthwise
1 kilogram 3% Salt Brine (page 438)

Remove all but 2 to 3 cm of the green tops of the
onions. Using your hands, separate the onion halves
into shells and sort all of the shells into three different
groups—small, medium, and large. Place each group
of onions into a separate vacuum bag, add one-
third of the Salt Brine to each, then vacuum-seal the
bags. Refrigerate overnight, then drain the onions in
a colander and blanch in boiling salted water until
softened and sweet, but not so soft that they don't
hold their shape anymore, approximately 1 minute for
the small onion shells and approximately 2 minutes
for the larger onion shells. Transfer to ice water to
cool. Once the onions are cooled, drain in a colander.
Slice the onion shells lengthwise into 3-mm strips, but
keep each onion shell intact by leaving approximately
0.5 cm of the tip uncut.

Diced Salted Fennel
1 large bulb of fennel, green tops trimmed and
    reserved
250 grams 3% Salt Brine (page 348)

Slice 1 cm off the bottom of the fennel and peel off
the two outer shells. Slice another 1 cm off the bottom
of the fennel and peel off the next two shells. Repeat
this process until all of the shells of the fennel have
been separated. Reserve the fennel trimmings and
the inner part of the fennel that does not separate
into shells for another use. Place the fennel into a
vacuum bag with the Salt Brine and vacuum-seal it.
Refrigerate overnight. Drain the fennel in a colander,
then cut into 3-mm pieces.

    Tear the leaves from the reserved green fennel tops
into 2- to 3-cm pieces, then finely chop the stems.

Sautéed Diced Onion
Vegetable oil
1 large new white onion, peeled and finely diced

Heat a sauté pan over medium-high heat and add
vegetable oil. Sauté the diced onions until soft,
translucent, and sweet, approximately 10 minutes. Stir
the onions frequently to prevent them from browning.

Crayfish
2 kilograms live crayfish
Vegetable oil
Freshly squeezed lemon juice
Fine-grain salt

Blanch the crayfish in boiling salted water very
quickly, just to kill them, approximately 10 seconds.
Transfer to ice water to cool. Once the crayfish are
cooled, drain in a colander. Remove the crayfish
claws, then separate the tails from the heads,
reserving the heads for later use. Bring another pot
of salted water to a boil and blanch the crayfish tails
for 1 minute, then the claws for 40 seconds. Transfer
to ice water to cool. Once the tails and claws are
cooled, drain in a colander. Using the back of a
knife or a nut cracker, gently crack the shells around
the crayfish tails and claws, just enough to be able
to peel them off. Peel the shells from the tails and
remove the claw meat from their shells. Finely dice
the cooked crayfish with a knife.

    Heat a sauté pan over high heat and add
vegetable oil. Sauté the heads of the crayfish until
browned, 6 to 8 minutes. Remove the pan from the
heat and cover it with a lid for 15 minutes. Set a very
fine-mesh cloth sieve over a bowl, put the crayfish
heads into a potato ricer, a few at a time, and crush
the heads to extract the juice. Allow the juice to strain
through the sieve into the bowl.

    In a bowl, mix the diced crayfish with the Diced
Salted Fennel, the Sautéed Diced Onion, and the
chopped fennel top stems and add enough of the
crayfish head juice to make a thick paste consistency.
Season with lemon juice and salt.

continued

Appendix

White Onions, Crayfish, and Fennel, continued

Cooked Onion Juice
Vegetable oil
1 large new white onion, peeled and roughly chopped

Preheat the oven to 70°C (160°F). Heat a sauté pan over medium-high heat and add vegetable oil. Sauté the chopped onions until soft, translucent, and sweet, approximately 10 minutes. Stir the onions frequently to prevent them from browning. Remove the pan from the heat and cover it with a lid for 15 minutes. Transfer the onions and their juices into an ovenproof bowl and seal tightly with cling film. Place the bowl in the oven for 1 to 2 hours. Remove the bowl from the oven and allow to cool slightly. Transfer the onions and their juices into a superbag set over a bowl and squeeze the onions to extract as much juice as possible. Discard the onions in the superbag. Cool the onion juice, covered, in the fridge.

Finishing
Fennel Puree, cold (page 410)
Fine-grain sea salt

Spoon 3 different-size piles of the crayfish mixture onto the plate in different places. Each of the piles should be different sizes corresponding to the sizes of the onion shells, small, medium, and large. Using a squeeze bottle, squeeze one large dot of Fennel Puree onto each of the piles. Place 2 pieces of fennel top leaves on top of the puree. Take a small Blanched White Onion Shell and tear off a slice. Place the slice around the small pile of crayfish. Tear off another slice and place it on the other side of the small pile of crayfish, making the tips meet and pointing off to one side. Keep on tearing off slices and placing it over the crayfish until it is completely covered and looks like a whole onion shell with a nice pointed tip. Do the same to the medium and large piles, with the corresponding-size Blanched White Onion Shells. Using a brush, brush a layer of Cooked Onion Juice onto each pile. Place 1 or 2 pieces of fennel top on each pile, tucking it between the slices of onion, and finish with a sprinkle of sea salt.

Turnips, Chervil, and Horseradish
Serves 6

Thick Butter Emulsion
250 grams unsalted butter, cut into cubes
250 grams boiling water
5 grams xantana

Combine the butter, boiling water, and xantana
in the Thermomix and process until emulsified,
approximately 2 minutes. (Note that this will make
more than you need for this recipe.)

Rehydrated Dehydrated Turnips
2 kilograms large turnips, peeled and trimmed
Thick Butter Emulsion, warmed
1 shallot, finely diced
1 bunch chervil, chopped
25 grams unsalted butter, cut into cubes
Freshly squeezed lemon juice
Fine-grain salt

Cut the turnips crosswise into 2-cm-wide slices.
Place the turnips in a single layer and dry at 65°C
(150°F) in a dehydrator. When they are completely
dried, transfer them to a large bowl, add enough
warm water to cover, and soak for 2 hours. Drain the
turnips in a colander and gently squeeze dry with your
hands. Slice the turnips into 1-cm strips.

 Blanch the turnip strips in boiling salted water
until the turnips are al dente, 1 to 2 minutes. Drain
the turnips in a colander. Transfer the turnips to a
saucepan, add the Thick Butter Emulsion, shallot,
and chervil, and stir over medium-high heat until
well mixed. Add the butter and stir until emulsified.
Season with lemon juice and salt.

Finishing
1 horseradish, peeled
12 grams black mustard seeds, toasted and
 slightly crushed

p.284

For each serving, place 3 large spoonfuls of
Rehydrated Dehydrated Turnips on the top quarter
of the plate, in a flat layer. Using a small knife,
scrape 8 or 9 pieces of horseradish and place them
on top of the turnips. Sprinkle with mustard seeds.

p.286

New Potatoes, Warm Berries, and Arugula
Serves 6

Arugula Sauce
45 grams fresh green sea lettuce, washed
210 grams arugula
30 grams water
15 grams Dijon mustard
50 grams pear vinegar, plus more for seasoning
325 grams vegetable oil, chilled
Fine-grain salt

Blanch the sea lettuce in boiling salted water until tender, 1 to 2 minutes, then transfer to ice water to cool. Drain in a colander and squeeze as dry as possible. Transfer the seaweed to a Thermomix, add the arugula, water, mustard, and vinegar, and puree until smooth. Decrease the speed to low and add the chilled oil in a fine stream. Press the emulsion through a fine-mesh sieve set over a bowl. Season with salt and pear vinegar.

Cooked New Potatoes
600 grams small new potatoes, scrubbed
1.5 kilograms Butter Emulsion (page 438)
Fine-grain salt
Green Sea Lettuce Powder (page 385)

Blanch the potatoes in boiling salted water until just cooked, but still slightly crunchy, 1 to 2 minutes, depending on the size. Transfer to ice water to cool, then drain in a colander. Put the Butter Emulsion in a saucepan and bring to a boil over medium-high heat. Add the blanched new potatoes and cook until they are warmed through, but not cooked further, approximately 1 minute. Using a sieve set over another saucepan, drain the potatoes, reserving the Butter Emulsion for further use. Season the potatoes with salt and sprinkle with Green Sea Lettuce Powder.

Finishing
Freshly squeezed lemon juice
24 Warm Unripe Strawberries (page 377)
Sea salt

In a saucepan, warm the Arugula Sauce over medium heat and season with lemon juice. For each serving, place a large spoonful of the Arugula Sauce in the center of a plate. Place 10 to 12 Cooked New Potatoes on top of the sauce, with the Green Sea Lettuce Powder side facing up. Place 3 or 4 Warm Unripe Strawberries, pointed side facing up, between the potatoes.

Potato, Seaweed, and Pecorino
Serves 6

Potato Noodles
1 kilogram large Marabel potatoes, peeled
1 kilogram 3% Salt Brine (page 438)
Clarified Butter (page 438), melted
40 grams Gracilaria seaweed, washed and julienned
Sea salt

Slice the potatoes on a Japanese turning vegetable slicer with the noodle attachment, making the longest noodles possible. As you cut the noodles, put them straight in a large bowl with the Salt Brine. Transfer the potatoes and the Salt Brine to a vacuum bag and vacuum-seal it. Keep in the fridge overnight. The following day, drain the potatoes in a colander, discarding the brine. Pull out 8 to 10 long potato noodle strands, bunch them together into one long line, and cut them into 50-cm lengths. Place the long bunch on a work surface and fold it in half crosswise. Brush the potatoes with Clarified Butter and place 4 small bundles of the julienned seaweed on top in different places. Using long tweezers, pinch the folded end of the line of potato noodles and tightly roll the noodles into a small bundle, then coil the bundle into a tight oval shape. Place the potatoes on parchment paper in a bamboo steaming basket. Repeat this process until you have 18 potato bundles. Place the steaming basket over a saucepan of boiling water over high heat and steam until the potatoes are just cooked, but not soft, approximately 3 minutes. Sprinkle the potatoes with salt.

p.288

Pecorino Sauce
125 grams Pecorino Romano cheese, cut into
    3-cm cubes
250 grams water
Fine-grain salt

Combine the cheese and the water in a Thermomix, set it to 60°C (140°F), and puree for 5 minutes until smooth and well combined. Season with salt. (Note that this makes more Pecorino Sauce than you will need for this recipe.)

Pickled Green Sea Lettuce
500 grams water
250 grams red wine vinegar
30 grams fresh green sea lettuce, washed

Preheat the oven to 180°C (355°F). Combine the water and red wine vinegar in a bowl. Dip the sea lettuce into the mixture for no more than 30 seconds, then place in a single layer on parchment paper. Place a baking sheet in the oven for 5 to 10 minutes, then transfer the parchment paper onto the hot baking sheet to warm but not cook the sea lettuce, approximately 1 minute.

Clarified Seaweed Butter
100 grams Clarified Butter (page 438)
5 grams Green Sea Lettuce Powder (page 385)

In a small saucepan, warm the Clarified Butter, then stir in the Green Sea Lettuce Powder. (Note that this will make more butter than you need for this recipe.)

Finishing

For each serving, place 3 bundles of Potato Noodles on a plate and top with 3 spoonfuls of the warmed Pecorino Sauce. Place 3 or 4 pieces of the warmed Pickled Green Sea Lettuce around the potato bundles and on the sauce. Drizzle with warmed Clarified Seaweed Butter.

p.290

Lettuce, Smoked Almond, and Olive Oil
Serves 6

Fermented Romaine Lettuce
3 small heads romaine lettuce, outer leaves removed
1 kilogram 3% Salt Brine (page 438)
30 grams Whey (page 438)
1 small horseradish, peeled and sliced

Halve the lettuce heads lengthwise and wash them carefully to remove all of the sand between the layers of leaves. Drain in a colander. Place the romaine lettuce in a glass jar or a food-grade plastic container and add the Salt Brine, Whey, and horseradish. Use a plate or something similar that fits inside the jar or container to weigh down the lettuce and horseradish to ensure that they are completely submerged in the liquid. Seal the jar or container with a lid fitted with an airlock. Place the jar out of direct sunlight, where the ambient room temperature is 16°C to 18°C (60°F to 64°F), to ferment for 5 or 6 days. The fermentation is complete when the structure of the lettuce breaks down, becomes soft, and tastes sour. Once fermented, you can seal the jar or container with a lid and store it in the fridge for up to 2 weeks.

Smoked Almond Sauce
40 grams Smoked Almond Milk (page 405)
10 grams reserved brine from Fermented Romaine Lettuce

In a saucepan, warm the smoked almond milk and the brine over medium heat slowly; do not boil.

Finishing
Freshly squeezed lemon juice
2 heads fresh romaine lettuce, darkest green leaves only, stems removed and leaves cut into chiffonade
Extra-virgin olive oil

Remove the Fermented Romaine Lettuce from the brine, reserving 500 grams of the brine. Cut the fermented lettuce in half lengthwise and then crosswise into 2-cm-thick pieces. In a saucepan, warm the reserved brine and the lettuce slowly over medium heat; do not boil. Drain in a sieve.

For each serving, place a large spoonful of the warmed lettuce in a pile in the center of the plate and spray with 2 sprays of lemon juice. Place 2 spoonfuls of the warmed Smoked Almond Sauce on top followed by a neatly placed pile of fresh lettuce chiffonade. Finish with a drizzle of olive oil.

Asparagus, Sunflower Seeds, and Mint
Serves 6

p.292

Fried Buckwheat
20 grams buckwheat groats
250 grams water
40 grams unsalted butter, melted
Fine-grain salt

In a large bowl, soak the buckwheat in the water overnight, covered in the fridge. The following day, drain the buckwheat in a colander and rinse under cold running water until the water runs clear. Allow to drain in the colander for 10 to 15 minutes. In a pan over medium heat, fry the buckwheat in the melted butter until golden brown, 10 to 15 minutes. Remove the buckwheat from the butter and drain on a layer of paper towels. Season with salt.

Pressure-Cooked Sunflower Seeds
100 grams raw sunflower seeds
1,500 grams water
1 kilogram Butter Emulsion (page 438)
Big handful of mint leaves, torn into halves
Extra-virgin olive oil
Fine-grain salt

In a large bowl, soak the sunflower seeds in 500 grams of the water for 30 minutes. Drain in a colander and transfer the seeds to a pressure cooker. Add the remaining 1,000 grams water, seal the lid, and cook over high heat until it starts to steam, approximately 10 minutes. When the pressure cooker starts steaming, decrease the heat to medium and cook for an additional 5 minutes. Remove the cooker from the heat and release the pressure. Drain the seeds in a colander and transfer to ice water to cool. While they are cooling, stir the seeds to allow the loose skins to float to the surface. With a fine-mesh sieve, remove the skins from the surface of the water and stir and remove the skins two or three more times until most of the skins have been removed. Once the seeds are cool, drain them in a colander.

The seeds should have some bite and texture, so it is best to cook the seeds the day before and refrigerate them overnight. Overnight, the seeds' structure will tighten and they become slightly firmer.

The following day, put the Butter Emulsion in a saucepan and bring to a boil over medium-high heat. Add the pressure-cooked sunflower seeds and cook until they are warmed through, but not cooked further, approximately 1 minute. Using a sieve set over another saucepan, drain the pressure-cooked sunflower seeds, reserving the Butter Emulsion. Mix the torn mint leaves in with the sunflower seeds and season with olive oil and salt.

Mint Puree
250 grams baby spinach
250 grams fresh mint leaves
2 ice cubes
300 grams cold water
Fine-grain salt

First, blanch the spinach in boiling salted water until tender, approximately 2 minutes, then transfer to ice water to cool. Next, blanch the mint in the boiling salted water until tender, approximately 6 minutes, then transfer to ice water to cool. Once the spinach and mint have cooled, drain in a colander and squeeze them with your hands, as dry as possible. In a Thermomix, puree the spinach, mint, ice cubes, and 150 grams of the cold water until smooth. You may need to add more cold water to ensure that the puree blends thoroughly, but be careful not to add too much, as it should not be runny. Press the puree through a tamis lined with very fine-mesh cloth into a bowl. The puree should hold a soft peak when spooned onto a plate. If the puree is too runny, pour it back into the tamis lined with very fine-mesh cloth and let it sit there, this time without pressing it through, which will allow some of the water to drip out until it reaches the desired consistency. Season with salt.

continued

399

Asparagus Rounds

550 grams medium to large green asparagus, tough
    ends trimmed
3 kilograms Butter Emulsion (page 438)
Fine-grain salt

To ensure that there is no sand on the asparagus, trim away the leaves on the asparagus stalks and wash well. Cut off the tips and set aside. Cut the stalks crosswise into 4-mm-thick rounds. Put the Butter Emulsion in a saucepan and bring to a boil over medium-high heat. Add the asparagus rounds and cook for 1 to 2 minutes, until tender but still crunchy. Using a sieve set over another saucepan, drain the asparagus, reserving the Butter Emulsion in the saucepan. Season the asparagus with salt. While the Butter Emulsion is still hot, add the asparagus tips and warm them through, 10 to 15 seconds. Drain in a colander and season with salt.

Finishing

12 mint leaves, torn into halves
75 grams Beurre Blanc (page 438), warmed
Lemon zest
Freshly squeezed lemon juice

For each serving, place an 8-cm ring mold in the center of a plate. In the center of the ring mold, put a spoonful of Mint Puree and place 2 torn mint leaves on top. Cover the Mint Puree and mint leaves with 3 spoonfuls of warmed Pressure-Cooked Sunflower Seeds, then sprinkle on a spoonful of the Fried Buckwheat. Fill in the rest of the ring mold with Asparagus Rounds, flattening the top of the pile with the back of a large spoon to even it out. Stick 2 asparagus tips on top, with the tips pointing upward and outward. Pour over 2 spoonfuls of warmed Beurre Blanc over the asparagus. Finish off with some fresh lemon zest on top and 2 sprays of lemon juice, then remove the ring molds carefully.

Jerusalem Artichoke, Quinoa, and Coffee
Serves 6

p.294

Roasted Jerusalem Artichoke Milk

100 grams Jerusalem artichokes, scrubbed and
    halved
5 grams vegetable oil
500 grams milk

Preheat the oven to 220°C (430°F). In a large bowl, coat the Jerusalem artichokes in vegetable oil. Place directly on the oven racks and bake until well caramelized and slightly charred, approximately 45 minutes. Allow the Jerusalem artichokes to cool, then place them in a vacuum bag with the milk and vacuum-seal it. Keep in the fridge for 2 or 3 days to infuse. Strain the milk through a fine-mesh strainer set over a bowl and discard the Jerusalem artichokes. (Note that this yields more milk than you'll need for this recipe.)

Puffed Quinoa

100 grams quinoa
1 kilogram vegetable oil

Cook the quinoa in boiling salted water until just cooked, approximately 12 minutes. Drain in a colander. Spread the cooked quinoa in a single layer and dry at 58°C (136°F) in the dehydrator until the outside surface of each quinoa grain is dried but the center is not, 3 to 5 hours.

In a saucepan, heat the vegetable oil over high heat until it reaches 200°C (400°F). Fry the dried quinoa until puffed and golden, 5 to 10 seconds. Drain the quinoa in a fine-mesh strainer, then transfer to a layer of paper towels.

Caramelized Yogurt
1 L yogurt
10 grams unsalted butter

In a saucepan, bring the yogurt and butter to a boil over medium-high heat, stirring occasionally. Boil the yogurt until it separates into curds and whey and keep the saucepan on medium-high heat until the whey reduces completely and the fat starts to caramelize the curds. Decrease the heat to medium and allow to caramelize evenly, stirring occasionally, approximately 2 hours. Strain the yogurt through a fine-mesh sieve set over a bowl and reserve the fat for another use. Transfer the yogurt to a layer of paper towels and place on trays in the dehydrator and dry overnight at 60°C (140°F). (Note that this yields more yogurt than you will need for the recipe.)

Roasted Jerusalem Artichoke Puree
650 grams Jerusalem artichokes, scrubbed and halved
55 grams vegetable oil
325 grams water
20 grams unsalted butter, cut into cubes

Preheat the oven to 220°C (430°F). In a large bowl, toss the Jerusalem artichokes in vegetable oil to coat. Place directly on the oven racks and bake until well caramelized and slightly charred, approximately 45 minutes. Allow the Jerusalem artichokes to cool, then place them in a single layer in a vacuum bag and vacuum-seal it. Place the bag in a large saucepan with enough water to cover and bring to a boil over medium-high heat. Boil the Jerusalem artichokes until they are completely soft, 35 to 45 minutes. Transfer the cooked Jerusalem artichokes, their juices, the 325 grams water, and the butter to a Thermomix and puree until smooth. Press the puree through a tamis lined with very fine-mesh cloth set over a bowl.

Aerated Roasted Jerusalem Artichoke Puree
100 grams baking potatoes, peeled
70 grams unsalted butter, cut into cubes
250 grams Roasted Jerusalem Artichoke Puree, warmed
100 grams Roasted Jerusalem Artichoke Milk, warmed

Preheat the oven to 180°C (175°F). Wrap the potatoes in aluminum foil with 20 grams of the butter and bake until completely soft, approximately 40 minutes. Transfer the cooked potatoes to a Thermomix, add the remaining 50 grams butter, the Roasted Jerusalem Artichoke Puree, and Roasted Jerusalem Artichoke Milk, and puree until smooth. Press the puree through fine-mesh sieve set over a bowl. Pour the puree into a siphon bottle and charge with two CO_2 cartridges. Shake the siphon until the puree is light and airy. Keep the siphon warm by placing it in a saucepan of water over low heat or in a water bath with an immersion circulator at 55°C (130°F).

Sautéed Crosnes
15 grams unsalted butter
90 grams crosnes, cleaned and cut into segments
Fine-grain salt

Melt the butter in a sauté pan over high heat until it starts to brown. Add the crosnes and sauté until just warmed through, approximately 1 minute. Season with salt.

Finishing
6 grams finely ground coffee

Siphon a 10-cm circle of the warm Aerated Roasted Jerusalem Artichoke Puree onto the center of a plate. Dot the foam with Sautéed Crosnes. Sprinkle on the Puffed Quinoa, Caramelized Yogurt, and coffee on top of the puree.

Sunflower Seeds, Kornly, and Pine
Serves 6

p.296

Sunflower Seed Puree
85 grams raw sunflower seeds

70 grams water

95 grams Reduced White Wine (page 439)

85 grams unsalted butter, melted

70 grams vegetable oil

Combine the sunflower seeds, water, and Reduced White Wine in a Thermomix and puree until smooth. Decrease the speed to low and add the melted butter in a fine stream. Increase the speed to maximum and blend for an additional 10 minutes, until all of the butter has emulsified. Decrease the speed to low and add the oil in a fine stream. Press the puree through a tamis lined with very fine-mesh cloth set over a bowl. (Note that this yields more puree than you will need for this recipe.)

Finishing
1.5 grams Butter Emulsion (page 438)

400 grams Pressure-Cooked Sunflower Seeds (page 399)

60 grams Beurre Blanc (page 438), warmed

Fine-grain salt

Freshly squeezed lemon juice

30 grams Kornly cheese

12 grams fresh pine shoots, picked off their stems

Put the Butter Emulsion in a saucepan and bring to a boil over medium-high heat. Add the Pressure-Cooked Sunflower Seeds and cook until warmed through but not cooked, approximately 1 minute. Using a sieve set over another saucepan, strain the sunflower seeds and reserve the Butter Emulsion for another use. In a saucepan, whisk the Beurre Blanc with the Sunflower Seed Puree over medium heat until smooth. Add the warmed Pressure-Cooked Sunflower Seeds and season with salt and lemon juice. For each serving, place a large spoonful of the sunflower seed mixture in the center of the plate and then shake the plate to flatten it out. Finely grate some Kornly cheese over the seeds and finish with a sprinkle of pine shoots.

Baked Potato Puree (Version 1)
Serves 6

p.298

Roasted Potato Milk
400 grams reserved roasted potato skins from
    Roasted Potato Puree
1 L milk

In the restaurant, we always save the potato skins from making the Roasted Potato Puree (below) so that we can make Roasted Potato Milk the next day. After we scoop out the cooked potato for the puree, we put the skins back in the oven until they are golden and crispy, 10 to 15 minutes. Allow the skins to cool to room temperature. Place the potato skins with the milk in a vacuum bag vacuum-seal, and allow to infuse in the fridge for 24 hours. Strain the milk through a fine-mesh sieve set over a bowl.

Roasted Potato Puree
1 kilogram large baking potatoes, scrubbed
500 grams Roasted Potato Milk
250 grams unsalted butter, cut into cubes
Fine-grain salt

Preheat the oven to 220°C (428°F). Place the potatoes on a baking sheet and bake until completely soft on the inside and crispy on the outside, approximately 1 hour. Meanwhile, in a saucepan, warm the Roasted Potato Milk and the butter over medium-high heat, until the butter is melted and the milk is hot, approximately 15 minutes. Using a kitchen towel to protect your hand from the heat of the potatoes, pierce each potato with a spoon, then break it in half. Scoop out the flesh and transfer to a bain-marie to keep it warm. Return the empty baked potato skins to the baking sheet and bake until crispy and golden brown, 10 to 15 minutes. Reserve these potato skins

to make Roasted Potato Milk for another day. Pour half of the warm Roasted Potato Milk mixture into the potatoes in the bain-marie and stir, breaking up any large chunks, making a chunky puree. Place a tamis over a second bain-marie and press the puree through the tamis. Stir in more of the warm potato milk mixture until the puree is the consistency of a thick pancake batter. Clean the first bain-marie. Press the puree, a second time, but through a fine-mesh sieve, into a the bain-marie. Season with salt and add more warm Roasted Potato Milk mixture until it becomes a smooth, thick puree. When stirring the puree, it is important not to stir too vigorously, since this will make the puree gummy. Instead, you should fold the puree slowly.

Thickened Buttermilk
150 grams buttermilk at room temperature
0.15 grams xantana

Blend the buttermilk and xantana together in the Thermomix until well mixed, approximately 15 seconds.

Finishing
30 grams dried black olives, crushed
30 grams Caramelized Buttermilk Powder (page 425)

For each serving, place a large spoonful of the Roasted Potato Puree on a shallow serving bowl, off center and to the left. Pour Thickened Buttermilk to the right of the puree. Sprinkle the black olives and Caramelized Buttermilk Powder to the left side of the puree.

p.298

Baked Potato Puree (Version 2)
Serves 6

Dried Bread Crumbs
1 loaf of day-old Sourdough Bread (page 370)

Cut off the crust and then cut the bread into 1-cm pieces. Place in a single layer and dry overnight at 65°C (150°F) in the dehydrator. The following day, transfer the bread to a Thermomix and process until it becomes a coarse powder.

Dried Citrus
1 small blood orange
1 small grapefruit
1 small orange
1 mandarin
6 kumquats, quartered
50 grams Brown Butter (page 438)
Freshly squeezed lemon juice

With a knife, trim the top and bottom of the blood orange. Set the blood orange on one end and cut away the peel. Cut the blood orange in half lengthwise, then roughly dice each half into 8 to 10 pieces, removing any seeds. Repeat the process with the grapefruit and orange. Peel the mandarin by hand, break apart the segments, and remove any seeds. Place the blood orange, grapefruit, orange, mandarin, and kumquats in a single layer and dry at 58°C (136°F) in the dehydrator. Remove the fruit when they are still chewy and not completely crispy and dried, 6 to 8 hours. In a saucepan, warm the Brown Butter over medium heat, add the dried fruits, and heat until they are just warmed through, 30 to 60 seconds. Season with lemon juice.

Finishing
420 grams Roasted Potato Puree (page 403), warmed

For each serving, place a large spoonful of the Roasted Potato Puree on the plate, off-center and to the left. Spread out some warmed Dried Citrus to the right of the puree and spoon over some of the Brown Butter. Sprinkle the Dried Bread Crumbs to the left of the puree.

Barley, Cauliflower, and Black Trumpet
Serves 6

p.300

Smoked Almonds and Smoked Almond Milk
Smoke powder
200 grams blanched almonds, peeled
100 grams water

Heat a saucepan with a thin layer of smoke powder in the bottom over high heat until it starts to smoke, 2 to 3 minutes. Place the almonds in a sieve and then position the sieve over the saucepan and cover with a lid. Keep the saucepan on high heat for approximately 30 seconds, until the whole saucepan fills with smoke. Remove the covered saucepan from the heat and let the almonds infuse with the smoke powder for 10 minutes, stirring the almonds around in the sieve occasionally. Repeat this process two or three more times, adding more smoke powder if it burns up, until the almonds are golden and smoky. Allow to cool.

Reserve 100 grams of the smoked almonds for Toasted Smoked Almonds. In a large bowl, soak the remaining 100 grams smoked almonds in the water overnight, covered in the fridge. The following day, transfer the almonds and water to a Thermomix and puree until smooth. Transfer the puree to a superbag and squeeze the puree into a bowl, extracting as much smoked almond milk as possible. Reserve the solids for another use and store the almond milk in the fridge.

Toasted Smoked Almonds
100 grams Smoked Almonds reserved from Smoked Almonds and Smoked Almond Milk
10 grams water
3.5 grams fine-grain salt

Preheat the oven to 150°C (300°F). Mix the Smoked Almonds with the water and salt and bake until golden and mostly dried, approximately 25 minutes. Decrease the heat to 80°C (175°F) and bake until completely dried and crunchy, 3 to 5 hours. (Note that this yields more almonds than you need for this recipe.)

Barley Porridge
600 grams water
80 grams rolled barley flakes
55 grams unsalted butter, cut into cubes
Fine-grain salt
Apple cider
Smoked Almond Milk

In a saucepan, bring 400 grams of the water to a boil. Reduce the heat to medium, add the barley, and cook, stirring every 5 minutes, for approximately 45 minutes. If the barley starts to look too dry, add up to 200 grams more water. After 45 minutes, the consistency should be fairly smooth and it should look like a liquid porridge. Stir in the butter, then remove from the heat and season with salt, apple cider, and Smoked Almond Milk.

Finishing
12 Cauliflower Stem Pieces (page 417), warmed in Butter Emulsion (page 438)
150 grams Cauliflower Rice (page 417), warmed in Butter Emulsion (page 438)
Fine-grain sea salt
9 Pickled Black Trumpet Mushrooms (page 440), torn into halves and warmed in Butter Emulsion (page 438)
Black Trumpet Mushroom Powder (page 440)

For each serving, place 3 spoonfuls of Barley Porridge on the center of the plate and flatten it out with the back of a spoon into a wide circle. Season the Cauliflower Stem Pieces and the Cauliflower Rice with salt. Place 2 Cauliflower Stem Pieces on top of the porridge and then 4 spoonfuls of the Cauliflower Rice in an even layer. Place 3 Toasted Smoked Almonds and 3 pieces of Pickled Black Trumpet Mushroom on top of the Cauliflower Rice. Sprinkle with Black Trumpet Mushroom Powder.

Carrot, Elderflower, and Sesame
Serves 6

p.304

Cooked and Dried Sesame Seeds
100 grams sesame seeds
500 grams 3% Salt Brine (page 348)

Place the sesame seeds and Salt Brine in a pressure cooker, seal the lid, and cook over high heat until it starts to steam, approximately 10 minutes. Decrease the heat to medium and cook for 30 minutes more. Remove the cooker from the heat and release the pressure. Drain the seeds in a fine-mesh strainer and transfer to ice water to cool. Once the seeds are cool, drain them again. Reserve half of the cooked sesame seeds for finishing. Place the remaining half of the cooked seeds in a single layer and dry overnight at 60°C (140°F) in the dehydrator. (Note that this makes more sesame seeds than you will need for this recipe.)

Dried Carrot Sheets
1 kilogram large, thick carrots, peeled and trimmed

Cut the carrots crosswise into 8- to 10-cm lengths so that they will fit into a Japanese-style turning vegetable slicer. Slice the carrots into the longest strips possible. Cut the carrot strips into pieces 15 to 20 cm long, then place in a single layer and dry overnight at 65°C (150°F) in the dehydrator.

Carrot Sauce
120 grams carrots, peeled and trimmed
45 grams fresh carrot juice, from peeled and trimmed carrots
75 grams white wine, preferably a chenin blanc or similar wine

Place the carrots in a single layer in a vacuum bag and vacuum-seal it. Place the bag in a large saucepan with enough water to cover and bring to a boil over medium-high heat. Boil the carrots until they are completely soft, 35 to 45 minutes. Transfer the cooked carrots, their juices, and the fresh carrot juice to a Thermomix and puree until smooth. In a small saucepan, bring the white wine to a boil over high heat and continue to boil until the alcohol flavor is gone, 3 to 5 minutes. Add the wine to the puree and blend to combine.

Sesame Cream
200 grams white sesame seeds
200 grams water

Combine the sesame seeds and water in a Thermomix and puree until smooth. Transfer the puree to a superbag set over a bowl and squeeze the puree to extract as much of the sesame cream as possible. Discard the solids in the superbag.

Reduced Carrot Juice
2 kilograms carrots, peeled and trimmed

Juice the carrots in a juicer and strain. In a saucepan, bring the carrot juice to a boil over medium-high heat. Decrease the heat to medium and simmer, occasionally skimming the foam from the surface, until the juice has reduced by two-thirds, 30 to 45 minutes.

Finishing
200 grams Reduced Carrot Juice
50 grams unsalted butter, cut into cubes
Fine-grain salt
Elderflower vinegar, reserved from Pickled Elderflowers (page 440)
10 bunches of Pickled Elderflowers (page 440), tender small stems and flower petals only
20 grams Cooked Sesame Seeds
20 grams Dried Sesame Seeds
Sea salt

In a saucepan, warm the Reduced Carrot Juice over medium heat and whisk in the butter until emulsified. Bring a large pot of salted water to a boil and cook the Dried Carrot Sheets until chewy but not soft, 15 to 25 seconds. Drain in a colander and add the carrot sheets to the carrot juice mixture and stir to glaze. Season with fine-grain salt and elderflower vinegar. Toss in the Pickled Elderflower stems and petals and the Cooked and Dried Sesame Seeds. Shape the Dried Carrot Sheets into tight bundles.

For each serving, place a large spoonful of warm Carrot Sauce in the center of a plate. Cover the sauce with a sprinkle of Cooked and Dried Sesame Seeds. To the bottom right of the Carrot Sauce, place a spoonful of the Sesame Cream. Place the Dried Carrot Sheet bundle on top of the carrot sauce. Sprinkle with sea salt and finish with 2 sprays of elderflower vinegar.

Charred Cucumber and Fermented Juice

Serves 6

Fermented Cucumber

3 large cucumbers, peeled, trimmed, and quartered
   lengthwise
3 kilograms 5% Salt Brine (page 438)
90 grams Whey (page 438)
35 grams horseradish, peeled and sliced lengthwise
   into 3-mm-thick pieces
25 grams garlic cloves, peeled

Using a knife, remove the seeds from each cucumber
quarter, reserving the seeds for the Salted Cucumber
Seeds. Place the cucumber quarters in a glass jar
or a food-grade plastic container and add the Salt
Brine, Whey, horseradish, and garlic. Use a plate or
weight to weigh down the cucumbers to ensure that
they are completely submerged in the liquid. Seal
the jar or container with a lid fitted with an airlock.
Place the jar out of direct sunlight, where the ambient
room temperature is 16°C to 18°C (60°F to 64°F), to
ferment for 5 or 6 days. The fermentation is complete
when the structure of the cucumber breaks down,
becomes soft, and tastes sour. Once fermented, you
can seal the jar or container with a lid and store it in
the fridge for up to 2 weeks.

Tapioca

120 grams tapioca pearls

Bring a large pot of lightly salted water to a boil.
Add the tapioca pearls and cook for 14 minutes,
until the pearls are clear all the way through. Drain in
a colander and submerge in ice water to cool. Once
the tapioca pearls are cool, drain in a colander.

Salted Cucumber Seeds

30 grams reserved cucumber seeds from Fermented
   Cucumber
1.5 grams fine-grain salt

p.306

Cut the reserved cucumber seeds crosswise into
5-mm-thick pieces. Mix them well with the salt.

Finishing

6 large fresh cucumbers, washed and trimmed

Remove the Fermented Cucumber from the brine,
reserving 100 grams of the brine. Cut the Fermented
Cucumber into 5-mm pieces. Cut the fresh cucumbers
lengthwise into 1-mm slices on a mandoline. In a
saucepan, warm but do not cook the Fermented
Cucumber, Salted Cucumber Seeds, Tapioca, and
the reserved brine over medium heat.

   For each serving, place 3 large spoonfuls of the
warmed mixture in the bottom of a shallow bowl.
Arrange the fresh cucumber slices on top, skin side
facing up, in a wavy and curly pattern. Using a gas-
powered kitchen torch, evenly char the exposed skin
of the cucumber slices.

p.308

Romaine, Egg Yolk, and Nettles
Serves 6

Poached Romaine
3 heads romaine lettuce, outer leaves removed
90 grams unsalted butter, cut into cubes

Place the romaine with the butter in a single layer in a vacuum bag and vacuum-seal it. Cook them in an immersion circulator at 68°C (154°F) for 18 minutes. Remove the romaine from the bag. Cut each head in half lengthwise.

Nettle Sauce
500 grams stinging nettles, washed
2 ice cubes
300 grams cold water
Reduced White Wine (page 439)
Fine-grain salt
Freshly squeezed lemon juice

Blanch the nettles in boiling salted water until tender, approximately 2 minutes, then transfer to ice water to cool. Drain the nettles in a colander and squeeze them as dry as possible. In a Thermomix, puree the nettles, ice cubes, and 150 grams of the cold water in a Thermomix until smooth. You may need to add up to 150 grams more cold water to ensure that the puree blends thoroughly, but be careful not to add too much, as it should not be runny. Press the puree through a tamis lined with very fine-mesh cloth set over a bowl. Season with Reduced White Wine and salt. In a saucepan, warm the puree over medium heat and season with lemon juice.

Finishing
6 Salt-Cured Egg Yolks (page 372)
50 grams dried black olives, crushed into pieces

For each serving, finely grate 1 Salt-Cured Egg Yolk onto the cut side of each Poached Romaine half, covering the romaine in a thin, even layer. Sprinkle some dried olives on top. Place the romaine on the plate and pour warmed Nettle Sauce to the right of the romaine.

Enoki, Kelp, and Seaweed
Serves 6

p.310

Mushroom and Kelp Broth
1 kilogram white button mushrooms, cleaned
30 grams fine-grain salt
12 grams dried kelp, rinsed
Reduced White Wine (page 439)
Mushroom Soy Sauce (page 440)

Cut the mushrooms into 1-mm slices on a mandoline. Place the mushrooms in a glass jar or a food-grade plastic container with the salt and mix well. Use a plate or something similar that fits inside the jar or container to weigh down the mushrooms to ensure that they are completely submerged in their own liquid. Seal the jar or container with a lid fitted with an airlock. Place the jar out of direct sunlight, where the ambient room temperature is 16°C to 18°C (60°F to 64°F), to ferment for 3 or 4 days. The fermentation is complete when the structure of the mushrooms has broken down, becomes soft, and tastes sour. Once fermented, strain the juice from the mushrooms through a fine-mesh sieve set over a bowl. Transfer the drained mushrooms to a superbag set over a bowl and squeeze as much liquid out as possible. Combine the mushroom liquids and discard the mushrooms.

Transfer 600 grams of the mushroom liquid to a vacuum bag with the kelp and vacuum-seal it. Cook the kelp in an immersion circulator at 60°C (140°F) for 1 hour. Strain through a fine-mesh sieve set over a bowl. Transfer the bouillon to a saucepan and warm over medium-high heat. Season with Reduced White Wine and Mushroom Soy Sauce. If the broth tastes too strong, add some water.

Steamed Enoki Mushrooms
600 grams enoki mushrooms
Pear vinegar
Mushroom Soy Sauce (page 440)
Fine-grain salt

Fit a saucepan pan with a bamboo steamer basket, fill with water, and bring to a boil over high heat. Place the enoki mushrooms in 6 bunches in the bamboo steamer. Steam until just cooked and slightly softened, approximately 1 minute, then remove from the steamer. Finish with sprays of pear vinegar and sprays of mushroom soy sauce. Sprinkle salt on the mushrooms.

Finishing
20 grams fresh green sea lettuce, washed
30 St. John's Wort leaves
20 purslane leaves
40 beach mustard leaves
6 beach mustard flowers
Green Sea Lettuce Powder (page 385)

For each serving, place 2 or 3 pieces of fresh green sea lettuce on the right side of a serving bowl. Place 5 St. John's Wort leaves, 3 or 4 purslane leaves, 5 or 6 mustard leaves, and 1 beach mustard flower around the seaweed. Place 1 bunch of Steamed Enoki Mushrooms on the left side of the plate, with the caps pointing left. Sprinkle the mushrooms with Green Sea Lettuce Powder. Serve the Mushroom and Kelp broth on the side to pour over the dish.

Fennel, Smoked Almond, and Parsley
Serves 6

p.312

Salted Fennel
3 large fennel bulbs or 24 small fennel side shoots
500 grams 3% Salt Brine (page 438)
3 kilograms Butter Emulsion (page 438)
Fine-grain salt

If you are using fennel bulbs, cut them in half lengthwise and separate them into layers. Place the fennel layers or fennel side shoots in a vacuum bag with the Salt Brine and vacuum-seal it. Store in the fridge for up to 6 hours, then drain in a colander. Put the Butter Emulsion in a saucepan and bring to a boil over medium-high heat. Add the fennel and cook until they are just cooked, but still slightly crunchy, 1 to 2 minutes. Using a sieve set over another saucepan, drain the fennel, reserving the Butter Emulsion for another use. Season with salt.

Fennel Puree
3 large fennel bulbs, roughly chopped
50 grams unsalted butter, cut into cubes
200 grams water
Reduced White Wine (page 439)
Fine-grain salt

Place the fennel in a single layer in a vacuum bag and vacuum-seal it. Place the bag in a large saucepan with enough water to cover and bring to a boil over medium-high heat. Boil the fennel until it is completely soft, 35 to 45 minutes. Transfer the cooked fennel, its juices, the butter, and 100 grams of the water to a Thermomix and puree until smooth. You may need to add up to 100 grams more water to ensure that the puree blends thoroughly, but be careful not to add too much, as it should not be runny. Press the puree through a tamis lined with very fine-mesh cloth into a bowl. The puree should hold a soft peak when spooned onto a plate. If the puree is too runny, pour it back into the sieve and let it sit there, this time without pressing it through, allowing some of the water to drip out until it reaches the desired consistency. Season with Reduced White Wine and salt. Keep warm.

Parsley Puree
250 grams baby spinach leaves
250 grams parsley leaves
2 ice cubes
300 grams cold water
Fine-grain salt

First, blanch the spinach in boiling salted water until tender, approximately 2 minutes, then transfer to ice water to cool. Next, blanch the parsley until tender, approximately 6 minutes, then transfer to ice water to cool. Once the spinach and parsley have cooled, drain in a colander and squeeze them as dry as possible. In a Thermomix, puree the spinach, parsley, ice cubes, and 150 grams of the cold water until smooth. You may need to add up to 150 grams more cold water to ensure that the puree blends thoroughly, but be careful not to add too much, as it should not be runny. Press the puree through a tamis lined with very fine-mesh cloth set over a bowl. The puree should hold a soft peak when spooned onto a plate. If the puree is too runny, pour it back into the sieve and let it sit there, this time without pressing it through, to allow some of the water to drip out until it reaches the desired consistency. Season with salt and keep in the fridge. (Note that this yields more puree than you will need for the recipe.)

Finishing
60 grams Smoked Almond Milk (page 405), warmed

For each serving, place a large spoonful of Fennel Puree on the plate and flatten it out with the back of a spoon. Splash a spoonful of Parsley Puree on top of the Fennel Puree. Place the Salted Fennel to the right of the purees and spoon over the warmed Smoked Almond Milk.

Dried Zucchini and Bitter Leaves
Serves 6

Dried Zucchini
6 large zucchini
3 kilograms Butter Emulsion (page 438)
Fine-grain salt

Peel the zucchini and reserve the peels for the
Mixed Green Powder. Place the zucchini in a single
layer and dry at 50°C (122°F) in the dehydrator for
approximately 6 hours, until semi-dried. Remove
the zucchini when the outer layer has dried to a
leathery texture and the flesh feels soft on the outside
but still firm on the inside. In a saucepan, bring the
butter emulsion to a boil over medium-high heat.
Using a very thin skewer, poke a lot of holes all over
the zucchini, then place it in the Butter Emulsion.
Reduce the heat to medium-low and simmer until the
zucchini are completely warmed through and plump,
approximately 25 minutes. Remove the zucchini from
the Butter Emulsion and drain on a layer of paper
towels. Sprinkle with salt.

Mixed Green Powder
50 grams reserved zucchini peels from Dried Zucchini
25 grams purslane stems
25 grams garden sorrel stems
40 grams Green Sea Lettuce Powder (page 385)

Place the zucchini peels, purslane stems, and
sorrel stems in a single layer and dry overnight at
65°C (150°F) in the dehydrator. The following day,
transfer to a Thermomix, add the Green Sea Lettuce
Powder, and process until it becomes a fine powder.
Sift the powder through a fine-mesh strainer. (Note
that this makes more powder than you'll need for
the recipe.)

Bitter Greens
Vegetable oil
50 grams Swiss chard leaves, cut into 4- to
    5-cm pieces
50 grams beet leaves, cut into 4- to 5-cm pieces
240 grams baby spinach leaves
50 grams red amaranth leaves
30 grams radicchio leaves, cut into 4- to 5-cm pieces
15 grams unsalted butter, cut into cubes
Freshly squeezed lemon juice
Fine-grain salt

p.314

In a large pan, heat a little vegetable oil over high heat.
When the pan is very hot, add the Swiss chard and
beet leaves and fry for 30 seconds. Add the spinach,
amaranth, and radicchio and fry for 30 seconds, then
add the butter. When all the leaves are softened and
just cooked, transfer the greens to a bowl and season
with lemon juice and salt.

Acidic Greens
24 small baby spinach leaves
24 purslane leaves
18 small garden sorrel leaves
18 small French sorrel leaves
12 red oxalis leaves
24 dragon's head leaves
12 arugula leaves
Extra-virgin olive oil
Freshly squeezed lemon juice
Fine-grain salt

In a large bowl, combine the spinach, purslane, the
sorrels, oxalis, dragon's head, and arugula. Dress with
olive oil, lemon juice, and salt.

Finishing

Place the Dried Zucchini on a baking tray and
sprinkle each one with the Mixed Green Powder to
cover one side completely. For each serving, place a
zucchini on the plate, off-center and to the right. To
the left of the zucchini, spread out the Bitter Greens
and Acidic Greens.

Fried Salsify and Bergamot

Serves 6

p.316

Salsify Puree

1 kilogram salsify, peeled and trimmed
100 grams water
50 grams unsalted butter, cut into cubes
Reduced White Wine (page 439)
Fine-grain salt

Place the salsify in a single layer in a vacuum bag and vacuum-seal it. Place the bag in a large saucepan with enough water to cover and bring to a boil over medium-high heat. Boil the salsify until they are completely soft, 35 to 45 minutes. Transfer the cooked salsify, their juices, and the water to a Thermomix and puree until smooth. Blend in the butter, cube by cube, until emulsified. Press the puree through a tamis lined with very fine-mesh cloth into a bowl. Season with Reduced White Wine and salt. (Note that this yields more puree than you will need for the recipe.)

Fried Salsify

24 salsify, scrubbed well and trimmed
3 kilograms vegetable oil
Brown Butter (page 438), warmed
Freshly squeezed bergamot juice
Fine-grain salt

In a wide shallow pot, heat the vegetable oil over high heat until it reaches 160°C (320°F). Fry 6 to 8 salsify at a time until they are cooked all the way through and the center of the salsify is soft, 12 to 15 minutes. Drain on a layer of paper towels and allow to cool. Peel small pieces of the skin off by pinching off the skin in different places all over the salsify, leaving about half of the salsify unpeeled. Break each salsify crosswise into halves. Heat the same oil until it reaches 200°C (400°F). Fry the salsify again until warmed through and caramelized on the outside, 10 to 20 seconds. Drain on a layer of paper towels, then transfer to a bowl and dress with the warmed Brown Butter and bergamot juice. Season with salt.

Bergamot Puree

325 grams skins from Salted Bergamot (page 440),
    rinsed well, pith and flesh removed
75 grams water
20 grams freshly squeezed lemon juice

Combine the bergamot skins, water, and lemon juice in a Thermomix and puree until smooth. Press the puree through a fine mesh strainer into a bowl. (Note that this yields more puree than you will need for the recipe.)

Finishing

120 grams Beurre Blanc (page 438), warmed
Freshly squeezed bergamot juice

For each serving, place a spoonful of the warm Salsify Puree on the plate, slightly off-center to the bottom right. Place 6 to 8 Fried Salsify pieces to the right of the puree, each one pointing in a slightly different direction from the others. Whisk a large spoonful of the Bergamot Puree into the warmed Beurre Blanc, season with a splash of bergamot juice, and pour a spoonful onto the center of the plate.

Salted Carrot and Oxalis "Béarnaise"

Serves 6

Salted Carrot Steak
1 kilogram purple carrots, peeled and trimmed
8 grams fine-grain salt
Vegetable oil
100 grams unsalted butter, cut into cubes
12 cloves garlic, unpeeled and roughly crushed

Aerated Béarnaise
40 grams water
0.04 gram xantana
120 grams egg yolks
20 grams egg whites
25 grams apple cider vinegar

p.318

Cut the carrots lengthwise into 2-mm slices on a mandoline. Reserve the first few slices for another use, since they will not be wide enough to use in the Carrot Steak. Take 800 grams of the carrot slices and sprinkle on the salt. Let stand for 15 minutes, until the salt softens the carrot slices, for approximately 5 minutes. Then mix the carrots and salt thoroughly with your hands. Transfer the carrots to a vacuum bag and vacuum-seal it. Place in the fridge for 20 minutes, then drain the carrot slices in a colander.

Stack 130 grams of carrot slices on top of each other, starting with a large slice. Continue to stack the slices until you make an even, oblong-shaped pile. Starting from one end of the stack, roll the carrot slices tightly into a round and secure with butcher's twine. Repeat the process until you have 6 carrot steaks.

Heat a large pan over high heat and add a little vegetable oil. Place the carrot steaks in the pan and cook for approximately 2 minutes. Add the butter and garlic and cook, basting every minute, until the bottom of each carrot steak is charred, approximately 5 minutes. When the garlic cloves begin to blacken, transfer 2 cloves to the top of each carrot steak to prevent them from becoming bitter. Decrease the heat to medium and continue cooking and basting every few minutes until the carrot steak has softened the whole way through, 40 to 45 minutes. When basting the carrots, increase the heat to high to make sure the butter is foaming, then lower it to medium to cook through.

Once cooked, carefully remove the carrot steaks from the pan, then drain on paper towels. Allow to rest for 2 or 3 minutes. Cut the butcher's twine and discard. Cut each carrot steak in half crosswise.

Combine all the ingredients together in a Thermomix and process on high speed until it reaches 65°C (150°F), approximately 15 minutes. Pour the béarnaise into a siphon bottle and charge with two CO_2 cartridges. Shake the siphon until the béarnaise is light airy. Keep the béarnaise warm in the siphon by placing it in a 56°C (132°F) water bath for up to 45 minutes.

Finishing
Sea salt
2 bunches oxalis, leaves picked and stems finely chopped

For each serving, place two halves of 1 Carrot Steak on the left side the plate, with the cut sides facing up. Sprinkle with sea salt. Shake the siphon and check that it is still light and airy. Siphon the warmed Aerated Béarnaise into a small bowl alongside the plate and sprinkle with oxalis stems and leaves.

413

Pork from Hindsholm and Rye
Serves 6

p.322

Sprouted Rye
100 grams whole rye grains, rinsed well

In a large bowl, soak the rye in cold water, covered, overnight at room temperature. The following day, drain in a colander, then spread it out in a single layer on a transparent tray or container, cover it with plastic wrap, and poke some holes in the plastic wrap. Put the tray in a warm place near a window that gets a lot of sunlight for 1 to 3 days. Rinse the rye in a large bowl of cold water, drain in a colander, and return to a clean transparent tray in a single layer, every morning and evening until each the rye grains have a sprout approximately 2 to 3 mm in length coming out of it. Every second time that you rinse the rye, add 2 drops of white vinegar to the rinsing water. When all the rye has sprouted, drain on a layer of paper towels.

Malted Buckwheat
50 grams buckwheat groats
White vinegar

In a large bowl, soak the buckwheat in cold water, covered, for 1 hour at room temperature, then rinse twice in a large bowl filled with water to remove the starch. Drain in a colander, then spread it out in a single layer on a transparent tray or container, cover it with plastic wrap, and poke some holes in the plastic wrap. Put the tray in a warm place near a window that gets a lot of sunlight for 1 to 3 days. Rinse the buckwheat in a large bowl of cold water, drain in a colander, and return to a clean transparent tray in a single layer, every morning and evening until all the buckwheat has sprouted. Every second time that you rinse the buckwheat, add 2 drops of white vinegar to the rinsing water. When all the buckwheat has sprouted, place in a single layer and dry at 65°C (150°F) in a dehydrator.

Sous-Vide Pork Shoulder or Neck
500-gram piece Hindsholm pork shoulder or neck, skinned
7.5 grams fine-grain salt
Sea salt

Sprinkle the pork with fine-grain salt, place in a vacuum bag, and vacuum-seal it. Cook the pork in an immersion circulator at 55°C (130°F) for 2¹/₂ hours. Remove the pork from the bag and pat dry with paper towels. With a knife, score the pork's fat with a crosshatch pattern. Place the pork, fat side down, in a cold sauté pan over medium heat and cook slowly until the fat has rendered slightly and becomes crispy, approximately 10 minutes. Increase the heat to high and continue cooking the fat side until it is golden brown, approximately 3 minutes. Then sear the meat on all sides until evenly browned. Remove the pork from the pan, transfer it to a rack, and let rest for 5 to 10 minutes. Cut the meat into 1-cm slices and sprinkle with sea salt.

Pork Fat and Cracklings
2 kilogram skinless pork fat

Grind the pork fat with a meat grinder and put it in a saucepan over low heat. Allow the fat to slowly render, stirring occasionally. Once all the fat has rendered, continue cooking the fat until the cracklings inside the fat have become a light golden-brown color. Strain the fat through a fine-mesh sieve set over a heatproof bowl. Remove the cracklings from the sieve and drain on a layer of paper towels. (Note that you will have more Pork Fat and Cracklings than you need for this recipe.)

<u>Cooked Rye</u>
60 grams whole rye grains, rinsed well
500 grams water

Bring the rye and the water to a boil in a saucepan over high heat. Once boiling, decrease the heat to low and simmer until the rye is cooked but not soft, approximately 30 minutes, stirring occasionally. Drain the rye in a colander, then transfer to ice water to cool. Once cooled, drain in a colander.

<u>Pork Sauce</u>
300 grams Pork Glaze (page 439)
300 grams Chicken Glaze (page 439)
Reduced White Wine (page 439)

Combine the Pork Glaze and Chicken Glaze in a saucepan and cook over medium heat until combined, 5 to 10 minutes. Season with Reduced White Wine and keep warm.

<u>Finishing</u>
Fine-grain salt

In a saucepan over medium-high heat, warm 500 grams of the Pork Sauce, the Sprouted Rye, and Cooked Rye and cook until warmed through, approximately 1 minute. Drain the ryes in a sieve, season with salt, and mix well.

For each serving, place a slice of pork slightly left to the center of the plate. Place a spoonful of Cooked Rye on the pork and flatten it into a single layer that covers most of the pork. Warm the remaining Pork Sauce in a saucepan over high heat until it just starts to boil, then pour it to the right side of the pork. Drizzle the pork with warmed Pork Fat, and finish with a sprinkle of Malted Buckwheat and Pork Cracklings on top.

p.324

Lamb, Turnip, and Samphire
Serves 6

Lamb
500 grams lamb loin, with skin on
Vegetable oil
30 grams Chicken Glaze (page 439)
Sea salt

With a knife, score the skin of the lamb with a
crosshatch pattern. Place the lamb in a vacuum bag
and vacuum-seal it. Cook the lamb in an immersion
circulator at 58°C (136°F) for 1½ hours. Remove the
lamb from the bag and pat dry with paper towels. In
a sauté pan, heat a little vegetable oil over high heat.
Sear the skin side of the lamb until golden and crispy,
1 to 2 minutes. Sear the remaining sides of the lamb
until evenly browned, approximately 30 seconds per
side. Turn off the heat and carefully pour out the fat
from the pan. Add the Chicken Glaze, return the pan
to the heat, and turn the lamb around in the glaze to
coat it evenly. Transfer the lamb to a rack and allow
to rest for 5 minutes. Cut the lamb, against the grain,
into 8-mm slices. Season with salt.

Lamb Sauce with Roasted Garlic
1 head garlic, halved crosswise
Vegetable oil
100 grams Lamb Glaze (page 439)
100 grams Chicken Glaze (page 439)
Reduced White Wine (page 439)

Preheat the oven to 200°C (400°F). Rub the garlic
with vegetable oil and place cut side down on a
baking sheet. Bake until roasted and caramelized,
approximately 15 minutes. Allow to cool and squeeze
the cloves out of the skin. Combine the Lamb Glaze
and Chicken Glaze in a saucepan and cook over
medium heat until combined, 5 to 10 minutes. Add
the roasted garlic and crush it with the back of a
spoon into the sauce. Season with Reduced White
Wine and keep warm. (Note that this yields more
sauce than you need for this recipe.)

Turnip Slices
4 large turnips
3 kilograms Butter Emulsion (page 438)

Blanch the turnips in boiling salted water until just
cooked but still slightly crunchy, 2 to 4 minutes, then
transfer to ice water to cool. Drain in a colander and
cut the turnips crosswise into 1-mm slices.
  Put the Butter Emulsion in a saucepan and bring
to a boil over medium-high heat. Add the turnips and
cook until just warmed through and slightly cooked,
approximately 1 minute. Using a sieve set over
another saucepan, drain the turnip slices, reserving
the Butter Emulsion for another use.

Finishing
60 grams samphire, picked into small pieces
Sea salt

Place 3 or 4 slices of Lamb in the center of the plate.
Top with 12 pieces of samphire. Pour 2 or 3 spoonfuls
of Lamb Sauce with Roasted Garlic over the meat and
samphire. Fold each Turnip Slice so that each one
stands on the plate and cover the meat completely
with 12 to 15 slices. Sprinkle with salt.

Cauliflower, Veal Sweetbread, and Basil
Serves 6

p.326

Veal Sweetbreads
550 grams veal sweetbreads
1 kilogram water
500 grams 3% Salt Brine (page 438)
Vegetable oil
50 grams unsalted butter, cut into cubes
50 grams Chicken Glaze (page 439)
Fine-grain salt

In a large bowl, soak the sweetbreads in the water for 24 hours, covered in the fridge. Drain the sweetbreads in a colander and place in a vacuum bag with the Salt Brine and vacuum-seal it. Keep in the fridge for 24 hours. Remove the sweetbreads from the Salt Brine, place them in a single layer in another vacuum bag, and vacuum-seal it. Cook the sweetbreads in an immersion circulator at 63°C (145°F) for 1 hour. Transfer the bag of sweetbreads to ice water to cool. Once cooled, remove the sweetbreads from the bag and pat dry with a paper towel. Carefully cut away the outer membranes of the sweetbreads, trying to cut as little of the meat as possible. Put the trimmed sweetbreads in a cold pan coated with vegetable oil and slowly cook over medium-low heat, on one side, until heated through and starting to brown, 15 to 20 minutes. Increase the heat to high, add the butter, and finish browning the one side until crispy, 4 to 5 minutes, basting the sweetbreads with the foaming butter. Turn off the heat and pour out all the fat from the pan, reserving the sweetbreads in the pan. Return the pan to medium heat, add the Chicken Glaze, and turn the sweetbreads to evenly coat them with the glaze. Once the sweetbreads are all evenly glazed, remove them from the pan and cut into 2-cm pieces and season with salt.

Veal Sauce
100 grams Veal Glaze (page 439)
100 grams Chicken Glaze (page 439)
Reduced White Wine (page 439)

Combine the Veal Glaze and Chicken Glaze in a saucepan and cook over medium heat until combined, 5 to 10 minutes. Season with Reduced White Wine and keep warm.

Cauliflower Stem Pieces
1 large head cauliflower
1 kilogram Butter Emulsion (page 438)
Fine-grain salt

Cut away the florets of the cauliflower from the stem. Reserve the florets for Cauliflower Puree (page 391) and Cauliflower Rice (below). Cut the stem crosswise into 5-mm-thick slices, then cut each of those pieces into four so that you have small pieces. Use only the tender parts of the stem and discard the fibrous parts. Put the Butter Emulsion in a saucepan and bring to a boil over medium-high heat. Add the cauliflower stem pieces and cook until warmed through but not softened, approximately 30 seconds. Using a sieve set over another saucepan, drain the cauliflower stem pieces, reserving the Butter Emulsion for further use. Season with salt.

Cauliflower Rice
500 grams cauliflower florets
2 kilograms Butter Emulsion (page 438)
Fine-grain salt

Finely chop the cauliflower florets until the size and texture is similar to couscous. You can do this in a Thermomix by pulsing a handful of cauliflower florets for 2 seconds at a time until it is evenly chopped. Put the Butter Emulsion in a saucepan and bring to a boil over medium-high heat. Add the cauliflower and cook until just warmed through and slightly

continued

417

Appendix

<u>Cauliflower, Veal Sweetbread, and Basil, continued</u>

cooked, approximately 1 minute. Using a sieve set over another saucepan, drain the Cauliflower Rice, reserving the Butter Emulsion for another use. Season with salt.

<u>Mixed Herbs</u>
1 bunch Thai basil
1 bunch lemon basil
1 bunch green basil
1 bunch red basil
1 bunch lovage

Pick the leaves and mix them all together.

<u>Finishing</u>
120 grams Cauliflower Puree (page 391), warmed
Freshly squeezed lemon juice

For each serving, place a large spoonful of warmed Cauliflower Puree in the center of a plate and top with 7 or 8 pieces of the Veal Sweetbreads. Tear some of the Mixed Herbs and put approximately 6 to 8 leaves on top of the sweetbreads. Tear the rest of the Mixed Herbs and mix them into the warm Veal Sauce, then season with a little lemon juice. Pour 2 or 3 spoonfuls of Veal Sauce over the sweetbreads. Place 4 Cauliflower Stem Pieces between the sweetbreads. Spoon on the Cauliflower Rice, making a rounded pile covering everything else on the plate.

Chicken Wings, White Asparagus, and Anchovies
Serves 6

p.328

Poached Chicken Wings
6 whole chicken wings, each divided into two pieces
    with wing tips removed
1 kilogram 3% Salt Brine (page 438)
Fine-grain salt

Place the chicken wings in a vacuum bag with the
Salt Brine and vacuum-seal it. Keep in the fridge for
24 hours. Remove the wings from the Salt Brine,
place them in a single layer in a large vacuum bag,
and vacuum-seal them. Cook the chicken in an
immersion circulator at 65°C (150°F) for 2 hours.
Remove the chicken from the bags and peel the skin
and meat from the bones with your hands. Season
with salt.

Sautéed Chicken Livers
60 grams chicken livers
250 grams 3% Salt Brine (page 438)
Vegetable oil
Fine-grain salt
1 shallot, finely diced
1 bunch chives, finely chopped
Freshly squeezed lemon juice

Place the chicken livers in a vacuum bag with the
Salt Brine and vacuum-seal it. Keep in the fridge for
24 hours. Remove the livers from the brine and trim
off the connecting membranes with a knife. Chop
the livers into 5-mm cubes. In a pan, heat a little
vegetable oil over high heat until very hot, then add
the chicken livers. Cook without stirring until browned
on the bottom, but still rare on the top, 30 seconds to
1 minute, then stir the chicken livers and add a pinch
of salt, the chopped shallot, and chives. Toss for 5 to
10 seconds, then deglaze the pan with a little lemon
juice and transfer to a small bowl. Season with
lemon juice and salt.

White Asparagus Slices
500 grams white asparagus, peeled and trimmed

Halve the asparagus lengthwise and then slice
lengthwise into 2-mm slices on a mandoline. Lay the
slices in a single layer on parchment paper. Place a
baking sheet in a 180°C (356°F) oven, then transfer
the parchment paper with the asparagus onto the hot
baking sheet to warm, but not cook, the asparagus,
approximately 1 minute.

Chicken Sauce
120 grams Chicken Glaze (page 439), warmed
80 grams water
Reduced White Wine (page 439)

In a small saucepan, warm the Chicken Glaze and
water, then season with Reduced White Wine.

Finishing
6 oil-packed anchovy fillets, drained and cut into
    5-mm pieces
Sea salt
Extra-virgin olive oil

For each serving, place 6 to 8 anchovy pieces
around the center of the plate. Cover the anchovies
with the Poached Chicken Wings and spoon the
Sautéed Chicken Livers on top. Place the White
Asparagus Pieces on top of the chicken, covering it
completely. Pour 3 spoonfuls of Chicken Sauce over
the asparagus. Sprinkle the asparagus with salt and
finish with 6 to 8 drops of olive oil.

Appendix

p.330

Wild Duck, Elderberries, and White Onions
Serves 6

Burnt Onion Powder
2 yellow onions, sliced into 5-mm-thick rounds

Preheat the oven to 300°C (575°F). Place the onion rounds in a single layer on a baking sheet and bake until burnt and completely dried, approximately 1 hour. Allow the onions to cool. Transfer the onions to a Thermomix and process into a fine powder. Sift through a fine-mesh sieve set over a small bowl.

Onion Noodles
3 large yellow onions, peeled
1 kilogram 3% Salt Brine (page 438)
3 kilograms Butter Emulsion (page 438)
Duck Fat (page 439), warmed
Fine-grain salt

Slice the onions on a Japanese-style turning slicer, making the longest strips possible. Place the onions and Salt Brine in a vacuum bag and seal. Refrigerate overnight, then drain the onions in a colander, discarding the brine. Boil the Butter Emulsion over medium-high heat, then add the onions and cook until tender, 1 to 2 minutes. Using a sieve set over another saucepan, drain the onions, reserving the Butter Emulsion for another use. Season the onions with a drizzle of Duck Fat and a sprinkle of salt. Shape the onions into 6 tight bundles and sprinkle with Burnt Onion Powder.

Grilled Onion Puree
1 kilogram yellow onions, peeled and halved
Reduced White Wine (page 439)
Mushroom Soy Sauce (page 440)
Fine-grain salt

Preheat a gas or charcoal grill to 300°C (575°F). Grill the onions until charred, 15 to 20 minutes, turning them every 5 minutes. Remove some of the extremely burnt pieces so it is not too bitter. Vacuum-seal the onions in a single layer in vacuum bags and boil in a saucepan of water until completely soft, approximately 45 minutes. Transfer the onions and their juices in the Thermomix with enough water to make a thick puree and let it reach 80°C (175°F).

Press the puree through a fine-mesh strainer set over a bowl and season with Reduced White Wine, Mushroom Soy Sauce, and salt.

Wild Duck Breast
Vegetable oil
2 wild grey ducks, wings, legs, wishbone, and backbone removed
Sea salt

Preheat the oven to 200°C (400°F). In a pan, heat a little vegetable oil over high heat. Sear the skin side of the ducks until golden brown and crispy, approximately 5 minutes. Put the ducks directly on the oven racks (setting a tray underneath to catch the drippings) and bake until the thickest part of the duck, next to the breastbone, reaches 52°C (126°F), 8 to 12 minutes. Remove the ducks from the oven and allow to rest for 10 minutes. Butcher the breasts off the bone and cut the meat lengthwise into 4-mm slices. Season with salt.

Duck Sauce with Elderberries
45 grams Duck Glaze (page 439)
45 Chicken Glaze (page 439)
60 grams ripe elderberries
Reduced White Wine (page 439)

Combine the Duck Glaze and the Chicken Glaze in a saucepan and cook over medium heat until combined, 5 to 10 minutes. Add the ripe elderberries and season with Reduced White Wine.

Finishing

Place a spoonful of the warmed Grilled Onion Puree on a plate, then layer 4 or 5 slices of Wild Duck Breast on top. Place 1 bundle of Onion Noodles to the top right of the Wild Duck Breast and pour 2 or 3 spoonfuls of Duck Sauce with Elderberries over the duck.

420

Salad, Beef, and Bronte Pistachio
Serves 6

p.332

Braised Beef Short Ribs
1.5 kilograms beef short ribs
15 grams fine-grain salt
150 grams red wine
1 carrot, peeled, trimmed, and roughly chopped
1 celery stalk, trimmed and roughly chopped
1 onion, peeled and quartered
1 head garlic, halved crosswise
Vegetable oil
Sea salt

Place the ribs, fine-grain salt, wine, carrot, celery, onion, and garlic in a flameproof casserole dish and add enough water to cover. Keep in the fridge, covered, overnight. The following day, preheat the oven to 100°C (212°F). Place the dish on the stove top, uncovered, and bring to a boil over high heat. Re-cover and bake until the beef is tender, 4 to 6 hours. Lift the beef out of the braising liquid and separate the beef from the bones. Discard the bones and allow the meat to cool in the braising liquid, uncovered, at room temperature for 1 hour, then transfer to the fridge to cool overnight. Remove the beef from the braising liquid and cut into 6 even portions. Reserve the braising liquid for the Meat Floss. Put the beef in a cold sauté pan with a little vegetable oil and slowly cook over medium-low heat, without turning, until heated through and starting to brown, 15 to 20 minutes. Increase the heat to high and finish browning one side until crispy, approximately 5 minutes. Cut each portion into 2-cm pieces and season with sea salt.

Meat Floss
1 kilogram reserved braising liquid from Braised Beef
    Short Ribs
1 veal shank
2 kilograms water
50 grams Chicken Glaze (page 439)
10 grams fine-grain salt
10 grams vegetable oil

Remove the pieces of hardened fat from the cold braising liquid. Combine the veal shank, braising liquid, water, Chicken Glaze, and salt in a large pot and bring to a boil over high heat. Decrease the heat to medium and simmer until the veal is tender

and falls off the bone, 3 to 4 hours, skimming away the fat and foam. Remove the bones and continue cooking the veal until it falls apart and the liquid evaporates, 4 to 5 hours. Once the liquid is evaporated, stir the veal constantly until it dries out and becomes fluffy, 45 to 60 minutes, making sure to scrape the bottom of the pot so the meat does not stick. Once the veal is dry, add the vegetable oil to the pot, increase the heat to medium-high, and fry until golden brown and crispy, approximately 20 minutes. Transfer to a layer of paper towels to cool.

Charred Romaine and Pistachio Sauce
6 heads fresh romaine lettuce, halved lengthwise
100 grams Pistachio Puree (page 371)

Heat a large sauté pan over high heat until smoking, then place the romaine in the pan, cut side down, until evenly charred, 5 to 10 minutes. Allow the romaine to cool. Juice the charred romaine in a juicer and strain through a fine-mesh strainer set over a bowl. Whisk in the Puree Pistachio.

Finishing
3 Poached Romaine (page 408), chopped into 1-cm
    pieces
Freshly squeezed lemon juice
Fine-grain salt
120 grams Pistachio Puree (page 371)
24 romaine lettuce leaves
Freshly squeezed lemon juice
Sea salt

For each serving, place the Beef Short Ribs in the center of the plate. In a saucepan, warm the Charred Romaine and Pistachio Sauce over medium-high heat and add the chopped Poached Romaine. Season with lemon juice and salt. Pour 3 spoonfuls of the Charred Romaine and Pistachio Sauce with a few pieces of the warmed Poached Romaine over the beef. Brush the Pistachio Puree in a thin layer onto the inside of the romaine lettuce leaves, then sprinkle the Meat Floss over the puree. Place 4 romaine leaves, Meat Floss side down, over the beef in a fanlike shape, so that it looks like a whole romaine lettuce. Finish with 3 sprays of lemon juice and a sprinkle of salt.

421

Veal, Grilled Sauce, and Anchovy
Serves 6

p.334

Veal Tongue
1 veal tongue
1 kilogram water
500 grams 7% Salt Brine (page 438)
5 grams Burnt Onion Powder (page 420)
Sea salt

In a large bowl, soak the veal tongue in the water for 24 hours, covered, in the fridge. Drain the tongue in a colander and place in a vacuum bag with the Salt Brine and vacuum-seal it. Keep in the fridge for 24 hours. Remove the veal tongue from the Salt Brine, place in another vacuum bag, and vacuum-seal it. Cook the veal tongue in an immersion circulator at 62°C (144°F) for 24 hours. Remove the veal tongue from the bag and, using a knife, cut off the skin of the tongue and discard. Sprinkle the veal tongue with Burnt Onion Powder and cut the tongue lengthwise into 3-mm slices. Season with salt.

Burnt Onion Pieces
1 yellow onion, cut into 5-mm rounds

Preheat a gas or charcoal grill to 300°C (575°F). Grill the onions until about 90 percent has charred, 10 to 15 minutes, turning them several times. The onion rings should be burnt in some places and still soft and chewy in others. Allow the onions to cool. Crumble the onions between your fingers to make a rough powder.

Salsify Discs
Freshly squeezed lemon juice
1 kilogram salsify, peeled and trimmed
3 kilograms Butter Emulsion (page 438)
Fine-grain salt

Set a mandoline over a large bowl of water and a little lemon juice and cut the salsify crosswise into 1-mm slices so that the slices fall straight into the lemon water. Drain the salsify in a colander. Put the Butter Emulsion in a saucepan and bring to a boil over medium-high heat. Add the salsify and cook until tender, 1 to 2 minutes. Using a sieve set over another saucepan, strain the salsify discs and reserve the Butter Emulsion for another use. Season the salsify with lemon juice and salt.

Finishing
60 grams Anchovy Emulsion (page 386)
180 grams Salsify Puree (page 412), warmed
150 grams Veal Sauce (page 417), warmed

For each serving, place 1 spoonful of Anchovy Emulsion in the center of the plate, then top with 2 spoonfuls of Salsify Puree. Slightly fold 3 or 4 slices of Veal Tongue and place on top of the Salsify Puree. Make 2 piles of the Salsify Discs on either side the tongue. Add the Burnt Onion Pieces to the Veal Sauce and pour 3 spoonfuls over the tongue.

Whipped Goat Cheese and Parsley
Serves 20

Liquefied Fresh Goat Cheese
250 grams fresh goat cheese

Place the goat cheese in a Thermomix and process on low speed until the cheese becomes a smooth liquid consistency, approximately 5 minutes.

Finishing
100 grams Parsley Puree (page 410)

For each serving, splash 2 large spoonfuls of the Liquefied Fresh Goat Cheese on the plate, then splash of 1 large spoonful of Parsley Puree on top.

p.338

Nordlys, Carrots, and Orange Zest
Serves 6

Carrot Chips
1 kilogram large, thick carrots, trimmed
50 grams Brown Butter (page 438), melted

Preheat the oven to 150°C (300°F). Cut the carrots crosswise into 8- to 10-cm lengths so that they will fit into the Japanese-style turning vegetable slicer. Slice the carrots into the longest strips possible. Cut the carrot strips into pieces 15 to 20 cm long. In a pan, cook the carrot strips in the Brown Butter over medium heat until just softened, stirring continuously, approximately 10 minutes. Place the carrot sheets on parchment paper–lined baking sheets in a single layer. Bake until they become crispy and slightly browned, 10 to 15 minutes. Transfer them to racks to cool.

Finishing
250 grams Nordlys cheese, at room temperature
Zest from 1 orange

For each serving, place a large spoonful of Nordlys cheese on the plate, slightly to the right of the center, and top with orange zest. Place 3 or 4 Carrot Chips to the left of the cheese, covering it slightly.

p.340

Chanterelles, Apple, and Granité
Serves 6

p.342

Dried Chanterelle Mushrooms
10 large chanterelle mushrooms, cleaned

Tear each chanterelle lengthwise into 3 pieces. Dry in a single layer in a 60°C (140°F) dehydrator.

Apple Granité
500 grams freshly pressed apple juice

Freeze the juice in a shallow container overnight. Once the juice is completely frozen, scrape it with a fork to create a flaky and airy granité.

Chanterelle Puree
50 grams unsalted butter
250 grams chanterelle mushrooms, cleaned

Melt the butter in a pan over high heat and cook the chanterelle mushrooms until well caramelized and browned, 8 to 10 minutes. Transfer to a Thermomix and puree until smooth. Transfer to a bowl and allow to cool, uncovered, in the fridge.

Chanterelle Mousse
270 grams heavy cream
5 grams fine-grain salt
240 grams Chanterelle Puree
125 grams sugar
30 grams water
145 grams egg whites

Fold 100 grams of the cream and the salt into the Chanterelle Puree. In a saucepan, combine the sugar and water, then bring it to a boil over medium-high heat. Boil until the sugar reaches 115°C (240°F). When the temperature of the sugar reaches 110°C (230°F) start to whip the egg whites on medium-low speed in an electric stand mixer until soft peaks form, approximately 8 minutes. When the sugar syrup reaches 115°C (240°F), increase the speed of the stand mixer to medium-high and slowly add the sugar syrup to the egg whites in a fine stream. After all of the sugar syrup has been added, increase the speed to high and whip until stiff peaks form and the meringue cools, approximately 8 minutes. Transfer this mixture to a separate bowl. Place the remaining 170 grams of cream to the stand mixer and whip until soft peaks form. Fold the egg whites into the Chanterelle Puree, then fold in the whipped cream. Cool the mousse for at least 2 hours, covered in the fridge. (Note you will have more mousse than you need for this recipe.)

Berry and Black Trumpet Crumble
200 grams skim milk powder
200 grams unbleached wheat flour
60 grams cornstarch
125 grams sugar
10 grams fine-grain salt
275 grams unsalted butter, melted
160 grams freeze-dried blackberry powder
150 grams Black Trumpet Mushroom Powder
    (page 440)

Preheat the oven to 160°C (320°F). In a bowl, stir together the powdered milk, flour, cornstarch, sugar, and salt. Pour the melted butter over the dry ingredients and stir until it comes together in crumbly 1- to 2-cm chunks. Transfer the crumble to a parchment paper–lined baking sheet and bake for approximately 10 minutes, until slightly browned. Allow the crumble to cool, then transfer to a bowl and mix in the blackberry and black trumpet mushroom powders.

Finishing
Fine-grain salt
Black Trumpet Mushroom Powder (page 440)

For each serving, put a large, round scoop of Chanterelle Mousse in the center of a frozen plate and sprinkle a little salt on top. Surround the mousse with a ring of the Apple Granité, then sprinkle the Berry and Black Trumpet Crumble on top of the mousse. Put a large pinch of Black Trumpet Mushroom Powder on top of the crumble in 3 different places and place 5 pieces of Dried Chanterelle Mushrooms on the granité.

Mandarin, Buttermilk, and Egg Yolk
Serves 6

p.344

Mandarin Curd
2 eggs
125 grams sugar
50 grams freshly squeezed mandarin juice
1 gram citric acid
150 grams unsalted butter, at room temperature and
    cut into cubes

Bring a saucepan of water to a boil and then decrease the heat to medium-low so that the water is at a low simmer. Combine the eggs, sugar, juice, and citric acid in a double boiler set over the simmering water. Whisk continuously until the mixture reaches 82°C (180°F), 20 to 25 minutes. Remove the bowl from the heat and place it over a bowl of ice water to cool until it reaches 60°C (140°F). Whisk in the butter, cube by cube, until emulsified. Allow the curd to cool in the fridge, approximately 2 hours.

Caramelized Buttermilk Powder
1 L buttermilk
250 grams unsalted butter, cut into cubes

In a saucepan, bring the buttermilk and butter to a boil over medium-high heat, stirring occasionally. Boil the buttermilk until it separates, then decrease the heat to medium and allow to caramelize, approximately 2 hours. After approximately 1 hour, the buttermilk will have reduced a lot and you will need to stir it continuously until it becomes dark brown. Strain the buttermilk through a fine-mesh sieve set over a small bowl. Transfer the buttermilk to a layer of paper towels and place on trays in the dehydrator and dry overnight at 60°C (140°F), changing the paper towels several times until the buttermilk is crispy. (Note that you will have more powder than you need for this recipe.)

Poached Eggs
8 large eggs

Poach the eggs in their shells in an immersion circulator at 62°C (144°F) for 25 minutes. (Note that you will have more eggs than you need for this recipe, so in case you break any egg yolks, there will be a couple of spare ones.)

Sweetened Buttermilk Snow
55 grams glucose
65 grams trimoline
135 grams water
500 grams buttermilk

In a saucepan, dissolve the glucose and trimoline into the water over high heat, 5 to 10 minutes. Allow to cool, then stir in the buttermilk. Freeze the mixture in a shallow, freezer-proof container overnight. Once completely frozen, remove it from the container and transfer the frozen block to a metal bowl. Using a heavy object, smash the block into smaller pieces, 1 to 4 cm in size. Transfer a handful of the frozen pieces to a Thermomix and process until it looks like a fine snow, approximately 30 seconds. Repeat with the remaining frozen buttermilk pieces. Transfer the snow to a freezer-proof container and freeze.

Finishing
1 mandarin, each segment cut in half crosswise and
    seeds removed
100 grams Mandarin Snow (page 431)

For each serving, place 2 spoonfuls of Mandarin Curd in the center of a frozen plate. Place 4 pieces of mandarin around the curd. Sprinkle 1 spoonful of the Caramelized Buttermilk Powder on top of the curd. Around the curd, place 3 spoonfuls of Mandarin Snow, followed by 3 spoonfuls of Sweetened Buttermilk Snow. Over a bowl, break a Poached Egg into your hand, and carefully allow the cooked whites to fall into the bowl, while holding on to the yolk. Reserve the whites for another use. Place the poached egg yolk in the center, on top of the curd.

p.346

Milk, Kelp, and Caramel
Serves 6

Milk and Kelp Ice Cream
700 grams milk
90 grams glucose
12 grams trimoline
30 grams sugar
1.5 grams guar gum
60 grams skim milk powder
240 grams heavy cream
57 grams dried kelp

In a saucepan, warm 150 grams of the milk over medium heat and add the glucose, trimoline, and sugar, stirring to dissolve them. Bring the milk to a boil. Transfer the hot milk mixture to a Thermomix, add the guar gum and skim milk powder, and blend until combined. In a large bowl, mix the remaining 550 grams of the milk and the cream and pour in the hot milk mixture. Mix well and allow to cool. Transfer the mixture to a vacuum bag, add the dried kelp, and vacuum-seal it. Allow to infuse in the bag for 13 minutes, then strain the mixture through a fine-mesh sieve set over a bowl. Reserve the kelp to make Candied Kelp. Freeze the ice cream mixture in 2 Paco beakers for at least 24 hours until completely frozen, then process in the Pacojet. (Note that you will have more ice cream than you need for this recipe.)

Caramel
200 grams sugar
450 grams heavy cream
100 grams unsalted butter, cut into cubes

In a saucepan, spread out the sugar in an even layer. Over medium-high heat, slowly melt the sugar, stirring until it completely liquefies, 1 to 3 minutes. Decrease the heat slightly if you see it starting to burn in some spots. Let the sugar caramelize until it has reached the color of Cognac, a reddish brown, 10 to 15 minutes. Slowly add the cream and butter and bring the caramel to just to a boil. Whisk well to combine. Transfer to a heatproof bowl and allow the caramel to cool overnight uncovered in the fridge. The following day, transfer the caramel to a piping bag and allow to come to room temperature, about 30 minutes, before serving. (Note that you will have more caramel than you need for this recipe.)

Candied Kelp
Reserved kelp from Milk and Kelp Ice Cream,
    rinsed well
300 grams powdered sugar
100 grams water

Bring a large saucepan of water to a boil over high heat and cook the kelp until tender, approximately 40 minutes. Drain the kelp in a colander, then rinse it under cold running water until all the slime is removed. Place the kelp in a single layer and dry overnight at 60°C (140°F) in the dehydrator. The following day, transfer the kelp to a Thermomix and pulse until the kelp becomes a rough crumbly texture. Preheat the oven to 140°C (285°F). In a bowl, mix the sugar and water, then add the crushed kelp and mix well. Transfer the mixture to a baking sheet and spread it out in a thin, even layer. Bake until dried, approximately 40 minutes. Allow the candied kelp to cool. (Note that you will have more candied kelp than you need for this recipe.)

Finishing
Pear vinegar

Make 6 quenelles of the the Milk and Kelp Ice Cream and place them on a frozen slate or flat plate. Draw thin zigzags of Caramel lengthwise on top of the quenelles and sprinkle Candied Kelp on top. For each serving, place a pinch of Candied Kelp in the center of a frozen plate. Carefully place the quenelle on top of the pinch of Candied Kelp and finish with 2 sprays of pear vinegar.

Rhubarb Compote, Almond, and Vinegar

Serves 6

p.348

Moscatel Vinegar Sorbet

90 grams trimoline
54 grams glucose
360 grams water
55 grams Moscatel vinegar

In a saucepan, dissolve the trimoline and glucose into the water over medium-high heat, approximately 5 minutes. Remove from the heat and allow to cool to room temperature, then stir in the vinegar. Freeze the sorbet mixture in a Paco beaker for at least 24 hours until completely frozen, then process in the Pacojet. (Note that you will have more sorbet than you need for this recipe.)

Milk Gel

1 gram gellan
1.2 grams agar
80 grams milk
20 grams heavy cream

Place the gellan, agar, and milk in a Thermomix and blend until well combined. In a saucepan, bring the milk mixture and cream to a boil over medium heat, then remove from the heat. Strain the gel through a fine-mesh sieve directly onto a baking sheet into a 1-mm-thin layer and allow to set at room temperature, approximately 10 minutes. Once set, cut the gel into 8 by 8-cm squares.

Rhubarb Compote

1 kilogram rhubarb, chopped in 1-cm pieces
320 grams sugar
Freshly squeezed lemon juice

In a saucepan, cook the rhubarb and sugar over medium heat until the rhubarb is tender, but not falling apart, 20 to 30 minutes. Transfer the rhubarb to a fine-mesh sieve and let it sit there, without pressing it through, allowing some of the liquid to drip out until it reaches the consistency of a thick compote. Season with lemon juice and keep warm. (Note that you will have more compote than you n eed for this recipe.)

Finishing

25 blanched almonds, peeled and finely grated
90 grams Fresh Almond Milk (page 382)
25 blanched almonds, peeled and halved lengthwise

For each serving, sprinkle some finely grated almond onto a frozen plate, slightly off-center and to the right. Scoop a large spoonful of the Moscatel Vinegar Sorbet onto the finely grated almond. Cover the sorbet with a square of the Milk Gel. Place a large spoonful of the warmed Rhubarb Compote to the left of the sorbet. Pour some Fresh Almond Milk to the left of the rhubarb and top with 8 almond halves.

Appendix

p.350

Jerusalem Artichoke, Malt, and Bread
Serves 6

Jerusalem Artichoke Ice Cream
400 grams Jerusalem artichokes, peeled
400 grams milk
200 grams heavy cream
50 grams sugar
70 grams trimoline
35 grams powdered milk
130 grams egg yolks

Place the Jerusalem artichokes in a single layer in a vacuum bag and vacuum-seal it. Place the bag in a large saucepan with enough water to cover and bring to a boil over medium-high heat. Boil the Jerusalem artichokes until they are completely soft, 50 to 60 minutes. Transfer the cooked Jerusalem artichokes and their juices to a Thermomix and puree until smooth. Press the puree through a tamis lined with very fine-mesh cloth set over a bowl and allow to cool. In a saucepan, warm the milk, cream, sugar, trimoline, and powdered milk over medium heat, stirring occasionally. Once the mixture reaches 60°C (140°F), remove it from the heat, pour a few splashes of the hot milk mixture into the egg yolks, and stir well. Continue to add small amounts of the hot milk mixture into the egg yolks and stir until the egg mixture slowly becomes warm. Once the egg mixture is warm, add the rest of the hot milk mixture.

Take 300 grams of the Jerusalem artichoke puree and 700 grams of the milk–egg yolk mixture and whisk together until well combined. Freeze the ice cream mixture in 2 Paco beakers for at least 24 hours until completely frozen, then process in the Pacojet. (Note that this will yield more ice cream than you need for this recipe.)

Candied Jerusalem Artichoke Skins
15 large Jerusalem artichokes, scrubbed
300 grams water
600 grams powdered sugar

Preheat the oven to 170°C (340°F). Place the Jerusalem artichokes directly on the oven racks and bake until completely soft, 1 to 1½ hours. Transfer the Jerusalem artichokes to a sealed container and allow to steam for 30 minutes. Cut each Jerusalem artichoke in half and scrape out the flesh, reserving it for another use. Mix the water with the sugar, then dip the Jerusalem artichoke skins in the sugar syrup. Decrease the oven temperature to 150°C (300°F), place the glazed skins directly on the oven racks, and bake until golden brown, 25 to 30 minutes. Remove the skins from the oven and allow to cool on the rack at room temperature. They should become crispy.

Bread in Toasted Malt Oil
100 grams vegetable oil
38 grams toasted malt powder
25 grams powdered sugar
3 slices day-old Sourdough Bread (page 370)

Combine the vegetable oil, toasted malt powder, and sugar in a Thermomix and process until well combined, approximately 4 minutes. Cut the crust off the bread and discard. Tear the bread into 1-cm pieces and place in a shallow container. Pour the malt oil over the bread and soak, covered, for 5 to 10 minutes.

Finishing

For each serving, place 3 pieces of Bread in Toasted Malt Oil in the center of a frozen plate. Quenelle the Jerusalem Artichoke Ice Cream and place it on top of the bread. Place another 2 pieces of Bread in Toasted Malt Oil on top of the ice cream. Cover the ice cream and bread pieces with 5 pieces of Candied Jerusalem Artichoke Skins, skin side facing up.

Sheep's Milk Yogurt, Beets, and Black Currant
Serves 6

p.352

Vanilla Ice Cream
2 vanilla beans
500 grams milk
500 grams heavy cream
150 grams sugar
160 grams glucose
240 grams egg yolks
10 grams skim milk powder
2.5 grams carob flour
40 grams unsalted butter, cut into cubes

Cut the vanilla beans in half lengthwise and scrape out the seeds with a knife. In a large bowl, combine the vanilla seeds and beans with the milk. In a saucepan, bring the cream, sugar, glucose, and the milk mixture to a boil over medium heat, stirring occasionally, approximately 15 minutes. Once the mixture comes to a boil, remove it from the heat, pour a few splashes of the hot cream mixture into a bowl with the egg yolks, and stir well. Continue to add small amounts of the hot cream mixture into the egg yolks and stir until the egg mixture slowly becomes warm. Once the egg mixture is warm, pour the rest of the hot cream mixture in. Transfer to a Thermomix and blend in the milk powder, carob flour, and butter. Strain the mixture through a fine-mesh sieve set over a small bowl. Freeze the ice cream mixture in 2 Paco beakers for at least 24 hours until completely frozen, then process in the Pacojet. (Note you will have more ice cream than you need for this recipe.)

Apple and Black Currant Gel
100 grams apple juice
1 gram gellan
Black currant vinegar

In a saucepan, bring the apple juice and gellan to a boil over medium-high heat, whisking continuously, approximately 5 minutes. Strain the gel through a fine-mesh sieve directly onto a baking sheet into a 1-mm-thin layer and allow to set at room temperature, approximately 10 minutes. Once set, cut the gel into 8 by 8-cm squares and brush with a thin layer of black currant vinegar.

Beet Reduction
1.5 kilograms red beets, peeled

Cut the beets into quarters, then juice the beets in a juicer and strain it through a fine-mesh strainer set over a bowl. In a saucepan, bring the beet juice to a boil over medium-high heat. Decrease the heat to medium and simmer until the juice has reduced by two-thirds, 25 to 30 minutes. Skim the foam from the surface.

Chewy Beets
15 small Chioggia beets, no larger than 4 cm in width, scrubbed
120 grams Beet Reduction
Black currant vinegar

Place the beets in a single layer in a vacuum bag and vacuum-seal it. Place the bag in a large saucepan with enough water to cover and bring to a boil over medium-high heat. Boil the beets until just cooked, but not too soft, 30 to 35 minutes. Transfer the bag to ice water to cool. Peel the beets and halve lengthwise. Place in a single layer and dry at 60°C (140°F) in the dehydrator for 6 to 8 hours, until half dried and chewy, with a moist center. In a saucepan, warm the Chewy Beets in the Beet Reduction over medium-high heat. Season with black currant vinegar.

Finishing
Sheep's Milk Yogurt Mousse (page 378)
30 grams freeze-dried black currants

For each serving, place a heaping teaspoon of the Vanilla Ice Cream onto the center of a frozen plate. Siphon enough Sheep's Milk Yogurt Mousse on top of the ice cream to cover it. Sprinkle freeze-dried black currants on top and cover the mousse with a square of the Apple and Black Currant Gel. Place 5 pieces of the warmed Chewy Beets on and around the gel and pour 2 spoonfuls of warmed Beet Reduction over the gel and the beets.

Hokkaido Pumpkin and Mandarin
Serves 6

p.354

Pureed Toasted Pumpkin Seeds
30 grams vegetable oil
150 grams pumpkin seeds

Preheat the oven to 200°C (400°F). Spread out 20 grams of the vegetable oil on a parchment paper–lined baking sheet. Add the pumpkin seeds and toss to coat. Bake until well toasted and puffed, approximately 20 minutes. Transfer the seeds to a Thermomix and puree until smooth, adding up to 10 grams more oil if necessary to blend. Allow the puree to cool.

Pumpkin Seed Ice Cream
8 poached eggs (page 425), cold
500 grams milk
75 grams sugar
35 grams trimoline
150 grams Pureed Toasted Pumpkin Seeds

Over a large bowl, break the eggs into your hands and carefully allow the cooked whites to fall into the bowl, while holding on to the yolk. Transfer the yolk to a container and reserve for another use. In a saucepan, warm the milk over medium heat and add the sugar and trimoline, stirring to dissolve them. Bring the milk to a boil. Transfer the hot milk mixture to a Thermomix, add the Pureed Toasted Pumpkin Seeds and 200 grams of the poached egg whites, and blend until combined. Freeze the ice cream mixture in 2 Paco beakers for at least 24 hours, until completely frozen, then process in the Pacojet. (Note that you will have more ice cream than you need for this recipe.)

Pumpkin Slices
250 grams Hokkaido pumpkin, peeled and cut into 1-mm-thick slices
500 grams fresh mandarin juice

Place the pumpkin slices in a single layer on a parchment paper–lined baking sheet, cover, and freeze overnight. The following day, remove the tray from the freezer and allow the pumpkin slices to defrost, approximately 1 hour. Transfer the defrosted pumpkin slices with the mandarin juice to a vacuum bag and vacuum-seal it. After 20 minutes, drain the pumpkin slices in a colander and reserve the remaining mandarin juice for another use.

Candied Pumpkin Chips
125 grams water
200 grams sugar
50 grams glucose
125 grams Hokkaido pumpkin, unpeeled and cut into 2-mm slices

In a saucepan, bring half of the water to a boil over high heat and add the sugar and glucose, stirring to dissolve them. Let the syrup caramelize until it has reached the color of Cognac, a reddish brown, approximately 20 minutes. Then stop the cooking by removing the saucepan from the heat and adding the remaining half of the water. Stir well and allow to cool. In a bowl, coat the pumpkin slices with the syrup. Place in a single layer and dry overnight at 65°C (150°F) in the dehydrator.

Sweet Pumpkin Pieces

1 kilogram water

250 grams trimoline

250 grams glucose

30 grams Hokkaido pumpkin, unpeeled and cut into
5-mm cubes

In a saucepan, warm the water over high heat and add the trimoline and glucose, stirring to dissolve them. Transfer half of the syrup to an uncovered bowl and place it in the fridge to cool. When the syrup is cool, bring the remaining half of the syrup to a boil, add the pumpkin, and blanch until very soft, but not falling apart, approximately 12 minutes. Drain the pumpkin in a colander, then transfer to the chilled syrup to cool.

Mandarin Snow

500 grams fresh mandarin juice

Freeze the juice in a shallow, freezer-proof container overnight. Once the juice is completely frozen, remove it from the container and transfer the frozen block to a large metal bowl. Using a rolling pin, pestle, or other heavy object, smash the ice block into smaller pieces, 1 to 4 cm in size. Transfer a large handful of the frozen mandarin juice pieces to the Thermomix and process until it looks like a fine snow, approximately 30 seconds. Repeat with the remaining frozen mandarin juice pieces. Transfer the snow into a freezer-proof container and place in the freezer. (Note you will have more snow than you need for this recipe.)

Finishing

For each serving, quenelle the Pumpkin Seed Ice Cream and place it in the center of a frozen plate. To the left side of the ice cream, place 6 Sweet Pumpkin Pieces and then 12 folded Pumpkin Slices. Place 3 spoonfuls of Mandarin Snow between the Pumpkin Slices and the ice cream, covering the Sweet Pumpkin Pieces. Place 5 Candied Pumpkin Chips on top of the ice cream.

Appendix

Corn, Bread Crumbs, and Marjoram
Serves 6

p.356

Dried Bread Powder
1 loaf day-old Sourdough Bread (page 370), crust
    removed

Cut the bread into 1-cm pieces. Place in a single layer
and dry overnight at 65°C (150°F) in the dehydrator.
The following day, transfer the bread to a Thermomix
and process until it becomes a fine powder. (Note you
will have more powder than you need for this recipe.)

Pan-Roasted Corn Kernels
200 grams unsalted butter, cut into cubes
6 large ears corn, peeled

In a large sauté pan, melt the butter over medium-
high heat. When the butter starts foaming and turning
brown, add the ears of corn. Turn the ears of corn
every few minutes and baste them with the butter
until evenly caramelized, 15 to 20 minutes. Once all
of the ears of corn are an even light brown color all
around, turn off the heat, cover the pan, and let the
corn steam for 15 minutes. Transfer the corn to a layer
of paper towels to drain and wipe off excess butter
with paper towels. Allow to cool. Using a knife, shuck
the roasted corn kernels from the cob. Set the cobs
aside for Roasted Corn Milk. (Note you will have more
than you need for this recipe.)

Roasted Corn Milk
6 corn cobs reserved from Pan-Roasted Corn Kernels
50 grams unsalted butter, cut into cubes
1.2 kilograms milk

Preheat the oven to 180°C (356°F). Place the cobs
on a baking tray with the butter and bake, turning
them occasionally as the butter melts, until they are
an even light brown color all around, approximately
20 minutes. Transfer the cobs to a layer of paper
towels to drain and cool. Place the cobs and the
milk in a vacuum bag and vacuum-seal it. Keep it in
the fridge for 24 hours to infuse. The following day,
strain the milk through a fine-mesh strainer set over
a bowl and discard the cobs.

Corn Ice Cream
660 grams Pan-Roasted Corn Kernels
800 grams Roasted Corn Milk
80 grams sugar
20 grams powdered milk
120 grams heavy cream

Blend the Pan-Roasted Corn Kernels and the
Roasted Corn Milk at high speed in a Thermomix
for 5 minutes at 60°C (140°F) until smooth. Strain
the mixture through a fine-mesh sieve set over a
small bowl, pressing on the corn pulp so that all of
the starch is extracted. Discard the pulp. Transfer
the hot corn milk mixture to a Thermomix, add the
sugar and powdered milk, and blend until the sugar
and powdered milk are well dissolved. Transfer the
mixture to a bowl and stir in the cream. Freeze the
ice cream mixture in 2 Paco beakers for at least
24 hours, until completely frozen, then before serving,
process in the Pacojet. (Note that you will have more
ice cream than you need for this recipe.)

Chewy Corn and Corn Powder
2 large ears corn, peeled and shucked

Blanch the ears of corn in boiling salted water until
you can remove whole corn kernels from the cob
without them bursting, approximately 10 minutes,
then transfer to ice water to cool. Drain in a colander.
Dry the ears of corn overnight at 65°C (150°F) in the
dehydrator. The following day, using your hands,
remove the dried corn kernels from the cob. Divide
the dried corn kernels in half. Transfer half to a
Thermomix and process until it becomes a fine
powder. Sift the powder through a fine-mesh sieve
set over a bowl. Blanch the remaining half of the dried
corn kernels in boiling salted water until they become
chewy, approximately 3 minutes. Drain in a colander,
then transfer to a layer of paper towels. (Note you will
have more corn powder than you need for this recipe.)

<u>Italian Meringue</u>
230 grams sugar
50 grams water
130 grams egg whites
Fine-grain salt
10 grams pear vinegar

In a saucepan, combine the sugar and water, then bring it to a boil over medium-high heat. Place a candy thermometer on the side of the saucepan to monitor the temperature of the sugar and continue to boil the sugar until it reaches 115°C (240°F). When the temperature reaches 110°C (230°F), start to whip the egg whites with a pinch of salt on medium-low speed in an electric stand mixer until soft peaks form, approximately 8 minutes. Add the pear vinegar. When the sugar syrup reaches 115°C (240°F), increase the speed to medium-high and slowly add the sugar syrup to the egg whites in a fine stream. Increase the speed to high and whip until stiff peaks form and the meringue cools, approximately 8 minutes. Transfer the meringue to a piping bag. (Note you will have more meringue than you need for this recipe.)

<u>Finishing</u>
Pear vinegar
Sea salt
6 sprigs marjoram, leaves picked

For each serving, pipe a small ring of Italian Meringue onto the center of a frozen plate. Spray the meringue with 2 sprays of pear vinegar. Quenelle the Corn Ice Cream and place it in the center of the meringue. Place a small pinch of salt on the quenelle. Sprinkle the ice cream and meringue with Chewy Corn, Corn Powder, Dried Bread Powder, and marjoram.

p.358

Elderflower and Rhubarb
Serves 6

Elderflower Vinegar Granité
1,200 grams water
150 grams glucose
250 grams trimoline
1 gram gellan
150 grams elderflower vinegar, reserved from
  Pickled Elderflower (page 440)

In a saucepan, warm 400 grams of the water,
the glucose, and the trimoline over high heat until the
mixture reaches 65°C (150°F). In a second saucepan,
stir the gellan into 400 grams of the water, then bring
to a boil. Boil for 45 seconds. In a third saucepan,
warm the remaining 400 grams water and the vinegar
until the mixture reaches 70°C (158°F). Mix all of the
liquids together and freeze in a shallow, freezer-proof
container overnight. Scrape the frozen mixture with
a fork to create a flaky and airy granité.

Yogurt Crumble
240 grams powdered milk
155 grams freeze-dried yogurt powder
200 grams unbleached wheat flour
60 grams cornstarch
125 grams sugar
10 grams fine-grain salt
275 grams unsalted butter, melted
300 grams white chocolate

Preheat the oven to 150°C (300°F). Combine
100 grams of the powdered milk, 100 grams of the
freeze-dried yogurt powder, the flour, cornstarch,
sugar, and salt in the bowl of a stand mixer. With the
dough hook attachment, mix on low speed while
slowly adding the melted butter, stopping when it
reaches a sandy consistency. Transfer the mixture to
a parchment paper–lined baking sheet and spread
in a thin layer. Bake until dried but not caramelized,
approximately 20 minutes. Allow to cool, then transfer
to a bowl. Add the remaining 140 grams powdered
milk and the remaining 55 grams freeze-dried yogurt
powder to the crumble. Melt the white chocolate in
a bain-marie over medium heat, approximately
15 minutes, then slowly pour into the crumble while
mixing. Spread onto a tray in a thin layer. Cool
overnight, uncovered in the fridge.

Elderflower Cream
150 grams milk
150 grams heavy cream
36 grams black cane sugar
13 grams fresh elderflowers
1 gram iota

In a saucepan, warm the milk, cream, sugar, and
elderflowers over medium-high heat to 70°C (160°F).
Remove from the heat and allow to infuse for
20 minutes. Strain the mixture through a fine-mesh
sieve set over a bowl and discard the elderflowers.
Allow the mixture to cool until it reaches 50°C (122°F),
then whisk the iota and bring to a boil over medium-
high heat. Boil for 30 seconds. Pour the mixture into
a heat-resistant container and allow to set at room
temperature, approximately 30 minutes. Once set,
spoon the mixture into a siphon bottle and charge
with one CO_2 cartridge. Shake the siphon bottle
several times until the cream is light and airy.

Rhubarb Leather
100 grams Rhubarb Compote (page 427)

Place the compote in a Thermomix and puree
until smooth. Spread the puree on a silicone pad
into a 2-mm-thick layer. Place the silicone pad in
the dehydrator and dry at 60°C (140°F) for 10 to
15 minutes, until the leather is set but not completely
dried. Peel the whole leather off the silicone pad and
rip into by 2-cm pieces.

Finishing
90 grams Rhubarb Compote (page 427), chilled
Flowers from 1 bunch fresh elderflowers

For each serving, place a spoonful of Rhubarb
Compote in the center of a bowl. Siphon enough
Elderflower Cream to cover the compote. Roll
5 Rhubarb Leather pieces into cone shapes and
stick them into the cream, with the open side facing
up. Sprinkle the Yogurt Crumble on top of the
Elderflower Cream and Rhubarb Leather, followed
by the Elderflower Vinegar Granité. Finish with a
sprinkle of the fresh elderflowers.

Jerusalem Artichokes, Coffee, and Passion
Serves 6

Passion Fruit Curd
165 grams passion fruit puree
60 grams powdered sugar
1 gram iota
60 grams unsalted butter, at room temperature and
cut into cubes

Divide the passion fruit puree in half. Put one half in
the fridge and the other half in a saucepan and bring
to a boil over medium-high heat. Whisk in the sugar
and iota. Transfer the hot passion fruit puree, the cold
passion fruit puree, and the butter to a Thermomix
and process until smooth. Allow to cool. (Note you will
have more curd than you need for this recipe.)

Jerusalem Artichoke Mousse
450 grams Jerusalem artichokes, peeled
50 grams water
2.5 grams fine-grain salt
150 grams egg whites
60 grams powdered sugar
325 grams heavy cream

Place the peeled Jerusalem artichokes in a single
layer in a vacuum bag and vacuum-seal it. Place the
bag in a large saucepan with enough water to cover
and bring to a boil over medium-high heat. Boil the
Jerusalem artichokes until they are completely soft,
50 to 60 minutes. Transfer the cooked Jerusalem
artichokes, their juices, and the water to a Thermomix
and puree until smooth. Press the puree through a
tamis lined with very fine-mesh cloth set over a bowl.
Stir in the salt and allow to cool.

Whip the egg whites on high speed in an electric
stand mixer until soft peaks form. Decrease the speed
to low and slowly add the sugar. Increase the speed to
high and whip until stiff peaks form. Whip the cream
until soft peaks form. Fold the egg whites into the
Jerusalem artichoke puree and fold in the whipped
cream. Refrigerate the mousse for at least 2 hours.
(Note that you will have more mousse than you need
for this recipe.)

Finishing
Liquid nitrogen
6 passion fruit, halved, seeds and flesh scooped
out and reserved
12 grams ground coffee

p.360

For each serving, place a large spoonful of the
Passion Fruit Curd in the center of a frozen plate.
Pour about 2 cups of liquid nitrogen into a bowl and
quickly scoop 3 spoonfuls of Jerusalem Artichoke
Mousse into the liquid nitrogen. Very quickly, use a
spoon to flip the scoops several times. Remove the
3 semi-frozen scoops from the liquid nitrogen after
1 or 2 seconds. Each piece of Jerusalem Artichoke
Mousse should have one side that feels as if about
3 mm of the exterior is frozen and the other side
should have about 1 mm of the exterior frozen.
Check by gently squeezing each piece. Place the
pieces around the Passion Fruit Curd and crush
slightly with a spoon so that about half of each piece
is crushed but the piece is still intact. Scatter the
fresh passion fruit seeds and flesh over the mousse,
followed by a sprinkle of ground coffee.

p.363

Mosaic of Leathers
Serves 6

Paradise Apple Leather
1 kilogram dark red Paradise apples
300 grams sugar
1 kilogram light red Paradise apples
1 kilogram yellow or orange Paradise apples

In a large saucepan, combine the dark red Paradise apples with 100 grams of the sugar, then cover and bring to a boil over high heat. Decrease the heat to medium and cook the apples until they are completely soft, 20 to 30 minutes, stirring occasionally. Transfer the apples to a Thermomix and puree until smooth. Press the puree through a tamis lined with very fine-mesh cloth over a bowl. Repeat the process for the light red and yellow Paradise apples and the remaining sugar. Spread each puree onto a silicone pad into a 2-mm layer. Place the pads in the dehydrator and dry at 65°C (150°F) for 35 to 45 minutes, until the leathers are set but not completely dried. Peel the leathers off the pad and store in airtight containers in the fridge.

Finishing

Tear the leathers into randomly shaped pieces that are 3 to 4 cm and arrange them, overlapping each other slightly, on a sheet of parchment paper, alternating the colors to form a mosaic pattern. Place another sheet of parchment paper on top of the leather and, using a rolling pin, flatten the leather so that the pieces stick together. Remove the top sheet of parchment paper and carefully cut the leather into 10 by 4-cm rectangles. Peel the rectangles off the parchment paper and place them on a plate.

Söl Tart
Makes 30

Söl Powder
250 grams *söl* seaweed, washed

Dry the seaweed in a single layer in a 65°C (150°F) dehydrator. The following day, transfer to a Thermomix and process until it becomes a fine powder. Sift the powder through a fine-mesh sieve.

Shortbread Tart
170 grams sugar
250 grams unsalted butter, at room temperature
1 large egg
450 grams unbleached wheat flour, plus more for dusting

Preheat the oven to 150°C (300°F). Combine the sugar and butter in the bowl of a stand mixer. With the whisk attachment, whip on high speed until pale and fluffy, approximately 5 minutes. Add the egg and mix well on a slower speed. Change to the hook attachment and mix in the flour until well combined. On a floured work surface, roll out the dough until it is 5 mm thick. Press the dough into 2 by 2-cm square tart molds and trim the excess dough from the edges. Prick holes in the bottom of each tart. Bake the tarts until golden brown, 5 to 10 minutes. Remove from the molds and cool.

Söl Toffee
80 grams water
30 grams *söl* seaweed, washed
215 grams heavy cream
150 grams glucose
250 grams sugar

Combine the water and *söl* in a Thermomix and puree until smooth. Mix in the cream. In a saucepan, heat the glucose and sugar over medium-high heat until it reaches 115°C (240°F), 10 to 20 minutes. Add the *söl* mixture and whisk well. Allow the toffee to cool, then transfer to a piping bag.

Finishing

Pipe Söl Toffee into a Shortbread Tart shell, then sprinkle with Söl Powder.

Bread Caramel
Serves 40

Bread Vinegar Powder
150 grams day-old Sourdough Bread (page 370), cut
    into 2-cm cubes
225 grams water
20 grams Sourdough Starter (page 370)

Combine the bread, water, and Sourdough Starter
in a container and let soak at room temperature for
1 hour. Transfer the mixture to a Thermomix and
puree until smooth. Cover with a kitchen towel and
let stand at room temperature for 5 days to ferment.
The fermentation is complete when the mixture
becomes slightly bubbly and tastes sour, fruity, and
alcoholic. Spread the puree on parchment paper into
a 2-mm-thin layer. Place the parchment paper in the
dehydrator at 65°C (150°F) overnight. The following
day, break the sheets into pieces that can fit inside the
Thermomix and transfer to a Thermomix to process
into fine powder.

Crystallized Fudge
300 grams water
80 grams glucose
75 grams sugar
20 grams unsalted butter, cut into cubes
15 grams heavy cream
Vegetable oil

Combine the water, glucose, sugar, butter, and cream
in a saucepan and cook over high heat until it reaches
115°C (237°F), approximately 12 minutes. Transfer the
mixture to the oiled bowl of a stand mixer and cool to
100°C (212°F). With the paddle attachment, mix on
slow speed until the mixture loses its sheen and starts
to look smooth and dry, 6 to 8 minutes. Transfer to an
oiled container and allow it to cool.

Bread Fudge
500 grams day-old Sourdough Bread (page 370),
    cut into 2-cm cubes
2.5 kilograms water
500 grams Sourdough Starter (page 370)
320 grams glucose
300 grams sugar

80 grams unsalted butter, cut into cubes
Vegetable oil
250 grams Crystallized Fudge, cut into cubes

Place the bread with 1.5 kilograms of the water in a
vacuum bag and vacuum-seal it. Keep in the fridge for
3 days. Cut a hole at the top of the bag and pour the
infused water into a container, discarding the bread.

Place the Sourdough Starter in a tall container
with the remaining 1 kilogram of water and let stand
at room temperature overnight. The following day,
combine 750 grams of the infused water, 750 grams
of the Sourdough Starter water, the glucose, sugar,
and unsalted butter in a large saucepan and cook
until it reaches 119°C (246°F), stirring constantly,
approximately 15 minutes. Transfer the mixture to the
oiled bowl of a stand mixer and allow to cool until it
reaches 110°C (230°F), approximately 5 minutes. Add
the Caramelized Fudge cubes to the mixture and,
with the paddle attachment, mix on slow speed until
the mixture loses its sheen and starts to look smooth
and dry, 6 to 8 minutes. Transfer to an oiled container.
Spread out into a 1-cm-thick layer and cover with
oiled parchment paper. Allow to cool overnight at
room temperature. The following day, using scissors,
cut the caramel into 1-cm-wide strips, then cut each
strip crosswise into 1-cm squares. Roll each square
into a flat round shape and coat each one with a thin
layer of the Bread Vinegar Powder by rolling the fudge
in the powder.

Finishing
Dried Bread Crumbs (page 404)

For each serving, cover the bottom of a small bowl
with a layer of Dried Bread Crumbs and place a few
Bread Caramels on top.

Appendix

Basics

Butter Emulsion
1 L water
750 grams unsalted butter, cut into cubes
2 grams xantham gum

Bring the water to a boil. Combine the water, butter, and xantham gum in a Thermomix and blend at high speed until emulsified, 1 to 2 minutes. Transfer to a saucepan to use immediately or transfer to an uncovered container to cool in the fridge for later use. Store for up to 1 week.

Beurre Blanc
250 grams Reduced White Wine (page 439)
350 grams unsalted butter, cut into cubes

Bring the Reduced White Wine to a boil in a saucepan over high heat. Transfer to a Thermomix and, at low speed, add the butter, cube by cube, until emulsified. Store in the fridge for up to 2 days.

Brown Butter
500 grams unsalted butter

Melt the butter in a saucepan over medium-high heat. Once melted, decrease the heat to medium and let brown slowly, stirring occasionally, 2 to 3 hours. When the butter has become a very dark brown, almost black, remove it from the heat and allow to rest until the burnt solids settle at the bottom of the pan and the butter cools slightly, approximately 1 hour. Gently pour the brown butter into a heat-resistant container, leaving the burnt solids behind. Discard the burnt solids. Store in the fridge for up to 2 weeks.

Clarified Butter
500 grams unsalted butter

Slowly melt the butter in a saucepan over low heat. Do not stir the butter or move the saucepan. After 10 to 12 minutes, the melted butter will separate into three layers: foam, fat, and milk solids. Skim the foam from the surface of the melted butter and discard.

Gently pour the fat into a heat-resistant container, leaving the milk solids behind. Discard the milk solids. Store in the fridge for up to 2 weeks.

3% Salt Brine
1 kilogram water
30 grams coarse-grain salt

Combine the water and salt in a Thermomix and process until well combined. Store in a sealed container at room temperature for up to 1 week.

5% Salt Brine
1 kilogram water
50 grams coarse-grain salt

Combine the water and salt in a Thermomix and process until combined. Store in a sealed container at room temperature for up to 1 week.

7% Salt Brine
1 kilogram water
70 grams coarse-grain salt

Combine the water and salt in a Thermomix and process until combined. Store in a sealed container at room temperature for up to 1 week.

Whey
1 kilogram milk
4 grams rennet
3 grams citric acid

Slowly warm the milk in a covered saucepan over low heat until it reaches 24°C (75°F), approximately 15 minutes. Add the rennet and citric acid and stir a few times until they dissolve. Remove the saucepan from the heat and let stand for 1 hour. Set a cheesecloth in a strainer set over a container and carefully pour the milk mixture into the cheesecloth. Leave to stand in the fridge overnight. The following day, you will have fresh cheese in the cheesecloth and whey in the container. Store the whey in the fridge for up to 3 days or freeze for up to 2 weeks.

Chicken Glaze
2.5 kilograms chicken wings
1.5 kilograms chicken bones

Place the wings and bones in a large stockpot and add enough cold water to cover. Bring to a boil over high heat and skim the foam and fat from the surface. Decrease the heat to low and simmer for 6 to 8 hours. Strain the stock through a fine-mesh sieve set over another stockpot and discard the bones. In a large saucepan, bring the stock to a boil over high heat and reduce to one-eighth of its original volume, approximately 3 hours. Store in sealed containers in the fridge for up to 1 week.

Pork Glaze
4 kilograms pork bones

Preheat the oven to 200°C (400°F). Place the bones in a single layer in a roasting pan. Roast the bones until golden, 35 to 45 minutes. Place the roasted bones in a large stockpot and add enough cold water to cover. Bring to a boil over high heat and skim the foam and fat from the surface. Decrease the heat to low and simmer for 6 to 8 hours. Strain the stock through a superbag set over another large stockpot and discard the bones. Bring the stock to a boil over high heat and reduce to one-eighth of its original volume. Cool, uncovered, in the fridge.

Veal Glaze
4 kilograms veal bones

Preheat the oven to 200°C (400°F). Roast the bones until golden, 35 to 45 minutes. Place the roasted bones in a large stock pot and add enough cold water to cover. Bring to boil over high heat and skim the foam and fat from the surface. Decrease the heat to low and simmer for 6 to 8 hours. Strain the stock through a fine-mesh sieve and discard the bones. In a large saucepan, bring the stock to a boil over high heat and reduce to one-eighth of its original volume, approximately 3 hours. Store in sealed containers in the fridge for up to 1 week.

Lamb Glaze
4 kilograms lamb bones

Preheat the oven to 200°C (400°F). Roast the bones until golden, 35 to 45 minutes. Place the roasted bones in a large stockpot and add enough cold water to cover. Bring to boil over high heat and skim the foam and fat from the surface. Decrease the heat to low and simmer for 6 to 8 hours. Strain the stock through a fine-mesh sieve and discard the bones. In a large saucepan, bring the stock to a boil over high heat and reduce to one-eighth of its original volume, approximately 3 hours. Store in sealed containers in the fridge for up to 1 week.

Duck Glaze and Duck Fat
4 kilograms wild grey duck bones

Preheat the oven to 200°C (400°F). Roast the bones in the oven until golden, 30 to 40 minutes. Reserve the fat that renders off the bones as they roast, allow to cool slightly, and transfer to a heat-resistant squeeze bottle. Place the roasted bones in a large pot and add enough cold water to cover. Bring to a boil over high heat and skim the foam and fat from the surface. Decrease the heat to low and simmer for 5 hours. Strain the stock through a fine-mesh sieve and discard the bones. In a large saucepan, bring the stock to a boil over high heat and reduce to one-eighth of its original volume, approximately 3 hours. Store in sealed containers in the fridge for up to 1 week.

Reduced White Wine
5 L dry white wine

In a large stockpot, bring the wine to a boil over high heat and allow it to reduce to 1 L, approximately 3 hours. Allow to cool. Store in a sealed container in the fridge.

Mushroom Soy Sauce

2 kilograms white button mushrooms, cleaned
60 grams fine-grain salt

Cut the mushrooms into 2-mm slices. Sprinkle the salt evenly on the mushrooms and mix them with your hands. Let stand for 1 hour, until the salt draws out some of the liquid in the mushrooms. Transfer the mushrooms to a superbag set over a bowl and squeeze the mushrooms as dry as possible to extract the juices. Discard the contents of the superbag. Store the mushroom soy sauce in the fridge for up to 2 weeks.

Black Trumpet Mushroom Powder

500 grams dried black trumpet mushrooms

Transfer the dried mushrooms to a Thermomix and blend until it becomes a fine powder. Store in a sealed container in dry storage.

Pickled Elderflowers

20 bunches elderflowers with stems attached
1 kilogram white wine vinegar

Gently rinse the elderflowers in a bowl of cold water. Sterilize a 1 L jar, then fill it with the elderflowers. Fill the jar with white wine vinegar all the way to the top, making sure that the elderflowers are completely covered by the vinegar. Seal the jar with a lid, submerge it in a large pot of water, and bring to a boil over high heat. Decrease the heat to medium and simmer for 5 minutes. Remove the pot from the heat and let the jar cool slowly in the water, approximately 45 minutes. Store the jar in a cool, dark place for at least 1 month and up to 1 year. Once opened, it keeps in the fridge for up to 3 months.

Salted Bergamot

1 kilogram bergamots, scrubbed
Coarse-grain salt, not iodized

Sterilize a 1 L jar. Trim the stem end of the bergamot off and cut an X halfway through the bergamot, from the stem end. Sprinkle a generous amount of salt into the X and rub it into the bergamot as deep as you can. Place the salted bergamot into the jar, along with a small handful of salt. Repeat the process for the remaining bergamots and pack them all into the jar, each time squeezing them in so that juice is pressed from the bergamots, filling the jar completely. Seal the jar with a lid, submerge it in a large pot of water, and bring to a boil over high heat. Decrease the heat to medium and simmer for 5 minutes. Remove the pot from the heat and let the jar cool slowly in the water, approximately 45 minutes. Store the jar in a cool, dry place for at least 3 months and up to 1 year. Once opened, keep in the fridge for up to 3 months.

Salted Mirabelle Plums

1 kilogram mirabelle plums, washed
500 grams 3% Salt Brine (page 438)

Sterilize a 1 L jar, then fill it with the plums. Fill the jar with Salt Brine all the way to the top, making sure that the plums are completely covered by the salt brine. Seal the jar with a lid, submerge it in a large pot of water, and bring to a boil over high heat. Decrease the heat to medium, and simmer for 5 minutes. Remove the pot from the heat and let the jar cool slowly in the water, approximately 45 minutes. Store the jar in a cool, dark place for at least 2 months and up to 1 year. Once opened, keep in the fridge for up to 2 weeks.

Pickled Black Trumpet Mushrooms

500 grams fresh black trumpet mushrooms, cleaned
200 grams vegetable oil
200 grams white wine vinegar

Place the mushrooms in a large bowl. In a saucepan, heat the vegetable oil and vinegar over medium-high heat until it reaches 90°C (194°F). In a heatproof bowl, pour the hot brine over the mushrooms and allow to cool. Transfer the mushrooms in a single layer with the brine to a vacuum bag and vacuum-seal it, then refrigerate. The mushrooms are ready to use after 2 or 3 days. Store in the fridge for up to 6 months unopened. Once opened, keep in the fridge up to 1 week.

Index

Index

Index

Index

Puglisi, Christian F.
  Relæ : a book of ideas / Christian F. Puglisi ; photography by
Per-Anders Jorgensen.
     pages cm
1. Cooking, European. 2. Relæ (Restaurant) 3. Cooking. I.
Title.
 TX723.5.A1P784 2014
 641.594—dc23
                              2014017923

Hardcover ISBN: 978-1-60774-649-2
eBook ISBN: 978-1-60774-650-8

Printed in China

Design by Homework

10 9 8 7 6 5 4 3 2 1

First Edition

Chef Christian F. Puglisi opened restaurant Relæ in 2010 on a rough stretch of one of Copenhagen's most crime-ridden streets. His goal was simple: to serve impeccable, intelligent, sustainable, and plant-centric food of the highest quality, in a setting that was devoid of the pretention and frills of conventional high-end restaurant dining. Relæ was an immediate hit, and Puglisi's "to the bone" ethos—which emphasized innovative, substantive cooking over crisp white tablecloths or legions of water-pouring, napkin-folding waiters—became a rallying cry for chefs around the world.

Today the Jægersborggade (where Relæ and its more casual sister restaurant, Manfreds, are located) is one of Copenhagen's most vibrant and exciting streets. And Puglisi continues to excite and surprise diners with his genre-defying, wildly inventive cooking.

Relæ is Puglisi's much-anticipated debut. Like his restaurants, the book is honest, unconventional, and challenges our expectations of what a cookbook should be. Rather than focusing on recipes, the core of the book is a series of interconnected "idea essays," which reveal the ingredients, practical techniques, and philosophies that inform Puglisi's cooking. Each essay is connected to one (or many) of the dishes he serves, and you are invited to flip through the book in whatever sequence inspires you—from idea to dish and back to idea again. The result is a deeply personal, utterly unique reading experience: a rare glimpse into the mind of a top chef, and the opportunity to learn the language of one of the world's most pioneering and acclaimed restaurants.

TEN SPEED PRESS
Berkeley
www.crownpublishing.com
www.tenspeed.com